BEYOND REAGANOMICS

Beyond Reaganomics

A Further Inquiry
into the Poverty of Economics

CHARLES K. WILBER
and
KENNETH P. JAMESON

UNIVERSITY OF NOTRE DAME PRESS
NOTRE DAME   LONDON

Library of Congress Cataloging-in-Publication Data

Wilber, Charles K.
    Beyond Reaganomics: a further inquiry into the
poverty of economics / Charles K. Wilber and Kenneth
P. Jameson.
        p.   cm.
    Includes bibliographical references.
    ISBN 0–268–00684–9
    1. Supply-side economics—United States. 2. United
States—Economic policy—1981–   3. Free enterprise. 4.
Keynesian economics. 5. Marxian economics. 6. Business
cycles—United States. I. Jameson, Kenneth P. II. Title.
HC106.8.W52 1990
338.973'00927—dc20   89–40745

For
KENNY, TERRY, MATT, ALICE, MARY,
ANGELA, AND LOUIE WILBER

REX AND MATTHEW JAMESON

Contents

Preface

We began working on this book as Ronald Reagan's presidency was coming to a close. He and his vision of the economy had largely dominated the 1980s, and it seemed to us important to assess the results and to look forward to the decades ahead.

We do not find much to cheer about in his legacy, and this is most clear in terms of income distribution and poverty, where the gains that had been made in prior decades were all but wiped out. Unleashing market forces can be destructive as well as creative. However, there is reason for optimism, for there are many indications that the Reagan presidency was simply a hiatus. There is a new awareness of the environmental problems we confront. There is a new willingness to admit that poverty is a problem, even if there is no new commitment to deal with that reality. The military-industrial complex, which provided the Reaganites their access to tremendous sources of wealth, is in retreat in the face of the changes in Eastern Europe even while the jockeying to capture the peace dividend has just begun. Thus, there is every reason to think we are going to reverse and begin to deal with our economic problems, rather than defining them away, ignoring them, or putting a positive spin on them as we did during the 1980s.

The Reagan revolution did generate some significant and positive changes in our economy. There is less willingness to rely solely on government to correct our economic problems. There is also a healthy willingness to look more critically at specific government policies. Unfortunately, no similar attitude toward the ability of the private sector to solve all of our economic problems has been generated. The limits to the naive faith in the private sector will soon be seen.

There is new awareness and willingness to encourage, man-

date, and move the economy to serve human beings. This was the
central message of the Catholic Bishops' pastoral letter, *Economic
Justice for All,* and it is the starting point for this book.

These changes reinforce our belief that the present economic
problems of the U.S. economy—low productivity growth, large
budget and trade deficits, growth of an impoverished underclass,
to name a few—can only be understood in light of the institutional
development of the economy and the history of economists' efforts to explain the workings of the economy.

The theoretical framework used is a combination of Joseph
Shumpeter's concept of creative destruction and the concept of
uneven development found in dependency theory.

Two things stand out in the history of capitalism in the U.S.,
and in the world generally. First, it has been successful in producing goods and services unprecedented in history; however, this
creativity has been coupled with the destruction of existing technologies, forms of business organization, and jobs. In the long run
there are more jobs, greater productivity, and higher levels of
output. In the short run industries are closed down, workers left
without jobs, and whole communities devastated.

Second, capitalist development has proceeded very unevenly
between countries, and among regions within countries. Historically, certain countries and regions became dynamic centers of
development while others stagnated on the periphery. Then the
process shifted, and once growing areas stagnated and stagnant
ones began new development. In addition, growth has proceeded
cyclically through booms and busts in each country and region.
This process extends to individual industries and even households.

Had these lessons from history been heeded, the headlong
rush in the 1980s to reform the economy into some image from
the past would have been seen for what it was—futile and destructive. We have tried to learn from history and think that we have
developed an analysis and a program that is consistent with the
lessons of the past.

While we hope that the work presented here is objective,
there is no artificial stance of neutrality. We are committed to
certain values that undoubtedly influence the choice of questions
asked and the variables considered for investigation. We are com-

mitted to the view that the economy should be the servant of peoples' goals. Further, we believe that these goals include the provision of life-sustenance, self-esteem and fellowship, and freedom. Finally, the economy should be evaluated on the extent to which it aids in the fulfillment of these goals. With these values in mind the reader can judge the degree of objectivity attained in this study.

In the process of writing this book we have incurred many debts and owe many a vote of thanks. Foremost is to the community of scholars at Notre Dame which has supported the type of inquiry we undertook despite its being outside the mainstream of economic orthodoxy. We also relish and appreciate the many colleagues with whom we have discussed and examined these ideas: James Weaver, David Richardson, Gene Ellis, Bryan Hehir, David Burrell, Michael Novak, and Ron Krietemeyer. Some were tough but friendly critics. They deserve special thanks.

This book is partly the outgrowth of work begun with the publication of *An Inquiry into the Poverty of Economics* (University of Notre Dame Press, 1983). It is a pleasure to continue working with a professional press such as Notre Dame's, and with its director, Jim Langford. We appreciate his support and interest in the project and thank him for the suggestions made in the process. In the actual book preparation, Teresa Anderson-Little provided able assistance, and many graduate students reacted to earlier drafts with helpful comments which we have incorporated.

But most of all we would like to thank our families who provide a constant source of support and stimulation for both of us, while they and we both grow and change. The bishops have a vision of society based on family values with those values emanating ever further from that familial center. Our vision is in many ways similar, though post-Keynesian institutionalism may seem a very long way to get there!

1. Introduction

Ronald Reagan imprinted his mark deeply onto the American economy. By direct attack or by evasion or by lukewarm responsiveness, his economic policy set out to undo the mixed economy which had developed since the Depression of the 1930s. Whatever mandate he could claim had derived from the turmoil and loss of direction of the 1970s.

After a golden age of economic prosperity, 1960 to 1973, guided by Washington economic policymakers, the American economy faced difficult times. From 1974 to 1980 the economic consensus, reached in the aftermath of the Depression and responsive to the influence of the economist John Maynard Keynes, came apart at the seams.

Our major industries—autos, steel, textiles, electronics—were routinely out-competed in the world marketplace by foreign firms, particularly the Japanese and Germans, and even the South Koreans and Brazilians. We began to worry about why our productivity growth was so slow—we who had been the world's leader! And we looked for someone to blame, usually labor, often the government, or on occasion our business firms.

The simultaneous appearance of high unemployment and double-digit inflation—the clearest manifestation of an economic crisis—questioned whether the accepted economic policy was still able to confront the challenges of the contemporary world. This deterioration took place against a backdrop of international instability in prices, exchange rates, growth rates, and indeed in all international economic relations.

One of the most confusing realities of the 1970s was the accelerating decay of the cities and of public services in general. Despite being richer than ever before, suddenly we could not afford to maintain our schools, public transit systems started going bankrupt, and cities fired large numbers of policemen despite rising crime rates. The troubles seemed endless.

As if this were not enough, questions of equity and freedom, which in the 1960s had been answered by economic success and by movement toward the "Great Society," resurfaced with a vengeance. As the government made greater efforts to control an economy that seemed to be slipping away, it taxed more, spent more, and regulated more. This led to a reaction against government control and the "welfare state" and to a demand for the greater economic freedom that it was believed earlier generations of Americans enjoyed.

The limits of the welfare state had been reached. The American Century with its New Frontier and Great Society had been mortally wounded in the jungles of Southeast Asia and the marketplaces of the world. Unease and foreboding stalked the land.

In 1980 Ronald Reagan represented an alternative. The American electorate opted to embrace him and the old-time religion of unfettered private enterprise under the guise of supply-side economics. They rejected Jimmy Carter, who was a slightly more liberal version masquerading as the descendant of the New Deal–Keynesian consensus that had dominated American economic policy since the 1930s.

Now the Reagan era is finished, and it is time to look beyond it. Perhaps its greatest success was abolishing any sense of crisis, putting a "spin" on any particular economic problem that made it seem minor or could even make it disappear. Only the "Black Monday" of the stock market, October 19, 1987, put a damper on the show, and that was only temporary. Thus in November 1988 the American electorate decided to continue the same course for another four years. Yet, when the Reagan record is examined closely, only in the case of inflation has the underlying problem been confronted. Unemployment has remained high, though it has gradually declined since 1984, productivity has not dramatically increased, and a host of other problems—huge budget and trade deficits, increased poverty, and in general a prosperity haunted by structural distortions in the economy and an underclass all too often hungry and homeless—have grown despite blithe denials.

Public discussion, including the 1988 presidential campaign, proceeds as if economic difficulties are temporary and subject to painless resolution. For example, it was clear that the savings and loan industry had been mismanaged to a crisis state, and yet in the election campaign neither side raised that situation as an issue, nor suggested steps that would be taken to confront it. Only after the election was the problem seriously addressed, and its magnitude quickly blossomed from a $40 billion bailout to one of $130 billion. Even then all sides attempted to mask the gravity of the situation by financing the relief without immediately forcing tax increases.

We must step out of this world of feeling good and of unreality to look in a hardheaded fashion at the contemporary American economy, at its many strengths as well as at its weaknesses and failures. We must take the Reagan administration's free enterprise policies as a given, for in certain areas they will never be reversed; and in a number of matters they should not be reversed. However, they have not lived up to their promise, and the issues of the 1970s continue today, demanding that new directions be sought in confronting them.

In this chapter we set out some points of departure for this effort. Later chapters present and evaluate the various traditions which have attempted to understand the capitalist economy, including a more detailed assessment of the program and policies of Ronald Reagan, of its several successes and of its many failures. We finally suggest an alternative understanding of the economy and a set of policies which can move it toward a more realistic confrontation with the 1990s.

All too often, public discussion of economic issues proceeds as if our economic difficulties recently and magically appeared and as if there is no precedent for dealing with such difficulties. As we begin the task of understanding these problems and what might be done to overcome them, it will help to provide some historical perspective.

THE HISTORICAL CONTEXT

Political democracy in the United States was founded on the assumption that contending political parties shared a minimum agreement on the core economic and social structure of the nation. We might argue about high or low tariffs, gold or silver backing for the money supply, or the appropriateness of child labor laws, but these could all be fought out as an intramural battle because the economic and social structure resulting from a commitment to a private enterprise economy would not be seriously affected by the outcome.

During the 1930s, however, this minimum agreement was threatened by the collapse of the economy into a prolonged depression. Glaring inequalities of income and wealth, widespread mortgage foreclosures and bankruptcies, the absurdity of idle men and idle machines in the face of obvious need, and the failure of the state to take responsibility for alleviating this massive suffering came near to tearing the very fabric of society. But New Deal politics and Keynesian economics rescued capitalist democracy by providing a new mainstream consensus. Potentially disruptive conflicts over massive income and wealth redistribution programs or major changes in the private ownership of productive property were sidetracked by policies designed to provide minimum economic security through old age benefits, unemployment insurance, minimum wage laws, and guarantees of the right of workers to organize. World War II provided the fiscal stimulus to restore full employment and the Employment Act of 1946 gave the federal government the right and responsibility to utilize macrostabilization policies.

In the wake of the recessions of the 1950s, an increased emphasis on rapid economic growth as a means to maintain full employment and to avoid conflicts over resource allocation was added to the existing economic security and full employment policies.

Economic growth required that the post–World War II economy be built upon an ever-expanding per capita consumption level. Thus was born the "high mass-consumption" society which had profound implications far beyond the economy itself. Producers had to entice consumers to spend at least at the same rate from an ever-expanding personal income. Thus advertising, product differentiation, and physical and stylistic obsolescence were developed to new heights to convince consumers that they needed the new products and had to discard the old. To accomplish this, consumption was turned into a virtue; and thrift—which had been one of the cardinal American virtues and part of the Puritan ethic—was demoted to at best a minor virtue for consumers.* At the same time the absence of thrift remained as the main explanation (along with laziness) for individual poverty.

The continuous expansion of new products resulted in a sharp increase in natural resource use and a concomitant increase in environmental pollution. Potential resource shortages were dismissed with the argument that science and technology would provide timely substitutes, and pollution was seen as the price of progress.

In this consumer society, government was called upon to play an increasingly active role. To aid this ever-expanding consumption and to attempt to ensure that the poor participated, at least marginally, in the American cornucopia, both the macromanagement functions of government and its economic security efforts expanded dramatically.

To fuel this consumer economy, the United States tapped the world's resources—oil, coffee, nickel, wolframite, and bauxite. As a result, foreign investments by United States' corporations increased fourfold between 1945 and 1965. To protect these investments and to prevent socialism from closing off areas of the world market to our resource needs and exports, Communism, first in its Soviet then in its Chinese versions, was opposed at all costs.** To this end the United States had to maintain a worldwide military network with all its attendant budgetary and foreign exchange costs. This system was built after World War II at a time when the other capitalist countries were economically prostrate and thus were no competitive threat. The U. S. export surplus allowed this overseas military burden to be financed without undue stress. The cost of a growing military establishment was made politically toler-

---

*Contemporary Japan is consciously moving in the same direction, encouraging the use of credit cards, reducing the work week, and creating "couples days" to get families to undertake activities which will spend money. This is necessary because the Japanese saving rate is so high and their balance of trade surplus is so great that it is disrupting the world economy.

**This does not deny that the United States opposed Communism for higher reasons—i.e., liberty—but the existence of the lower reasons strengthened its resolve.

able through the pork barrel of military public works such as army and air force bases.

The "golden age" of American capitalist democracy was 1960–1973. Per capita income and consumption expanded dramatically. Keynesian economics seemed to meet its test, for full employment and stable prices were achieved. In the euphoria of the moment, "fine-tuning" was expected to banish forever the twin evils of inflation and unemployment. In addition to successful macromanagement, the period saw the launching of the Peace Corps and the War on Poverty. It was the era of the New Frontier and the Great Society. The Achilles heel of democratic capitalism—unemployment—was finally conquered, and few were concerned with the first rumblings of inflation.

But cracks in the facade began to appear in 1965, spreading through 1968, changing directions in 1969–70, resulting in 1973–75 with the longest and deepest recession/depression since the 1930s and culminating in seemingly endless stagflation. First came the war in Vietnam, then the revolt of the young, inflation, pollution, food and oil shortages, recession, and stagflation. Economists began to talk about a wide variety of new institutional developments that somehow seemed to have an ominous role in all these crises—the rise of multinational corporations with their transfer pricing and cross-subsidization; the development of foreign multinational firms as competitors; the coincidence of the business cycles of the United States, Japan, and the Western European capitalist countries; OPEC, the oil cartel; and the apparent impotence of government. And as if this were not enough, the whole Keynesian consensus was shattered by the simultaneous appearance of massive unemployment and double-digit inflation—stagflation.

The Reagan administration conquered the inflation half of stagflation at the cost of the deepest recession since the 1930s. The subsequent recovery after 1982 covered up a number of problems that will challenge policymakers in the 1990s: the record budget and trade deficits; an unprecedented increase in consumption expenditures and decline in savings; a tragic deferral of infrastructure maintenance; the deindustrialization of the U.S. economy with a consequent growth of a two-tiered wage system; and growth of an "underclass" of poor trapped inside the lowest wage sectors of the economy or pushed outside the economy, frequently hungry and homeless.

Thus our current economic problems have their roots in the changes of the last twenty years, in the unwillingness to deal with these changes in the 1970s, and in the unwillingness to admit their existence in the 1980s. This suggests as a starting point an examination of the fundamental nature of our economic system, for that will condition any policy steps which might be taken in the future.

THE NATURE OF CAPITALISM

To understand the economic problems we face requires us to realize that the economic system is a human creation. As a human creation it solves certain problems for us while causing other ones. For example, market competition increases productivity thereby enabling us to produce more. However, if another nation learns to produce that item even more productively, or with lower wage costs, they will put our producers out of business, resulting in our producing less. In the long run the resources (human and natural) used to produce the first item will be transferred to the production of something new, or will go unused. This process keeps repeating itself.

Two facts stand out from an examination of the history of capitalism. Capitalism has been successful in producing amounts of goods and services unprecedented in history; *and* it has done so in a temporally and spatially uneven manner, i.e., capitalist development has proceeded very unevenly between countries, and among regions within countries. The capitalist system developed both North America and South America, but one more so than the other. Certain countries and regions became dynamic centers of development while others stagnated on the periphery. Then the process shifted, and once growing areas stagnated and stagnant ones developed. And, of course, development has proceeded cyclically through booms and busts in each country and region. This process extends to individual industries and even households. These imbalances are naturally generated by the process of capitalist development.

One of the great economists of the twentieth century, Joseph Schumpeter captures the positive side of this dynamic process in his concept of "Creative Destruction":

> The fundamental impulse that sets and keeps the capitalist engine in motion comes from the new consumers' goods, the new methods of production or transportation, the new markets, the new forms of industrial organization that capitalist enterprise creates.... [These developments] incessantly revolutionize the economic structure *from within,* incessantly destroying the old one, incessantly creating a new one. This process of Creative Destruction is the essential fact about capitalism.[1]

While such a vision is magnificent, it is scant solace to the skilled worker thrown out of a job or the town which progress left behind. So the strengths of the economic system are also its weaknesses. There are three possible responses to this reality. The first proclaims that there is no alternative to allowing the "natural" laws of the economy to work themselves out. Attempts to reform capitalism, or even worse to replace it, will only cause greater harm. This is the basic position of Conservative Economic Individualism (CEI) and the economists advising the Reagan and Bush administrations.

The second proclaims that capitalism is not reformable, its very structure defeats any such attempt. This is the basic position of most Marxists and other radical socialists. A similar stance is found in the cycle theorists who see a recurrent pattern of booms and busts endemic to capitalist society.

The third argues that, in fact, capitalism can be reformed, though for the reforms to be effective they must take into account the dynamics of the system. This is the stance of the Keynesians, as well as ours.

A specific example will be helpful. A dominant concern of the 1980s is to increase international competitiveness by raising productivity. Why? The U.S. economy is very productive, more than ever before in its history. However, if another country becomes even more productive, the U.S. becomes less competitive. In turn if the U.S. then becomes even more productive, the other country becomes less competitive. The expansion of markets as the central international coordinating mechanism removed governments' abilities to cushion the impact of these changes on their domestic economies.

The problem is that competition increases productivity but in the process creates losers—those who are out-competed. This is both a creative and destructive process. In the long run it creates expanded productivity and wealth, though unevenly, while in the short run it destroys firms, jobs, and communities.

People always have attempted to subordinate economic forces to their values as embodied in social, religious, and political institutions (see chapter 8). During the past fifty years citizens turned ever more to government as the social institution with the task of softening the destructive side of economic forces. The great economic debate in the U.S. has been and still is: Can the destructive side of the capitalist growth process be mitigated while doing minimal damage to the creative side? Free market economists have said no and Keynesian economists have said yes. Classical Marxists and cycle theorists, though rarely included in policy debates, see this destructiveness as inevitable, and costly in human terms.

We believe that economies are human creations, and thus can be improved through human action. Many steps to affect the economy can be taken by individuals, and the fulfillment of human needs must be an essential goal of every economy. However, government as a social institution must play an important role. Clearly not all government actions are positive, but we believe that a positive role for government is indeed possible and is the result of a well-functioning democracy. Government can be the instrument wielded by men and women to attenuate the effects of the destructive side of economic growth.

However, individual self-interest and government actions are still inadequate to meet the challenges of the 1990s. Single-minded pursuit of self-interest as adulated in the CEI theory is often detrimental to others and in many instances prevents even greater gains from occurring. Cooperative behavior through cooperative institutions can be fulfilling to the individuals involved, can encourage such behavior on the part of others, and can be much more successful in confronting the challenges of the modern economy. Recall that one of the successes of Japanese production management is the high level of productivity it attains by involving workers in the decision-making process.

So the successful economy will combine all three varieties of action. And it will do so to ensure that the economy serves the goals that the human beings set out for it.

GOALS AND THE ECONOMY

The variety of "economies" in the world today is vast, ranging from that of the Amazonian Indian tribes to the sophisticated and integrated Swedish or Swiss economies. If we can escape the bounds of our enthnocentrism, it may come as a surprise that a clear ranking in terms of success or desirability may not be possible when we compare economies. An Amazonian Indian given the opportunity to live in New York might die rather than benefit from the opportunity.

How can we evaluate the operation of different economies and of our own United States economy? The first step is to realize that there is no single criterion, that success can only be assessed in reference to the needs of the human beings who constitute the economy. Thus we often hear that "efficiency" is the highest goal of the economy and that certain steps must be taken to encourage it. This may be true, but it can only be judged so if efficiency leads to the attainment of peoples' needs. Too often efficiency is used as an ideological weapon to defend the free market and its underlying values. The claim that economic theory can provide a scientific, value-free means of evaluating the performance of economic institutions and policies, thus obviating the need for social goals, misunderstands the nature of economics. Despite its claim to be value-free, standard economic theory contains within its very structure a vision of the good society based on the attainment of individual goals. That is, economic theory embodies an individualist philosophic position that both damages its credibility as a science and frequently places it in opposition to the very idea of social goals.

In addition economic theory ignores a central element necessary for a well-functioning economy, a shared conception of the moral base of the economy. Without an agreed upon set of moral canons, any economic system would degenerate into a struggle where raw power would win out, and where no holds were barred.

The individualist conception of the economy encourages self-interested behavior, which in turn often results in actions inconsistent with the assumed moral base of the economy. So one element which must be considered in viewing any economy is the existence and vibrancy of its moral base.

What can be said about indicators of successful performance of an economy? One approach would identify the natural laws of the economy and then assess its performance in conformity to these laws. This would be a return to an Aristotelian conception of society that might convince some by its sheer logic. We feel that there would be little agreement on the identity of these laws and thus reject this perspective.

Another approach would survey persons and their views on what the economy should do. This would yield some surprising results. For example, Richard Easterlin discovered that a crucial component of such an evaluation was the perception of one's relative situation.[2] Thus it would seem to be exceptionally difficult for an economy to improve its performance, for every relative gain would imply a relative loss, or no net gain! This reality and the confusion in our society between growth, which we place as a preeminent goal, and affluence, which by all standards we have clearly obtained, suggests that one of the problems of our society is to deal with "the poverty of affluence."[3]

We think that to begin to deal with this problem we must look at broader psychological studies and at information which is gathered across different societies. We draw upon cross-cultural studies which have attempted to find absolute needs or needs that are expressed in a variety of societies. Following the work of Denis Goulet,[4] three goals can be specified for an economy.

The first is what Goulet calls "life-sustenance," which corresponds generally to physiological needs or what we call basic material goods. Every society strives to provide its citizens with the basic goods that are necessary for life—adequate food, water, housing, clothing, education, and health care—and an economy is successful if it can provide them. The satisfaction of this goal is quite directly linked with overall economic performance. Unemployment will affect the ability of those without jobs to satisfy their need for life-sustenance, inflation can erode the purchasing power of portions of the population, and some elements of growth may

be necessary to provide life-sustaining jobs. Instability in the economy, the economic cycle, can also affect the provision of basic
material goods.

We must also ask how we can specify basic material goods.
One manner is to differentiate among three types of goods. The
first are necessities such as food and water. Within some limits
needs in this realm can be specified. The second type of goods are
"enhancement goods," which make life more vital, more interesting, more worth living. Examples might be music, various forms
of entertainment, some household goods, and so on. The third
level of goods involves what are commonly known as luxury
goods. Driving a Cadillac instead of a Chevrolet, buying a marble-
topped table instead of a wooden one, and walking on a llama rug
instead of polyester are all instances of consuming luxury goods.

We can all agree that basic needs must be met. Most believe
that enhancement goods are worthy of pursuit. There is less accord on luxury goods. Traditional economics in the U.S. has
claimed that individual wants are unlimited and that luxury goods
satisfy wants, as do basic goods. If individuals want Cadillacs and
llama rugs, and if the economy can produce such luxuries, it ought
to. There are voices which dispute this view. A study by Scitovsky
found that the simple increase in the amount of consumption in
the U.S. has not increased peoples' happiness.[5]

A second component of societal goals found in most societies
is esteem and fellowship. The system should provide a sense of
worth, of dignity to its citizens. One's goods can be a measure of
societal esteem, but surely there are other important elements.
The institutions in which citizens work should support them physically and give them a sense of belonging and of contributing to
an important undertaking. Society should have clubs, churches,
or other entities which support the individual. If the family is the
basic social and economic unit, as is the case in the U.S., the economy should provide support and encourage in families a sense of
self-esteem that can help sustain them. Another term for this is
fellowship; the economy should promote right relations among its
participants, and to the extent it can, should keep life from being
"nasty and brutish," while providing basic material goods to
lengthen it.

For no society can function smoothly, without disruptive tensions, if there is no fellowship among its members. If people are alienated from one another and society is fractured into myriad self-interested and self-centered individuals or groups, society will not long survive. If no genuine concern for one's neighbors exists and if empathy for others disappears, then each small self-reliant entity (whether this be family, occupational group, or individual) will eventually withdraw unto itself and live at odds with others. No social system can prevail which endorses or engenders such self-centeredness. Even if material economic well-being were at the heart of social success, surely fellowship would be the life blood that sustains the community, the cohesion that makes one individual feel a closeness and a unity of purpose with all others in that society, whether known personally or not. Consequently, we insist that one goal of an economic system, in addition to providing for the material needs of its members, is to encourage the growth of widely shared esteem that yields a life-giving and life-sustaining fellowship.

This implies an element of equity among citizens. No modern society could provide esteem or fellowship which gave minimal income to most of the population, but fabulous wealth to a few families. Equity, of course, does not necessarily mean equality, but it does mean that there be some consensus regarding the justness of the distribution of wealth and income.

The third goal of the economy is freedom. The desire for freedom has played a major role in our own history beginning with the drive for independence from England. However, freedom is still a difficult goal to specify clearly. It obviously does not mean that all individuals may do whatever they wish, for that would be anarchy and the death of society. At its weakest, an increase in freedom means that the range of options open to the individual or the group has increased, that there are more choices available. This has its physical side in choice of goods, but it can also operate in other spheres such as the political or religious.

There are three component parts to the goal of freedom. The first, and the one which is usually at the center of much economic theorizing in the United States, is the provision of consumer sovereignty. Individuals should be able to choose the goods that they wish to consume.

The second part is worker sovereignty. People must have a

choice of jobs, jobs they find meaningful and that enhance their human capacities. There must be mechanisms for finding peoples' preferences on work and creating the types of jobs required. A variety of mechanisms could satisfy this need: labor mobility among jobs of widely different character, control by workers over their job situations, or provision of capital resources to laborers to allow them to establish their own undertakings. Whatever the mechanisms, this characteristic is important because work plays an important part in human development.

Third, a society must provide citizen sovereignty, a mechanism to aggregate peoples' preferences for community. What kind of community do people want? What kind of environment do they want? The concept of citizen sovereignty implies that a way to express preferences and to control communities is provided to the citizen. A number of mechanisms may be found which satisfy this requirement, in addition to the democratic voting procedures used in the U.S. One way of enhancing citizen sovereignty could be through strengthening local groups for citizen participation in decision making, e.g., parent-teacher organizations, zoning boards, and citizen review boards of police departments and other public agencies. Or perhaps local residents might participate in the operation of local industries in their areas, by electing representatives to firms' boards of directors to minimize the negative aspects of industrial production such as noise and pollution. The absence of real citizen sovereignty generates conflicts among groups in society. The reality of such conflict has been denied over the last decade, but will be a central element in the coming decade. It can be either a destructive or a constructive force in charting the course of the economy.

As we set out to examine the U.S. economy and its performance, we have as criteria three goals which seem to characterize all societies: life sustenance, esteem and fellowship, and freedom. They are broad goals which will aid us in evaluating economic performance. The existence and acceptance of such goals is central to our examination of various approaches to the economy and of the possible policy options for dealing with our current economic crisis.

We suggest that attaining these goals requires reestablishing a common moral base which will allow us to deal with the latent conflicts in our society, conflicts that will become manifest in years to come. We suggest that the moral constructs of stewardship, jubilee, and subsidiarity can provide a basis for economic policy and economic behavior that will aid our efforts to attain the three goals of our economic society.

A LOOK AHEAD

The remainder of this book is devoted to analyzing both the successes and failures of the U.S. economy in achieving these goals and to suggest how we can be more successful in the future. This requires us to look at the history of economic policy and of the theories that underlie those policies.

Part I provides an overview of different approaches to understanding how the economy works and an evaluation of the results of the economic theories that guided economic policy at different times. Chapters 2 through 4 concentrate on the two major views of the economy that dominate public debate and on the results of their policy advice. These are the Conservative Economic Individualist (free market) and Keynesian theories. Chapter 5 is an extensive review of the recent embodiment of the free market theories, the administration of Ronald Reagan from 1981 through 1988. In Part II, chapter 6 outlines a set of formal cycle theories—long swings, chaos theory—which have little role in the contemporary debate in the U.S. but which provide a very appealing explanation for the cycles which have characterized our capitalist economy. The Marxian analysis presented in chapter 7 also plays little role in contemporary policy debates. However, there are a number of useful insights from these theories and they have substantial influence outside of the U.S., so they must be presented for completeness.

Part III originates in the failures of the alternative theories and policies which the first part has specified. It insists that adequate economic policy for the future must take as its starting point the fact that capitalism is both creative and destructive and that the role of public policy is to contain the destructiveness, both human and environmental, while not losing the creativeness. Conservative Economic Individualism downplays the destructiveness and highlights the creativeness. Keynesianism's macroeconomic approach to controlling capitalism no longer appears to be viable.

Our approach, which we call "Post-Keynesian Institutionalism" (PKI), attempts to provide the basis for a new social consensus to control capitalism's uneven development. The goal is to harness its creativity to achieve the three goals of life-sustenance, self-esteem and fellowship, and freedom, while its human and environmental destructiveness is minimized. It requires the reestablishment of a common moral base as well as the development of a more effective and consistent set of economic policies.

America is at a crossroads in its history where the destructiveness of international capitalist development is overwhelming its creativeness. We are now on the short end of its uneven development. The challenge is great. Let us begin.

PART ONE

The Reigning Orthodoxies

2. Free Enterprise
and Laissez-Faire Economics

Despite the apparent prosperity of the last half of the 1980s, there is a widespread sense that the American economy is in trouble, that good feelings can not hide underlying problems. The persistent and intractable budget and trade deficits contribute to this uneasiness, as does the continued existence of poverty and homelessness. George Bush's now hackneyed call for a "kinder, gentler society" responded to this sense. Despite many promises, economists have been unable to present convincing solutions to our economic problems. Surely they have had enough time to study, reflect on, and understand the intricacies of the economy, so why are they not able to tell us what to do to escape the difficult circumstances of the eighties and nineties? The short answer is that one large group of economists, the laissez-faire theorists, believe that economic problems are best solved by benign neglect, while the other major group, the Keynesians, at one time believed that most of these problems had been solved. The longer answer is presented in this and the next three chapters.

Until the mid-1930s, most economists believed a "free market" economy would solve whatever problems arose. If goods and services and inputs into production were bought and sold in markets, the economy would function as well as possible. Thus they called on public authorities for a laissez-faire policy of "hands-off" of markets. With the breakdown of the economy in the 1930s, laissez-faire economics seemed discredited and the activist policies of Keynesian economics dominated until the doldrums of the 1970s. In the 1980s a renewed version of laissez-faire economics regained ascendency. This chapter examines the original laissez-faire economics and its eclipse. Chapter 3 focuses on Keynesian economics, chapter 4 charts the revival of laissez faire in its new form of "conservative economic individualism," and chapter 5 evaluates the successes and failures of the Reagan administration's version of CEI.

THE CLASSICAL ORIGINS OF LAISSEZ-FAIRE ECONOMICS

Modern economics is usually dated from the 1776 publication of Adam Smith's *The Wealth of Nations*.[1] This book initiated a tradition in economic thought which continued through John Stuart Mill in the mid-nineteenth century and has become known as the classical school. The core of classical economic analysis is the model of competitive market capitalism. The classical school believed that an uncoerced person could be depended upon to act rationally to maximize his or her individual self-interest; and more importantly, that an automatic, self-regulating mechanism to manage economic affairs was possible if it were built on basic human nature. Free individual choices were expected to overcome scarcity and result in the common good through the automatic adjustments of free exchange in markets. The forces of competition ensured that the economy produced those goods which people desired and that those goods were produced in the most efficient way. This was the result of the "invisible hand" of competition.

Thus, from Adam Smith to this day, mainstream economists have argued that the best way for economic problems to be confronted is to rely on the individual's pursuit of self-interest in a private property system, regulated by the forces of market competition. The government should simply act as the neutral umpire of the rules of the economic game. In order to have an income each person has to provide something (product, service, or labor) which others want and are willing to pay for; and through a process of voluntary exchange, overall production would be maximized while at the same time protecting individual freedom.

But what prevents a system of private property based on self-interest from degenerating into a jungle, where the powerful oppress the weak? According to classical economists, competition is the great regulator of economic life. The forces of competition ensure that the economy produces those goods which people desire and in the quantities desired. Although they were not blind to the faults and machinations of business people, they argued that little harm could be done in a society dominated by freely competitive enterprise. If producers tried to sell products at a higher price than the market price, consumers would buy from others. No one would buy at a price above the market price. On the other hand, if one attempted to pay workers less than the going wage, they would leave to take higher-wage employment. Therefore, the forces of competition would ensure that workers were paid the going wage and that consumers got their products at the lowest possible price.

As each individual attempts to maximize individual well-being, society, the sum of these individuals, benefits. Thus, private profit and public welfare become reconciled through the automatic and impersonal forces of competition.

The fact that all economies, including the most advanced industrial ones, were characterized by widespread poverty, unemployment, and low wages posed a problem to the classical economists, just as the persistence of these conditions is problematic for today's laissez-faire theorists. The claim that free competition ensured life-sustenance seemed to ring hollow. Classical economists explained these problems in two ways. First, there were countries which restricted the free operation of markets. If these countries would remove the restrictions to the free play of self-interest, much of the poverty would be eliminated by the resulting economic growth. Second, in those countries with free market systems, continuing poverty was explained as the result of the niggardliness of physical nature and the improvidence of human nature. The first was enshrined as the law of diminishing returns and the second as the law of population.

Adam Smith, Thomas Malthus, David Ricardo, and John Stuart Mill all thought that poverty resulted from the interaction of physical scarcity and population growth. In each version of classical economic theory, economic growth culminates in a stationary state where growth in per capita income is zero and wages have settled at the subsistence level. The wage level tends to subsistence because of the behavior of population, or the supply of labor, in the long run: an increase in wages brings forth a proportionate increase in population which drives wages back down through the forces of competition. Higher wages increase population through lower mortality because families can afford better nutrition and health care.

The origin of this dismal view of life's prospects is often attributed to Malthus. However, the notion that improved living conditions would be swamped by a resultant increase in population had been a familiar one in England for some time. In 1761 the Reverend Robert Wallace, famous minister of Greyfriars' church in Edinburgh and good friend of Adam Smith, published *Various Prospects of Mankind, Nature, and Providence*. He argued that people were always inclined to marry and multiply their numbers until the food supply was barely enough to sustain all of them. This book was so well known that Richard Godwin spent considerable space in his *Political Justice* refuting the population argument. It was Godwin's book in turn that Malthus's *Essay on Population* was directly aimed at countering.

Adam Smith's views were not quite so pessimistic as Wallace's. He did believe that economic growth eventually led to a stationary state where wages would return to subsistence. Smith softened this picture, however, by arguing that people do not breed to their physiological capacity, but are regulated by customary living standards. Thus the subsistence level in England is much higher than in China. In addition, as long as economic growth is maintained wages will stay above subsistence since the demand for labor will be growing faster than the supply of labor. Since the threat of the stationary state is off in the distant future, the basic tenor of Smith's work is one of optimism. Wages will remain high if investment continues at a rapid rate; investment will be maintained if the free market economy is not restricted domestically or internationally.

But Smith's optimism was not shared by Malthus, who was to have a much greater influence over classical economists on this issue. The success of Malthus's *An Essay on the Principle of Population, as It Affects the Future Improvement of Society, With Remarks on the Speculations of Mr. Godwin, M. Condorcet, and other Writers* (1798) must be understood in terms of a latent pessimism in the whole body of economic liberalism which Adam Smith epitomized.[2] The problem of the scarcity of resources lay at the core of Hobbes's *Leviathan* (1651), where the scarcity of nature meant that one person's gain was another's loss. Nonetheless, from the time of the supremacy of Parliament in 1688 to the French Revolution in 1789, the battle of wits between people and nature was generally regarded with optimism, for English thought was dominated by the theory of progress. This optimism can be seen in the complete title of Smith's work, *An Inquiry into the Nature and Causes of the Wealth of Nations.* It was Malthus who transformed the contest from a lighthearted sparring match into a struggle to the death. His essay on population could have been entitled "An Inquiry into the Nature and Causes of the Poverty of Nations." To the Hobbesian scarcity of physical nature, Malthus added the improvidence and perversity of human nature. Whereas Smith had focused upon how a free economy would channel the acquisitive aspect of human nature to overcome scarcity, Malthus found the roots of poverty in that same human nature.

The classical economists and their later laissez-faire followers have continued to use arguments about the perversity of human nature to explain free market economies' inability to overcome poverty, and these same arguments have been used to demonstrate that major changes in the social and economic institutions of a free market society are impossible.

Since the analytical positions of the 1980s are the direct descendents of the arguments of the nineteenth century it is worth spending time to review the classical arguments.

An important goal of Malthus's theory was an attack on the English Poor Laws. This set of laws had originated in an Act of Parliament in 1536 during the reign of Henry VIII and had been extended many times thereafter. They provided for relief of the poor by local government units with the cost covered by taxes levied on landed property. In 1795 the Speenhamland Act amended the laws to provide supplementary assistance to employed workers whose wages were below a minimum subsistence calculated by the Poor Law commissioners. By Malthus's time increased relief rolls had greatly raised the burden of the tax rates. Malthus maintained that the Poor Laws damaged not only the rich but the poor as well, and he argued his case with such eloquence and effectiveness that Pitt dropped his plan for family allowances and Whitbread his plan for public housing.[3] The new Poor Law of 1834 embodied the spirit of Malthus[4] as expressed in his eloquent criticism of the previous law:

> The poor-laws of England tend to depress the general condition of the poor in these two ways. Their first obvious tendency is to increase population without increasing the food for its support. A poor man may marry with little or no prospect of being able to support a family in independence. They may be said therefore in some measure to create the poor which they maintain.
>
> Secondly, the quantity of provisions consumed in workhouses upon a part of the society that cannot in general be considered as the most valuable part diminishes the shares that would otherwise belong to more industrious and more worthy members.
>
> Hard as it may appear in individual instances, dependent poverty ought to be held disgraceful. Such a stimulus seems to be absolutely necessary to promote the happiness of the great mass of mankind, and every general attempt to weaken this stimulus, however benevolent its apparent intention, will always defeat its own purpose.[5]

The implication of these comments is central to understanding the laissez-faire treatment of poverty. While there may be some hope for the poor, they will derive no benefit from policies which tamper with the institutions of a free market society. Any radical change in the institutions would be even worse, a view influenced by the French Revolution which first attracted, then repelled, Malthus and most middle- and upper-class Englishmen. It was not only the Terror that worried Malthus but also that the Revolution encouraged a belief in the perfectibility of human nature. His essay's title even refers to Godwin and Condorcet, two of the best-known French "Perfectibilians." Malthus's distaste for the French Revolution and all its works was stated with force and passion.

> To see the human mind in one of the most enlightened nations of the world, and after a lapse of some thousand years, debased by such a fermentation of disgusting passions, of fear, cruelty, malice, revenge, ambition, madness and folly, as would have disgraced the most savage nation in the most barbarous age must have been such

a tremendous shock to [Godwin's] ideas of the necessary and inevitable progress of the human mind that nothing but the firmest conviction of the truth of his principles, in spite of all appearances, could have withstood.[6]

Godwin had posited that human nature was infinitely perfectible and all present-day evils could be traced to the corrupting influence of bad social institutions. He envisioned a future communitarian society where love was the guiding principle of human behavior. Malthus found these ideas particularly unacceptable because they contradicted Adam Smith's position that self-interest led to the common good and because they were based on the abolition of private property, which Malthus considered the very basis of civilization. Malthus used his population theory to prove that Godwin's vision was unworkable and undesirable. His position was simple and clear:

> Population, when unchecked, increases in a geometrical ratio. Subsistence increases only in an arithmetical ratio.
>
> ... This natural inequality of the two powers of population and of production in the earth and that great law of our nature which must constantly keep their effects equal form the great difficulty that to me appears insurmountable in the way to the perfectibility of society.[7]

Malthus's belief in private property derived from his view that only the necessity of supporting one's self and family drives people to work and makes them limit their family size. He argued "there can be no well-founded hope of obtaining a large produce from the soil but under a system of private property." It is visionary to believe that "any stimulus short of that which is excited in man by the desire of providing for himself and family and of bettering his condition of life" can overcome the "natural indolence of mankind."[8] In a communal society, "the corn is plucked before it is ripe, or secreted in unfair proportions.... Provisions no longer flow in for the support of the mother with the large family.... at length self-love resumes his wonted empire and lords it triumphant over the world." Thus, the most perfect society imaginable would necessarily degenerate into "a society divided into a class of proprietors, and a class of labourers, and with self-love the mainspring of the great machine."[9]

According to Malthus there is very little hope indeed, and perfectibility is an illusion. In the first edition of the *Essay* he saw only vice and misery as restraints on population growth, concluding one discussion with "It has appeared that from the inevitable laws of our nature, some human beings must suffer from want. These are the unhappy persons who, in the great lottery of life, have drawn a blank."[10] In the second edition (1803) he introduced moral restraint as a possible, but not probable, limitation on population growth and therefore on poverty. The only hope was in moral education of the poor by the middle- and upper-classes:

> Among the poor themselves, its effects would be still more important. That the principal and most permanent cause of poverty has little or no direct relation to forms of government, or the unequal division of property; and that, as the rich do not in reality possess the power of finding employment and maintenance for the poor, the poor cannot, in the nature of things, possess the right to demand them; are important truths flowing from the principle of population, which, when properly explained, would by no means be above the most ordinary comprehensions. And it is evident that every man in the lower class of society who became acquainted with these truths, would be disposed to bear the distresses in which he might be involved with more patience; would feel less discontent and irritation at the government and the higher classes of society, on account of his poverty; would be on all occasions less disposed to insubordination and turbulence; and if he received assistance, either from any public institution or from the hand of private charity, he would receive it with more thankfulness, and more justly appreciate its value. The mere knowledge of these truths, even if they did not operate sufficiently to produce any marked change in the prudential habits of the poor with regard to marriage, would still have a most beneficial effect on their conduct in a political light.[11]

Both of the other major classical economists, David Ricardo and John Stuart Mill, incorporated Malthus's population principle into their economic theories. It aided Ricardo's attack upon the Poor Laws and was an important pillar of his income distribution theory. Mill was an ardent social reformer who believed that education of the poor and technological development in contraception would allow the poor to restrict their numbers and thus overcome poverty. Mill's sense of optimism echoed the earlier views of Smith, adding the possibility that conscious policy could diminish the scourge of poverty. Economic analysis in the classical tradition ended with Mill, and without a resolution of the poverty issue.

There was a similar standoff in the debates over other economic problems. Is the free market economy stable and able to ensure maximum employment over time, or is it unstable and given to gluts or recessions when unemployment rises and goods cannot be sold? Malthus held that gluts were not only possible but common, while Jean Baptiste Say maintained that free market economies could not generate gluts for "the mere circumstance of the creation of one product immediately opens a vent for other products."[12]

Nonetheless the view that the free market economy embodied the solution to economic problems had a firm foundation; it remained for the neoclassical economists to turn attention to understanding the workings of the market economy in greater detail. Their technical contributions were substantial, but they also served to distract attention from the persistence of problems such as poverty, instability, and unemployment.

THE NEOCLASSICAL ORIGINS OF
LAISSEZ-FAIRE ECONOMICS

"Neoclassical" economics, beginning in the 1870s, turned away from the concern with growth and poverty and concentrated instead on the problem of efficient resource allocation. In the static neoclassical world, input supplies, including labor, were taken as given and ideas about population receded into an ad hoc explanation whenever the free market was blamed for continuing poverty. For example, in 1870, W. Stanley Jevons commented on the continued existence of "pauperism" in England one hundred years after the industrial revolution began:

Such a melancholy fact ... is a verification of the [economists'] unheeded warnings; it is precisely what Malthus would have predicted of a population supplied with easily earned wealth . . . and bribed by mistaken benevolence of the richer classes into neglect of the future. . . . The wise precautions of the present poor law are to a great extent counteracted by the mistaken humanity of charitable people. . . . Nothing so surely as indiscriminate charity tends to create and perpetuate a class living in hopeless poverty. It is well known that those towns where charitable institutions and charitable people most abound are precisely those where the helpless poor are most numerous.[13]

It did not occur to Jevons that the causation might run in the reverse direction: an abundance of poor people might call forth a large number of charitable institutions and good works.

Alfred Marshall held that Malthus's "position with regard to the supply of population . . . remains substantially valid."[14] However, he believed that in England technological change in agriculture, education of the working classes, and improved birth control techniques had combined to raise living standards.[15]

With population as their explanation of the anomalous continuation of poverty, neoclassical economists turned their attention to a different concern, the development and articulation of the technical characteristics of the market economy. This effort required a number of choices in how to view the economy. The choices were made partly for their simplicity, partly for their descriptive realism, and partly for the kinds of analysis they facilitated; and they determined the course of the development of neoclassical economics.

Perhaps the central idea was "equilibrium." The market economy was treated as a system which was stable, and if it were shocked out of its given state, perhaps by a crop failure, automatic forces would be generated to restore stability or equilibrium. Equilibrium is an "end-state," and its use in economic analysis focused thinking on that end state, making the problems of disequilibrium, the persistence of poverty, and the causes of economic growth less central. In addition there was a natural tendency to focus on the creative elements of market operation, rather than its destructive elements. For example, if the disequilibrium or instability is caused by a new technical innovation, one assumes the destruction of older and less efficient industries is outweighed by the creative elements of the innovation.

A second technical category is "marginal analysis," the analysis of the effect of small, incremental changes. On the one hand, marginal analysis using the calculus allows a rigorous view of the problem faced by an individual attempting to maximize personal satisfaction (or "utility" as economists call it) or of the firm wishing to maximize profit. On the other hand, its effect is very similar to that of Malthus's views on radical institutional change in the economy: the entire issue of structural change is defined to lie outside of the concerns of economics. The focus for these economists was literally on marginal or very small adjustments in the economy. The motto inscribed on the title page of Marshall's *Principles* was *Natura Non Facit Saltum* (Nature Makes No Leaps).

Neoclassical economists analyzed the conditions of the supply of goods to a market, and the demand for goods in that same market, again using equilibrium and marginal constructs to frame the analysis. The process of buying and selling would drive a product's market price to the level where the amount sellers wanted to sell equalled the amount that buyers wanted to buy. So supply and demand determined the price and quantity sold of every good and service in the economy, including labor.

By analogy with the market for wheat or for pencils, neoclassical economists held that the macroeconomy was also guided by supply and demand. In particular, in what came to be called "Say's Law" after J. B. Say, supply was seen to create its own demand in the national economy. That is, it was assumed that a seller sold in the market to get the funds necessary to buy other goods or services. Since every seller was also a buyer, given free markets, the operation of Say's Law would lead economies to equilibrium at full employment of resources; any unused resource, such as labor, would see its price drop until enough of it was used in production to provide full employment. Only if the owner of a resource refused to supply it at the free market price would it remain unemployed.

In his equilibrium and marginal analysis of the behavior of firms in markets, Marshall distinguished between short-period and long-period equilibrium. Because he was concerned with influencing business behavior, Marshall concentrated on problems of short-period equilibrium. He considered long-period equilibrium of purely theoretical interest with no practical use. It remained to Leon Walras, the inventor of general equilibrium analysis, to cast the theory in terms of the long period. He demonstrated mathematically that in the long period (a conceptual time period defined as the time required for all production inputs to be perfectly variable), a free market system will attain Adam Smith's optimal welfare equilibrium. The assumption and conditions necessary for this "ideal state" are so restrictive that the theory was considered of little practical significance. However, as we will see later, it has played a major role in shaping the vision of economists in the mid-twentieth century. Since neoclassical economists constructed their models on the pattern of the physical sciences, economics became ever more mathematical and general in its formulations as it built on the work of Marshall and Walras.

These concerns combined with the earlier views on competition and elements of classical analysis to yield a particular economics, but also a particular social philosophy. We term it the "free enterprise" or "laissez-faire" tradition within economics. This was the dominant view of economics in both England and the United States until the 1930s, and can be summarized under a few propositions held by these economists.

(1) People are motivated primarily by self-interest, described best by Adam Smith as an "innate propensity to truck, barter, and exchange."

(2) A free market economy, through the forces of competition, converts that self-interested behavior into the common good by forcing profit-maximizing firms to produce what utility-maximizing consumers demand, and to do so in the most efficient way.

(3) A free market economy requires freedom of choice—of where to invest, of what job to take, of what product to purchase, and so on.

(4) Problems in the economy, including poverty, are due either to government interference with the free market or are the result of physical and human nature. The scarcity in physical nature requires time to overcome. The perversity of human nature means some people will always fail and thus be poor; some people are lazy, immoral, or improvident.

(5) Public authorities can and should do little besides enforce the rules of the game and provide those goods, e.g., defense, that the private sector is unable to produce.

(6) There is an inherent stability in the market economy, and since supply will create its own demand, that equilibrium stability will generally be at a position of full employment. What may appear as destructive effects of market operation, the loss of jobs or industries, are transitory by-products of the markets' creativity in constantly forcing increases in efficiency and productivity.

(7) The propositions that hold for national economies hold in the international sphere as well. A regime of free trade through international markets with little government involvement will be most successful in improving world income.

ECONOMIC THEORY AS SOCIAL PHILOSOPHY

In the case of the free competition–laissez-faire view of the economy, the technical and analytical became intermingled with personal interests and underlying views on society. As a result, this tradition, just as other economic traditions, is also at least partly a social philosophy.[16] As a social philosophy, or ideology, the laissez-faire economic theory that had been dominant in the industrialized West served two essential and related functions. It acted to restrict the scope for "scientific" inquiry and it served as a policy stance for molding society in its image, while legitimating certain aspects of the status quo.

By restricting the scope of economic inquiry to marginal analysis and equilibrium, neoclassical analysis downplayed the importance of instability, destructive effects, unemployment, and poverty. The first three were either temporary, short-run phenomena or were manifestations of the creativity of capitalism's drive for efficiency. In the case of poverty, laissez-faire economic theory focused attention on the niggardliness of physical nature and the improvidence of human nature, just as Malthus had. Universally applicable hypotheses were devised which transcended institutional, systemic, and historical variations. The theory focused potential economic research upon and effectively constrained attention to the behavior of individuals and households. Thus, people were poor because they had made the wrong decisions on questions such as family size, lacked the necessary ambition, or simply had bad luck in their choices. This provided a universal explanation for poverty which exonerated particular economic institutions from blame.

Concentration on the actions of atomistic actors camouflaged the existence and exercise of power in the economic system and failed to admit the possibility that poverty was perpetuated if not created by social institutions which benefit certain social classes at the expense of others. It overlooked the possibility that creative and hard-working individuals might be forced into poverty and unemployment by the instability of the market system or by the destruction of their livelihood through the march of the market. Ultimately, the theory became a conservative defense of the status quo. Poverty, caused by the improvidence of human nature, can be reduced only by encouraging people to overcome their natural indolence. Changing economic structures will make no difference, unless existing social institutions misdirect the decision making of rational individuals. Indeed, efforts to change economic structures would simply interfere with the market's creativity and would only heighten instability since markets are inherently stable.

Economics developed primarily within the individualist-rationalist societies of England and the United States which emphasize achievement and responsibility of the individual. Free market views certainly resonated well within this tradition. An explanation of poverty as a result of flaws in human nature fit very well with its values. Hard work, thrift, and prudence had always been seen as the keys to success and failure had been attributed to an absence of these virtues. Systemic causes of the failure to overcome poverty had been ignored; instead, blame had been placed on personal characteristics.

According to free market economics an absence of self-esteem has nothing to do with the social conditions, but results from the failure of the individual. In hard times, when one loses a job or when one's business is forced into bankruptcy, there is no societal obligation. Individuals must pick themselves up and enter the job market to find any job which is available. Freedom must be exercised.

Government must avoid interfering with the stability of the

economy and its natural tendency to equilibrium at full employment. Cyclical ups and downs of the economy might be necessary to reallocate resources more efficiently, and government intervention in past cycles merely made things worse.

Freedom must also be fostered, and government interference in the economy must be avoided. Any effort to control the growth of markets, such as the stock market during the 1920s, should be avoided, for freedom of choice in a competitive economy will lead to the best possible economic results.

During the 1920s this strain of economic philosophy became linked with a conservative Republicanism best exemplified by Calvin Coolidge.[17] And the boom of the 1920s, with its high growth rates, increasing consumption, creation of ever newer financial mechanisms and consequent growth of the financial sector, seemed to validate this economic and social philosophy. Reality conformed to the model's assumptions and there could be no questioning such a success story. The creativity of the market system was manifest to all.

THE DECLINE OF LAISSEZ-FAIRE ECONOMICS

The theory of a free market economy dominated the thought of economists until the 1930s. Actual policy was never so completely laissez faire as economists would have wished, for policymakers were more realistic. They and the voting public were influenced not only by the individualist strain in American culture, but also by its communitarian elements.[18] Despite the theories of economists, government had participated in the economy from the beginning: it built canals, gave land to settlers under the Homestead Act, passed the Sherman and the Clayton Antitrust Acts, and regulated the railways and the airways. And no government, not even imperial England, operated under a regime of free international trade.

From the 1930s until the 1980s the laissez-faire theory of macroeconomics was pushed to the margins of mainstream economics.[19] Certainly a major factor in this eclipse was the Depression which fundamentally challenged the claims of that social philosophy, both on the causes of poverty and on the assumption of full-employment stability. Those who were thrown into poverty during the Depression had not changed overnight from thrifty and industrious workers to lazy and indolent loafers. Could the rash of bank failures, farm foreclosures, and business bankruptcies occur in an economy that was truly characterized by stability and efficiency? In addition it became apparent that the theory could not account for the major problems faced by actual economies: monopoly, externalities, unequal opportunity, in addition to unemployment.

The market economy as it actually developed had an Achilles' heel: competition tended to self-destruct. It turned out to be a foot race with the winner getting larger and larger and the losers dropping out of the race. This process accelerated during the late 1800s and again in the 1920s. The U.S. economy became characterized both by largeness and by the concentration of activity among a few firms in each industry. As a result, price competition was replaced by competition in advertising and product differentiation. To the classical economists, competition was the key force ensuring that the market economy was efficient, so the decline of competition was a severe blow to the credibility of laissez-faire theory. This led to calls from those outside the laissez-faire social philosophy for government intervention to restore competition through antitrust and pro-competition policies, or through the imposition of government regulation as a substitute for competition.

Externalities were the second free market problem that laissez-faire theory failed to address. An externality is a cost or benefit not included in the prices determined by the market. For example, a firm's cost of producing an auto might be $3,000. With a $1,000 markup, the sales price would be $4,000. However, in producing the auto the firm dumps waste in the local river that will cost $500 to clean up. This $500 is a cost to those who use the river for swimming, fishing, or drinking. As industrialization and population density increased during the growth of the U.S., so did externalities. And again, without government intervention the market failures were not corrected nor the external costs taken into account.

Economists also came to realize that for a free market to allow self-esteem and real freedom, as well as encourage efficiency, some degree of equality of opportunity was necessary. Inequalities in income, power, and wealth made claims to equality of opportunity highly dubious. All citizens ostensibly had ample freedom of choice; however, only those with an income adequate to implement their choices fully enjoyed the freedom. Someone without skills or a stable job had few decent choices: a little more to eat or a few more clothes, to continue in a dead end job or try to get some type of dole, to vote for someone who would neglect her interests or to abstain. And, of course, the poor family's child had little equality of opportunity when compared with the rich family's child. Again, this realization led to calls for public policies that would tend to equalize economic opportunities.

The most serious problem that plagued the free market economy was periodic recurrence of massive unemployment, the clearest manifestation of the failure of a free market system. To worry over the efficiency of resource allocation in the face of large-scale and prolonged unemployment seemed as important as rearranging the deck chairs on the Titanic. When the U.S. unemployment rate hit 25 percent in 1933, economists and policymakers were ripe for a new vision and a new social philosophy. In the public's eye the fundamental problem was that after 150 years of economic growth under a free market economy, two-thirds of the population were still "ill-housed and ill-fed." The easy assumption about the individual's sole responsibility for poverty rang hollow as millions of hard-working persons suddenly found their life-sustenance severely threatened.

In addition, this failure occurred not just in the U.S. but throughout the whole market system. Rather than growth and progress being transmitted by market-based international institutions, these institutions were a central factor in propagating a world-wide depression.

The New Deal–Keynesian economics consensus that emerged out of the 1930s provided a theory and program to save the market economy by utilizing government intervention to correct the first of its four failures—unemployment.* It is to that story we turn in chapter 3.

---

*The other three failures of the unfettered market system have been dealt with—however inadequately—piecemeal during the past forty years.

3. The Triumph of Keynesianism

When the classical and neoclassical analyses failed to provide acceptable answers to the Depression and the problems of monopoly, externalities, and equality of opportunity, there was a vacuum. And policy making, like nature, abhors a vacuum. In the process of recovering from the Depression, a new analysis and set of policies took form, based on the work of the English economist, John Maynard Keynes. His followers, the Keynesians, inherited the influence and respect which had been the neoclassical economists' before them. They also inherited responsibilities for the economy which they shouldered quite successfully, at least through the 1960s.

This chapter traces the development of economic theory and policy from the thirties, when a new era in economic thought commenced, to 1973–75, when the Keynesian dominance waned. Gradually during these four decades Keynesian economic ideas permeated the thought of the majority of economists and government policymakers, and all was well with the economic world—or so it seemed.

UNSTABLE BACKGROUND—STABLE ADVANCE

The period from 1930 to 1975 was hardly placid. These forty-five years of the mid-twentieth century saw the first days of a depression in the Western world that threatened the collapse of the entire free market system. Unemployment in the U.S. rose sharply, hit astronomical figures, and refused to drop, averaging 18 percent from 1930 to 1939. Glaring inequities of wealth and income became stark realities in the face of bread lines and wide-spread poverty. Meeting basic needs was only a dream for many. There was a rash of mortgage foreclosures that expelled countless small farmers from their land and sent them west out of desperation only to find the bitter taste of *Grapes of Wrath* and to lose what pride and self-esteem they had. All of this occurred in the midst of an absurd idleness of capital equipment, despite the obvious need for production.

The problems of this first critical period were then exchanged for new ones in another cataclysmic event: World War II. This truly world-wide war ravaged the whole of Europe, much of Asia, and left few "neutral" countries unscathed. While carried out mainly on foreign soil, the war nonetheless had a major impact on the lives and livelihood of North Americans.

The fifties provided something of a breathing spell in spite of the Korean War and three Eisenhower recessions; and the final decade of these forty-five years brought the first days of Camelot, attractively bedecked with the apparel of an upswelling idealism and the belief in the possibility of a better world and a better life for all peoples. But while engaged in an all-out war on poverty at home, Camelot and the Great Society were caught offguard and destroyed in the distant swamps of Vietnam.

From another perspective, these four decades comprised a period of steady progress for the profession of economics: these were years of increasing knowledge about the American economy and improving policy skills designed to avoid major disruptions like the crash of 1929 and the Depression of the thirties. These were the halcyon days of the Keynesian economists, who convincingly showed that government could have a beneficial stabilizing impact on a growing economy. While support for Keynesianism may have been tentative in the 1930s, the recurring success and reinforcement of the Keynesian approach prompted even Richard Nixon, himself an inheritor of Republican laissez-faire tradition, to concede that "we are all Keynesians now." So a seemingly impregnable consensus on theory and policy was built from its fledgling days during the Depression years to its triumphal achievements of the sixties. What follows is the story of the construction of this consensus.

CONCEPTION AND CONSTRUCTION OF THE NEW DEAL–
KEYNESIAN CONSENSUS: THE STORY UNFOLDS

The story begins in October and November of 1929, the months of the stock market crash and the initial phase of the Depression. A three-year period followed when bank failures would become commmonplace (9,000 out of the 24,700 banks in existence in 1930 had gone under by the end of 1933);[1] when jobs would dissipate as if into thin air (unemployment rose to 25 percent in 1933);[2] when debts would become insufferable, and when prices would begin to drop (wholesale prices in the U.S. dropped 16 percent by the summer of 1930). The price decline was a major obstacle to recovery because business expectations of profits, which influence orders to manufacturers, were continually lowered since no one could foresee when, and at what level, the fall would come to an end.[3] It also meant that the real value of debts rose, making repayment more difficult. The most frightening aspect of all was that the system could apparently do nothing to help itself.

Traditional economists of the day believed sincerely that the free market economy was self-regulating, self-stabilizing, and self-sustaining. While the industrial world was suffering this disaster, economists were busy writing about the theoretical implications of assuming perfect competition versus imperfect competition in their models of static resource allocation. During 1932–35 the main British economics journal, the *Economic Journal,* published only three articles on the subject of unemployment. The same was true of the *American Economic Review* and of doctoral dissertations in the United States.[4] In 1932, Professor Edwin Cannan of the London School of Economics said in his presidential address to the Royal Economic Society, " ... more persons can be employed if they work for less remuneration. General unemployment appears when asking too much is a general phenomenon ... [the world] should learn to submit to declines of money-income without squealing."[5] Thus their only answer to the Great Depression was that workers lower their wage demands, and they assumed that the economy would then return to a full-employment equilibrium. In reality they were at a total loss to explain this seemingly perpetual downspin, and they were even less able to prescribe appropriate remedies.

In the United States it was not until 1933, when Franklin Delano Roosevelt assumed the presidential helm, that the deterioration in living conditions and economic understanding began to turn itself around. This was certainly not because Roosevelt had been blessed with a vision of the intricate workings of the economic system, but because he was a creature of his times and realized, along with his counterparts in European capitols, that only one economic agent could possibly provide an avenue of escape for the system: the central government itself.[6]

It had by then become acutely obvious that the isolated, atomistic activity of individual producers and consumers was not going to generate the motive force for economic recovery, at least not in any acceptable time frame. Although there had been a long history of government involvement in the economy, Roosevelt proceeded to inject the government into previously unacceptable areas. For example, during the Roosevelt years the government checked industry's abuse of labor by establishing minimum wages and maximum hours. Labor unions were endorsed and protected in the wide-ranging National Labor Relations Act (Wagner Act). Various public works projects were supported and the government employed people in activities previously handled exclusively by private industry. Public utilities came under strict and far-reaching regulation to prevent abuse of their monopoly position. The government intervened in agriculture to protect farmers by introducing legislation to support prices. The Social Security Administration was organized. And finally the government began to play a role in the extraction and use of the nation's natural resource and power supplies, as evidenced in the Tennessee Valley Authority.[7]

And even as Roosevelt was hard at work getting the government involved intimately in the economy, John Maynard Keynes was establishing the intellectual underpinnings of this approach to recovery. Roosevelt was aware of neither the substance nor of the potential impact of Keynes's work when the two met in 1934; he nevertheless was implementing the very types of policies suggested in the economist's revolutionary volume *The General Theory of Employment, Interest, and Money*, which was published in 1936.

Indeed, Roosevelt's reaction after the meeting with Keynes was, "I saw your friend Keynes. He left a whole rigamarole of

figures. He must be a mathematician rather than a political economist." Keynes's reaction was similarly laudatory, saying that he had
"supposed the President was more literate, economically speaking."[8]

The General Theory

Keynes's argument in *The General Theory* was economic her-
esy. Economists had believed that free market economies were
self-stabilizing; but Keynes was now arguing that such laissez-faire
systems were inherently unstable. His argument, in essence, was
rather simple. The classical economists before Keynes's time had
assumed and had even abstractly "proven" that through the medium of markets, tens of thousands of economic participants
would go about their daily economic activities in such a way as to
achieve, unknowingly, a full-employment economy. But Keynes
now argued that this theory was only a special case of a more
general theory; and that equilibrium with unemployment was the
general expectation.

One of the cornerstones of Keynes's theory was his treatment
of investment. Classical and neoclassical economists believed that
the level of investment was closely tied to the interest rate, that as
the interest rate dropped borrowing for investment would increase. If an economy started to fall into a recession, the interest
rate would decline, causing investment to increase, thus preventing the recession. Keynes, on the other hand, argued forcefully
that investment decisions were much more closely linked with
what he called "animal spirits." The term suggested fragility and
instability, even when it was, in large measure, narrowed to refer
to profit expectations or business optimism. Keynes had ample
evidence for his case in the Depression, for even though investment was sorely needed and the interest rate had fallen below one
percent, there was still minimal investment. No sane business
would invest, regardless of the interest rate, if convinced that the
project would incur losses.

In addition to his argument about the interest rate and investment, Keynes rejected the neoclassical notion that wage reductions would lead to increases in employment. Instead, he argued
that wages are a part of aggregate demand, in addition to being

production costs. If wages fall, aggregate demand and sales will fall. If sales fall, profits will decline and firms will demand less labor. The Depression experience made these points convincing to all who were not wedded to classical or neoclassical economics.

Thus Keynes argued that decentralized decision making by millions of consumers and businesses would add up to full employment only by accident. There are no automatic mechanisms pushing the capitalist economy toward full employment. To Keynes it was not at all surprising, therefore, that the economy was mired in a state of high unemployment with no mechanism to lift itself out.

Keynes, however, did not leave the economy to flounder. He proposed that the necessary ingredient for stability was appropriate government fiscal intervention, consisting primarily of expenditure and/or taxation policy. He showed that such policies could have a "multiplier" effect on the economy; so the government could ease the recession-racked economy back toward a full-employment equilibrium by providing the initial stimulus to restore confidence and return some much-needed purchasing power to participants in the economy. As a result, any unemployment caused by deficient aggregate demand could be overcome by government action to increase aggregate demand.

A hypothetical example can provide a clear illustration of how such a government program would work. Suppose a town has several industries, none producing at capacity because they simply cannot sell their wares. As a result unemployment has risen. In an effort to forestall layoffs, workers have allowed wages to be lowered, but the layoffs continue. Banks, which have excess money to loan out, reduce the interest rate in hopes that some businesses will find an opportunity to invest the funds, create jobs, and start the system on the road to recovery; but there are no takers. The town's economy is stagnant and a spirit of pessimism is pervasive. But the town council has an idea (let us assume this town is autonomous and thus has control over the money supply); they want to restore peoples' optimism by pumping purchasing power into the economy. They plan to hire some workers to build a much-needed bridge over the local river. To carry out this plan they need workers, cement, steel, lumber, and assorted other products. There is now an increased product demand for the industries producing cement, steel, and lumber; and in order to meet the new demand, they must increase production by using some of their presently excess plant capacity and by hiring workers to operate the machines. This may not seem like a long-term answer to the problem, but now the newly hired workers have received paychecks and they in turn go out to buy goods they have done without. The multiplier effect of the bridge expenditures comes into operation. Surprisingly, the cement, steel, and lumber industries do not experience the expected fall in demand when the town council project comes to an end. Instead the workers are now refurbishing their homes, buying new furniture, appliances, and cars, and the industries find that they can continue their increased level of production. The people begin to feel that the bad times are behind and the good times are ahead. As optimism rises, new investment takes place because now businesses anticipate realizing a profit over and above the interest rate of their loans; and unemployment is diminished further. Eventually, with the appropriate council policies the town will achieve a full-employment economy and the citizens will have left behind their hopelessness and despair. Also, and importantly, the town's project will have paid for itself through higher tax revenues from the new activity. Thus there will be no deficit for the council to pay off.

This hypothetical town illustrates some crucial aspects of Keynes's prolific and creative writings. For our purposes, he contributed two vital concepts that permeated the new mainstream economic analysis until the seventies. First, he argued that the market economy was by itself fundamentally unstable. Second, responsible and discretionary government intervention could stabilize the economy and maintain full-employment equilibrium. This macroeconomic stability would allow free markets to play their role as the most efficient mechanism for allocating scarce resources. Our own work and that of a group called "Post-Keynesians" take Keynes's insight of inherent market instability as our point of departure. Keynes's argument for the stabilizing role of discretionary policy became the basis of "Keynesian" analysis in the U.S.[9]

It must be emphasized that Keynes focused on the immediate deficiency of aggregate demand that made full-employment production unprofitable. In that situation, government borrowing and spending of idle funds would set the economy in motion again. The policy analysis was clearly focused on the short run and did not deal with long-run questions. But with 25 percent unemployment, Keynes was justified in declaring "in the long run we are all dead."

Before examining in greater detail U.S. Keynesianism, Keynes's other contributions to economic thinking should be noted. He did not confine his thinking to issues existing within national boundaries. He had written critically of the reparations agreement that was forced on Germany at the end of World War I, predicting the instability it would engender. And at the end of World War II he was a central figure in establishing at Bretton Woods the institutions that have guided the world economy in the postwar period, the International Monetary Fund (IMF), the World Bank, and the proposed International Trade Organization which became GATT (General Agreement on Tariffs and Trade). He envisioned institutions which would foster world stability by facilitating the maintenance of aggregate demand in the industrial countries. The current world instability underlines the importance of the international financial system.

The New Deal-Keynesian Consensus

Though FDR engaged the government more deeply in traditionally private-sector activities than ever before, and though conditions were improving slowly, the real proof of the Keynesian demand-management propositions came with the monumental spending requirements of World War II. In short order the vacant factories were taken out of mothballs, dusted off, and retooled, and were soon producing the equipment needed for the U.S. war effort. Idle men and women were either handed a rifle to use or were put at the seat of a rifle-making machine. There was practically no unemployment. The war experience was thus the first piece of clear evidence that the government could have a major impact on aggregate demand and could offset the demand deficiency of the private sector.

Production for war, however, did not serve the daily needs of consumers in the U.S., and many feared that with the end of the war the economy would lapse back into a depression. But the high employment levels during the war had brought money into the hands of people which they had not been able to spend because of the comprehensive rationing programs. Therefore, when the war ended, the pent-up consumer demand that had been building during the war years was unleashed and resulted in such a flurry of economic activity that the economy easily maintained its healthy full-employment position, aided in some degree by the complex process of women leaving the labor force. Once again the experience bore witness to the primacy of demand and proved that sufficient aggregate demand was the vital component in maintaining a healthy economy.

Keynesian ascension hit a lull in the 1950s. To start off the decade the power of aggregate demand was once again eminently clear as a recession during the Truman years was washed away by spending for the Korean War. Then began eight years of a nostalgic return to the principle of the balanced budget. President Eisenhower sincerely believed that "deficits were bad for the character, public spending was wasteful, and the national debt was a burden unfairly imposed by one generation on the generations which succeeded it."[10] Eisenhower believed the free market, based on individual economic decision-makers, would lead to the best economy possible. Such an opinion is exemplified in comments of George Humphrey, the Secretary of the Treasury:

> I just do not believe that there is any group of men who are so smart that they can tell everybody in America what to do and be wiser than the great bulk of our people who are actuated by an incentive free choice system.[11]

In other words, intervention in the economy would be kept to an appropriate minimum. There would be no effort on the part of government to maintain the economy at some approved level of growth, unemployment, and inflation.

Such an apparent reversal of Keynesian economics might be interpreted as a setback had the Eisenhower policies been successful. This was far from the case, for in "seeking balanced budgets, free markets, active competition, and price stability, Republican policy had achieved instead deficits, inflation, recession, and lagging growth."[12] So Keynesian tactics, instead of suffering a strategic defeat, were vindicated by the failure of the non-Keynesian approach. The three recessions of the Eisenhower years were powerful evidence that without government intervention in the economy, there would be continual instability, low growth, and social unrest. The Keynesian policy mix appeared successful in attaining the desired economic goals.

The stage was thus set for the new, vigorous, and idealistic leadership of John F. Kennedy, who adroitly recognized the centrality of economic well-being in the lives of common Americans. This was not surprising, since it was the coincidence of the presidential race and the third Eisenhower-Nixon recession that paved the way for the narrow Kennedy victory in 1960. Naturally, Kennedy was well aware of the importance of understanding, monitoring, and controlling the economy in postwar society. For a political figure to be associated with economic prosperity meant reelection and public praise; but to be identified with economic recession heightened the probability of defeat. Although somewhat reluctant at first, Kennedy was eventually won over by the Keynesian theoreticians on his Council of Economic Advisers and was instrumental in introducing a 1962 tax cut proposal, which finally passed in 1964. Such a tax cut would have been considered suicide by pre-Keynesian economists because it was enacted in the face of a sizable budget deficit. However, far from causing budgetary problems, this tax cut appeared to initiate a long period of growth and low unemployment.* This was the first authentic Keynesian experiment carried out in complete contradiction to pre-1930 economic doctrine. And it had all the appearances of a smashing success: output rose, unemployment fell, inflation was negligible, and the deficit did not worsen, but actually improved by 1965.

The success of the experiment was important in developing the Keynesian approach to stabilization. Recovery from the Depression had relied upon increases in government expenditures to fuel demand. Now it was shown that changes in tax policy could

---

*This tax cut should be distinguished from that proposed and enacted in 1981 by "supply side" economists. The Keynesians propose personal tax cuts when there is idle capacity and stable prices. This provides an incentive to put idle plants back into production and satisfy increased demands. The supply siders see tax cuts as providing incentives for making new investments in plant and equipment.

have similar effects. So the economic policymaker had two tools which could be used for the same end, and the potential for mixing them increased the likelihood of success in "fine-tuning" the economy.

This experience made Kennedy's successor, Lyndon B. Johnson, extremely optimistic (with hindsight, overly so) about the ability of appropriate government policy to ensure full employment and rapid growth. This doctrine of fiscal activity was just what Johnson needed, because his vision of the "Great Society" could never become reality without massive government-spending efforts. Indeed the spending required by these programs combined with the increasing expenditures on arms for the Vietnam War reduced the unemployment rate to 3.3 percent in 1968. The combination of low unemployment and the Great Society programs directly aimed at poverty promised an answer to the scourge of poverty that had beset capitalism from its infancy. However, there were limits to the stimulation the economy could easily absorb as unused capacity disappeared.

Johnson balked from 1965 to 1967 at the suggestion of his Keynesian advisers that federal spending was too high for the tax revenues being collected. They warned that with the economy growing vigorously, unemployment very low, and a budding inflation showing signs of flowering, taxes ought to be increased to balance the high levels of spending. Their model suggested that the budget should be balanced over the cycle, that fiscal deficits in times of recession should be counterbalanced by fiscal surpluses in times of growth and low unemployment. Keynesians now argue that had their call for increased taxes been heeded, the inflationary pressure would not have built up as it did. But Johnson feared that a tax increase would dissolve support for the Vietnam War and for his social programs. As a result he did not request it until 1967, and it was enacted in 1968, when it was too late to stem the tide of a rising inflation.[13]

Nevertheless, the 1960s was a period of growth and expansion, the longest single period of continual growth in the nation's history. It was initiated by the Kennedy-Johnson tax cut; and the economy was kept hot, perhaps too hot, by expenditures for the Vietnam War and the Great Society. Despite the higher than desired inflation rate, there was still little doubt by the end of the decade that Keynes had squarely hit the head of the macro-economic nail when he suggested that government influence on aggregate demand was a key factor in the economy. Government had been instrumental in bringing about a successful economic era, though it had also contributed to the inflation of the late sixties. Still, with better management such errors in policy could certainly be minimized. The road to economic prosperity, self-esteem, and freedom seemed to be marked out by Keynesian analysis.

And the rosy pattern in the U.S. was reflected in the world economy which experienced an unprecedented period of prosperity and growth, not just in the industrialized countries but also in developing countries. Many factors accounted for this, but the Bretton Woods institutions made a definite contribution. The system of fixed exchange rates provided a stable context for international economic relations. The IMF used its resources to help countries in temporary difficulties. The World Bank was a growing channel for resources which were to be used in projects in developing countries where returns should be high. And barriers to trade were gradually lowered under the GATT accords. This was an exceptional period which seemed to vindicate Keynes's perceptions.

The Coming of Age of the Council of Economic Advisers

The previous paragraphs alluded to the new and increasing influence of the Council of Economic Advisers. Both Presidents Kennedy and Johnson turned to their councils for advice on economic trends and policy proposals. This group engineered the 1964 tax cut and finally convinced President Johnson of the necessity for increased taxes in the late sixties. Given its importance in economic policy making, we should look briefly at the rapid rise of the council to domination of national economic policy.

Presidents, monarchs, and other world leaders have rarely been able to handle the myriad duties of governing their lands without the liberal use of a corps of counselors. Two of the more famous historical figures were Machiavelli and Rasputin. On a less sinister level one might add Thomas More and Rexford Tugwell. We are interested in less-renowned names: Charles Schultze, Paul McCracken, and Arthur Okun.

These advisers are part of a new breed who came to prominence in recent years in most, if not all, countries around the world. Perhaps Schultze, McCracken, and Okun will never command the historical attention accorded Machiavelli and More, but they represent a group which has gained progressively more power in national and international political and economic arenas. These are the economic advisers, and in many ways, they are doing for the economic what Machiavelli did for the political: developing a framework in which economic considerations have an independent existence open to policy manipulation, but always under the guidance of professional economists. Charles Schultze was an influential economic adviser during the 1960s and was named chairman of the council by President Carter in 1977. Paul McCracken was the chairman under President Nixon, and Arthur Okun chaired the council under President Johnson. They found important niches for economists in the executive branch of government.[14] A similar role has been staked out on the legislative side with the Congressional Budget Office under economists Alice Rivlin, Rudolph Penner, and Robert Reischauer.*

What process led to such an important role for economists? As the new Keynesian era dawned, and faith in automatic economic stability was shaken, those best equipped to monitor economic performance and suggest appropriate economic interventions were naturally those trained in economics. Therefore, when Congress passed the Employment Act of 1946 and officially legitimated a role for government in attaining the main economic objectives, one of the provisions was for the appointment of a Council of Economic Advisers, a group of three economists headed by a chairman. The initially prescribed role for the council was to prepare the "Economic Report of the President." While operating in the shadows during the Truman and Eisenhower years, the council began to gain more influence during the Kennedy administration and the remainder of the sixties.

---

*Rivlin, a liberal democrat, and Penner, a mainstream republican, were appointed with bipartisan support, indicating the overriding importance of good technical analysis. Political differences over the economy resulted in a two-year stalemate over a new director until Reischauer was appointed after the 1988 elections.

Under Kennedy, who had realized that the state of the economy influences political success or failure, the role of the council expanded substantially. It now began advising the president of trends in the national economy as well as on policies which might aid in attaining growth and stability.

At the same time the new advisers were improving their capacities for this role. One of the main developments was new, highly sophisticated mathematical models to represent the U.S. economy. Such models used economic theory to manipulate massive amounts of economic information. Using the techniques of statistics and the capacities of ever more powerful computers, the economy could be represented in a series of equations. Of course, it would be a simplification in some degree, but if the simplifications of a good model were only in unimportant areas, the results would not be distorted. From their beginnings in the fifties, the models became more complex and detailed and by the late sixties there were several models of the entire economy, each with hundreds of equations. They could be used by the policymaker to simulate a policy maneuver and determine the probable results. Alternatively, an appropriate goal for the economy could be defined and policy actions to achieve that objective could be isolated from the model. Consequently it was not necessary to use the real economy as a guinea pig, for what worked in the model ought to work in the economy and ill-conceived policies need not burden the public. The policy advisers could experiment with these model economies until they found just the right policy mix to attain the desired goals.

The main agents in these developments were the Keynesian economists who have supported an active role for government in stabilizing economic affairs. The activist doctrine was ideally suited to the politician, for in politics nothing succeeds like success; and here was promise of success in the sphere of life that increasingly dominates citizens' concerns in our mass-consumption society. It is no wonder that economists and their "simple" models became the handmaidens of the politicians, and first the council and then the Congressional Budget Office became central players in national policy development.

The strength of this process was shown most obviously during the Nixon and Ford administrations when advisers such as

Herbert Stein and Alan Greenspan, who would never admit to Keynesianism, continued the central role of the council in economic policy. Indeed their use of the Council was so clear and successful, that Congress felt unable to play an independent role in such an important area and so created the Congressional Budget Office. It was not until the Reagan administration of 1981 that the status and importance of traditional economic advisers was challenged.

Nonetheless, a number of issues remained for the Keynesian analysts. The dominant one was the appropriate tools for demand management. This question sparked the lengthiest debates of the 1960s. While Keynes had emphasized fiscal policy and his followers heightened this emphasis, experience showed that monetary policy was certainly not passive, and so could not be ignored as irrelevant. In fact, monetary policy had a key role in certain instances such as the credit crunch of 1966 when restrictive policy raised interest rates and paralyzed construction activity. In addition, special problems were posed by the fact that monetary policy was vested in the Board of Governors of the Federal Reserve System, not in the executive. Coordination of fiscal and monetary policy became a concern, particularly when the philosophies of the Board and the administration differed, not an unusual situation since the seven governors were each appointed to fourteen-year terms and could only be removed by impeachment. So they were independent of any president.

Just as monetary policy was not as passive as had originally been thought, so the operation of fiscal policy raised a series of issues for the Keynesians. For example, tax laws could not be altered without time-consuming legislative processes. It was possible to recognize the need for a tax action in one year, but to be unable to effect that action until the next year, when it may have been too late. Furthermore, to be effective, tax changes had to be permanent, otherwise consumers would tend to ignore their effect on disposable income and not perceptibly alter their consumption patterns. Finally, since businesses base investment decisions primarily on criteria other than tax rates, tax cuts to business in the form of accelerated depreciation had very little impact on the level of investment, and therefore a minimal impact on the economy as a whole. Naturally, this has not diminished the fervor with which businesses lobby for "job-creating" tax cuts, nor has it lowered public faith in their efficacy. But complete success in fine-tuning the economy could not be attained until these difficulties with policy implementation could be solved. Such problems were amenable to research and improvement, though there were some other areas that had more serious implications for the Keynesian mainstream.

As the Keynesian star reached its zenith in the 1960s, intellectual interest in macroeconomic problems waned; the Keynesian task seemed simply one of slowly perfecting the analysis and fine-tuning the use of policy. Since the Keynesian approach had now assumed the mainstream position, it also took over in the classrooms where a new generation of students focused on the lessons, the issues, and the achievements of the Keynesian approach to macroeconomics.

Events would soon shatter this Keynesian complacency and would point to a number of weaknesses in the Keynesian understanding of the macroeconomy.

Clouds on the Horizon: The Phillips Curve and International Pressures

Although Keynesians had discovered much about the inner working of the economic system, there were areas that went almost completely untouched. The first was the supply side of the economy. With primary attention accorded to demand, questions relating to long-run supply decisions and incentive effects remained largely unexamined. The second major omission was the behavior of prices. Keynesians tended to treat prices as a subsidiary component of demand analysis. The theory assumed that if demand were too high there would be a tendency for prices to rise; but it was also implictly assumed that rising prices were a concomitant of low unemployment. The answer to rising prices was simply to utilize contractionary policies, thereby cooling off an overheated economy by lowering aggregate demand.

The paucity of research in these two areas is not surprising since Keynesian economics was a child of the Depression. Supply was not an issue, because in the thirties the producers' willingness to produce was restricted primarily by the shortage of demand. Also, in that period there was no danger of inflation, so that question was given low priority.

The environment in which Keynesianism grew offered little chance for learning how to cope with either supply shock phenomena or major price increases that were not demand-related. In the seventies these omissions caused the mature Keynesian analysis initially to demur and then to scramble for ad hoc explanations of apparently unexplainable phenomena.

While the seventies exposed these Keynesian weaknesses and continued to threaten the very heart of the theory, the Keynesians had earlier warnings. The first intimation that there might be more to a stable and growing economy than mere demand management came in 1958 from the Englishman A. W. Phillips. He noted that there was a definite relation between wage increases and rates of inflation which was not confined to periods of full employment. This implied that there was a trade-off between unemployment and inflation across the broad range of states of the economy. Phillips found that lower rates of unemployment were generally associated with higher rates of inflation. This meant that fighting inflation by restricting aggregate demand would create unemployment and possibly even trigger a recession. This posed a discomfiting political choice—either more inflation or more unemployment.

This trade-off existed because in reality the economy did not mirror the perfectly competitive model underlying both neoclassical and Keynesian theories. The economy had large areas of monopoly power, labor and natural resources were not highly mobile, and other inflexibilities slowed down the adjustment mechanisms of the market system.

Robert Solow and Paul Samuelson, two of the foremost counselors of the sixties, investigated this phenomenon and found that a rate of unemployment of 3.5 percent would result in a rate of inflation of 4 percent and unemployment of 2 percent would lead to 7 percent inflation.[15] Thus life was made a bit more complicated. The sanguine view that Keynesian tools were equally effective against both inflation and unemployment was no longer tenable: some mix of these two undesired phenomena would have to be chosen. The estimates indicated that the mix would be acceptable in the American context, but it was still a cloud on the Keynesian horizon.*

A second cloud was the growing pressure on international economic institutions, especially the system of fixed exchange rates. The U.S. generally had balance of payments deficits, but dollars were quite welcome throughout the world. One exception in the mid-sixties was France under Charles DeGaulle who began to trade the dollars accumulating in France for gold. By the end of the decade other countries were absorbing large amounts of dollars whose value would decline greatly if the relation of the dollar and gold were ever changed. Adjustments to the system should have been made, but it had worked well during the entire postwar period, so it was easier to assume that international economic stability would continue. This was another cloud on the horizon of Keynesian economics.

THE END OF ORTHODOX KEYNESIANISM

While in the sixties Keynesians could offer the benign alternatives of 5 percent unemployment and 3 percent inflation or 3.5 percent unemployment and 5 percent inflation, in the seventies the alternatives were more likely 12 percent inflation and 7 percent unemployment or 8 percent inflation and 9 percent unemployment. Such choices are akin to choosing between suicide and execution: neither is very palatable. Keynes and the post-Keynesians expected instability. However, the events and the many economic problems of the 1970s threatened the very foundation of the mainstream Keynesian analysis, placing American Keynesianism on the defensive and providing an opening for the revival of free market economics.

In general the Keynesian defense is that the decade of the seventies was unusual, one in which totally unexpected events cropped up, which dramatically increased the instability of the

---

***In the 1980s 3.5 percent unemployment and 4.0 percent inflation would be heaven itself. The worsening of the trade-off is the story of the 1970s and the lowering of our expectations the story of the 1980s.

economic system beyond the ability of policy to cope. One of the preeminent Keynesians, Franco Modigliani, a highly respected economist from M.I.T. who firmly believes in the ability of the government to promote economic stability and growth, offered the following explanation:

> The serious deterioration in economic stability since 1973 must be attributed in the first place to the novel nature of the shocks that hit us, namely supply shocks. Even the best possible aggregate demand management cannot offset such shocks without a lot of unemployment together with a lot of inflation. But, in addition, demand management was far from the best. The failure must be attributed in good measure to the fact that we had little experience or even an adequate conceptual framework to deal with such shocks; but at least from my reading of the record, it was also the result of failure to use stabilization policies, including too slavish adherence to the monetarists' constant money growth prescription.[16]

So his explanation is that supply shocks were one factor in the apparent Keynesian ineptitude, and errors in demand management were the other.

Supply Shocks: Jet Streams, Anchovies, and OPEC

In the early seventies our economy was hit blindside by some tremendous shocks, most of them international in nature. The weather patterns in this period, largely dependent on the jet streams in the upper stratosphere, became temporarily disrupted and brought drought to large sections of world agriculture. Crop losses in many countries were high and world food supplies became uncertain. On the home front there was no drought but American consumers still felt the bite of higher food prices due largely to huge grain sales to Russia and China and sales of other food goods to countries adversely affected by the droughts. As food supplies all over the world fell, prices rose.

This food shock was exacerbated by the untimely disappearance of the anchovy schools off the Peruvian coast, because of perennial overfishing and changing ocean current. A scarcity of anchovies seems hardly to merit a prime spot in the economic problems of the 1970s, but it is not mentioned flippantly. Anchovies were a major source of protein in livestock and chicken feed and when producers in the mid-seventies had to turn to soybeans, the price of meat and chicken rose accordingly. These were not the only shocks of the decade.

In 1973 the Arab affiliates of OPEC (the Organization of Petroleum Exporting Countries) decided to embargo sales of oil to the U.S. and Europe. During and after the embargo, prices of oil shot up. Soon the price of oil had increased by 400 percent and as the oil cartel consolidated and exercised its power, periodic price hikes became the norm for the 1970s. These steps were intimately linked to the demise of the fixed exchange rate system and the chaotic reorganization of the world economy. There was no Keynes to provide a vision of how to attain orderly policies which could benefit all economies.

In the U.S. the effects of the price hikes were profound, for postwar growth had been directly founded on cheap energy sources. One immediate effect was that businesses passed along their increased costs to consumers and general price rises became the rule as other businesses and workers tried to recoup their losses. As contractionary policies were enacted to fight the rising inflation, workers were thrown out of their jobs and the seeds of stagflation started to bear their fruit. After 1973 the rising price of energy continued to be a prime cause of the unabating inflation, according to Keynesians. The combined effect of the oil shock and the temporary food shock accounted for 60 percent of the inflationary binge of 1974. In 1979 OPEC imposed another large price increase.

In their defense Keynesians argue that government policies helped the economy adjust to these shocks. Changes in agricultural policy limited the effect of international supply problems on U.S. inflation. And conservation efforts were so successful that by the early 1980s the energy savings resulting from smaller autos and other conservation measures had led to a substantial, if temporary, oil glut and had prevented OPEC from making their price increase effective. So we may now be more successful in adjusting to external shocks, despite the flawed record of the 1970s.

Policy Problems: Errors, Shortcomings and What to Do About Them

While these unexpected shocks wreaked havoc on the U.S. economy, there were also a number of policy failures which are more threatening to the Keynesians. In a 1977 *Wall Street Journal* article Paul McCracken said, "Our problems of recent years are not, as has sometime been alleged, that economies no longer respond to fiscal and monetary policies. Economies were responding only too faithfully, but to the wrong policies."[17] The disregard of advice by presidents is certainly one of the sources of misguided policies. We already mentioned the reluctance of President Johnson to impose a necessary tax increase in the late sixties.

Besides contrary-minded presidents Keynesians have had their troubles with the Federal Reserve Board. Because the Fed is independent of other government offices, neither the Keynesian advisers nor the president himself can insist that the board behave in any prescribed manner. So the task of coordinating monetary and fiscal policy becomes much more difficult, for the Fed controls the former while the President and Congress control the latter. If the Fed had been populated with Keynesians this problem would have diminished, but that has not been the case. Chairman of the Board Arthur Burns (1970–79) was certainly no advocate of government intervention in the economy and neither was Paul Volcker (1979–1987) nor Alan Greenspan (1987—).

Ample evidence of the failure to coordinate policy was given during October 1977, when the country was treated to an executive office statement decrying the monetary restraint of the Federal Reserve. Less than a week later Arthur Burns delivered a speech which characterized the Carter policy on the economy as weak and ineffective. Similar exchanges also transpired between Paul Volcker and the Carter administration. Even the Reagan administration blamed some of its major problems on Fed policy, and there was almost immediate disagreement between the Bush administration and the Fed over the need to raise interest rates to slow inflation.

Modigliani noted the ineffective use of monetary policy in the seventies. His prime example was the 1973–74 supply shock, and the coincident decision of the Fed to maintain a fairly constant money supply growth rate. This made the subsequent inflation and recession much worse than was necessary. Had the Fed increased the growth rate when the shocks hit and then reduced it again when the initial shock had passed, the repercussions would have been substantially smaller. Another example would be the Volcker decision in 1979 to restrict money growth which led to rocketing interest rates and a recession.

There are other technical problems with macropolicy efforts as well. Perhaps the most significant barrier to appropriate policy implementation is the inability to control fiscal and monetary policy instruments effectively. All too often there have been wide divergences between the desired and actual rates of money supply growth, or between planned taxation or expenditure levels and the actual levels. At one point in 1977 it was estimated that real disbursements were running at least 20 billion dollars below what had been programmed. Such an inability to control outlays could obviously undercut the Keynesian insistence on the stabilizing role of fiscal spending.

In much the same way the money supply cannot be controlled precisely. Not only is there hot disagreement over what constitutes the money variable to control, but even when some measure of money is chosen, there is no guarantee that the Federal Reserve Board can control that quantity over periods shorter than six months. This is a recurring problem which has been exacerbated in the 1970s and now the 1980s by the creation of new monetary instruments such as NOW accounts or money market funds. These difficulties led Frank Morris, who was President of the Federal Reserve Bank of Boston, to declaim "we can no longer measure the money supply with any kind of precision."[18] In the long run it still appears that the money supply can be fairly well controlled, but the wild and apparently uncontrollable gyrations in the short and medium run can have a significant impact on the performance of the economy; so the solace of long-run controllability may be scant indeed and this is one reason the Fed has returned to using the level of interest rates as one policy target.

Another technical problem is the time lag between the onset of a problem and the use of appropriate policy tools. When lags are prevalent there is no guarantee that policy action will have the desired effect on the economy. In fact, if the lags are long enough

the policy may serve to do exactly the opposite of what it is supposed to.

In addition, the highly touted mathematical models of the
economy designed to predict future economic trends were of little
help in the seventies with its instability. While one was predicting
a downturn, another was predicting an expansion, and when the
future "arrived" the economy had done neither. Experience with
the models found that they did not differ greatly in the short run,
but beyond two years or so the variation in predictions was substantial. And any one model could give very different predictions
if some of its embedded assumptions about the behavior of the
economy in the face of external events were slightly changed.
Thus the experience in the seventies with the models produced
in the sixties was disillusioning; and the role that models could
play in assisting the formulation of policy came into doubt.

The potentially most damaging problem for the Keynesian
approach of an activist government is the role of expectations. For
example, one critique claims that Keynesian policies built expectations of inflation into the structure of the economy in the late
sixties and seventies. This contributed to perpetually rising prices
and wages, and engendered inflation-hedging behavior. As a result of this reaction to inflation and its expected continuation, the
Phillips trade-off became less favorable than it was in the early and
mid-sixties. Unemployment could still be reduced to traditionally
low rates, but now only at the expense of higher inflation.

So the policy problem becomes more complex if it has to
affect peoples' expectations as well as the economic variables.
Given the wide popularity of business reports and the intense
interest in economic indicators, there is every reason to think that
expectations play an increasing role in economic behavior, compli-
cating the policy problem.

The Keynesian Defense

The response of the Keynesians to these admitted difficulties
is that they are not evidence against an activist government policy.
They claim that the history of activist economic policy in the post–
World War II period demonstrates a more successful economic
performance than either the prewar period or the 1980s. Average

annual economic growth was higher, the decline in poverty was greater, and the unemployment rate lower. If the last five to seven years of the 1970s were excluded, we would all proclaim it a "Golden Age." The failures of those few years do not disprove the Keynesian project of using an activist federal government to promote social goals such as full employment, stable growth, reduced poverty.

It must be remembered that many of the problems since 1973 were due to the external supply shocks, such as the OPEC oil price increases, that were unique to the period and cannot be blamed on Keynesian policy. In fact we have learned from those experiences and are able to provide better policy recommendations if such supply shocks should occur again. Also many of the policy failures were the result of politicians' failure to heed economists' advice, and coordination problems in monetary and fiscal policy are amenable to political solution.

Lags are clearly a more difficult problem. Policymakers can work to minimize the importance of lags, to some extent, by trying to reduce them, but they will never be removed completely. Therefore, Keynesians have become more cautious and are willing to resort to vigorous policy actions only when there are strong and continuous trends in one direction or the other. This view is represented in a macroeconomics textbook written at the end of the 1970s. The authors say: "there are still clearly definable circumstances in which there can be no doubt that the appropriate policy is expansionary or contractionary. An administration coming to power in 1933 should not have worried about the uncertainties associated with expansionary policy...."[19] Stabilization policy is also essential during wars and periods when unemployment rises too high, e.g. the year 1975, when unemployment was 8.2 percent and on an upward trend.

With respect to fine-tuning, however, the authors are equivocal. They are reluctant to abandon the whole concept, but they make no hard and fast case in favor of it either. "The major lesson ... is not that policy is impossible, but that policy that is too ambitious in trying to keep the economy always at full employment [with zero inflation] is impossible. The lesson is to proceed with extreme caution, always bearing in mind the possibility that policy itself may be destabilizing."[20]

One other experience which supports the importance of fiscal policy and demand stimulation is the record of the Reagan
administration which will be discussed in chapter 5. Keynesians
can point to the long and sustained recovery from the 1982 recession and note that the historically high budget deficits during the
period were certainly strong contributors, that indeed any success
of the Reagan years was a vindication of the Keynesian emphasis
on government fiscal policy.

So the Keynesians are alive, if not as well as before. The experience of the 1980s can only cause their influence to grow, and their
base in academe and in research institutes such as the Brookings
Institution places them at the ready. There is interesting and important work which they are undertaking, for example, Robert
Eisner's effort to redo the national income accounts to reflect the
dramatic changes that have occurred in past decades.[21] Nonetheless they are certainly chastened and are much more careful in
their promises. This may be realistic in a time when the international influences over the U.S. economy have grown so substantially, and when any success in creating a stable international economy seems to require the advent of another Keynes.

Externalities, Monopoly, and Unequal Opportunity

So far we have focused on Keynesian attempts to correct just
one of the four major flaws of a free market economy—unemployment—and the resulting stagflation of the 1970s. Keynesian failures in this area obscure substantial, if mixed, successes in correcting the other three flaws: externalities, unequal opportunity, and
monopoly.

Keynesian economists joined the fight to correct the worst
externalities in our economy. As a result we breathe cleaner air,
enjoy purer lakes and rivers, and work with greater safety. The
undoubted benefits, however, were tarnished by costs of implementation. Costs of production were increased by antipollution
and safety regulations. In addition, the bureaucracy created by
regulation was quite inefficient and caused a public outcry that
helped defeat the Carter government along with his Keynesian
advisers. The positive contribution of government policy in this
area ensured that it would survive later active efforts to remove

government; nonetheless, the proper role for government was certainly not clearly defined in this experience.

A whole series of policies that were at least coincident with the Keynesian era expanded equality of opportunity. Voting rights laws gave blacks equal access to the political system. Equal employment laws banned job discrimination against minorities and women. School systems were required to equalize per pupil expenditures where before they had been heavily weighted in favor of the well-to-do. Head Start tried to reach the young to help them overcome the lack of opportunities caused by disadvantaged backgrounds. These programs were seen as making a "free" market economy more free by increasing equality of opportunity. The fruits of these policies are being seen today.

However, the clear benefits were once again obscured by the public outcry against certain programs, particularly busing and affirmative action. In addition, welfare programs tended to be confused with those aimed at equal opportunity, to the detriment of both.

In the case of the fourth major flaw of a free market economy—monopoly—Keynesians paid lip service to competition but did little to stem the tide of industrial concentration. In fact, the greatest merger movement in American history to that point—the conglomerate mergers—took place during the 1960s and 1970s. And the 1980s have continued that process in somewhat different form.

IN CONCLUSION

The Keynesians have three rejoinders for those who criticize them and contend that their message is obsolete. Supply shocks, policy errors, and technical policy issues, say the Keynesians, are the culprits of the economic malaise that infected our country in the second half of the 1970s. They hope no more supply shocks would threaten us; they are sure that policy errors could be reduced as bureaucratic flaws were weeded out and a better understanding of policy effects was gained; and the progress of economics itself will ensure that policymakers could improve the technical elements of policy. But all of this filled the economic cup of the

future with just a little more wishful thinking than the typical
American wished to drink. The result was a repudiation of
the New Deal–Keynesian consensus with the election of Ronald
Reagan as president in 1980.

Needless to say, these difficulties and the electoral decision
did not demonstrate the superiority of free market theories to any
Keynesian's satisfaction. Their view of how the economy operates
remained intact. With its origins in the Great Depression, Keynesians believe in the inherent instability and the tendency toward
substantial market failure within an unregulated market economy.
This view fits comfortably with an optimistic belief in the efficacy
of active intervention by government through the use of fiscal and
monetary policy.

Although the evidence on whether Keynesian policies improved performance during the 1970s in the face of the shocks is
inconclusive, the Conservative Economic Individualists (CEIs)
clearly won the debate; and many Keynesians became more conservative and less interventionist. There were several reasons for
this development. The CEIs had one very important advantage:
their policies had not had to face the test of implementation until
the Reagan administration. The Keynesians, by contrast, suffered
from their identification with an activist government—one which
takes responsibility for the stability and growth of the economy—
at a time when that government could not deliver acceptable results.

A second advantage for the CEIs was that, since empirical
tests are inconclusive, and since both groups are believers in the
free market system, the burden of proof is always on the Keynesians to show why government is needed. Each government policy
failure was interpreted as evidence *against* Keynesianism and also
for the CEI worldview. This forced Keynesians to take a more
conservative stance. More and more of them began calling for
government deregulation, the use of market incentives for government programs, a less activist fiscal policy, and so forth, all
without convincing empirical evidence, though certainly in harmony with their belief in free markets.

Clearly the Keynesian record was mixed. The balance of success appears to depend on who is doing the evaluation. Nonetheless, having reached the inner circles of the government, the

Keynesians did not pull back in quiet splendor to review the decade of the sixties as grandparents might savor home movies of times gone by. In fact, much of the rhetoric from high level economists and from the White House itself during the Carter years retained heavy vestiges of the Keynesian influence. This changed with the Reagan electoral victory. His economic advisers were of the CEI school. But if, as Keynesians anticipated, the CEIs promoted policies out of step with what the economy and the country needed, then Americans would again be on the prowl for new economic understanding. They might turn once again to the Keynesians. In the meantime the Keynesians patiently waited, readying themselves for a return to Washington.

In the next two chapters we look at the arguments of the renewed free market school of economics, the CEIs and their record as advisers to the Reagan administration during the years 1980–88.

4. The Assault on the Keynesians: Free Enterprise Once Again

As the 1970s drew to a close economists turned from arguing with each other to persuading the public. Two of the prime examples of such efforts were television series also published as books, one by John Kenneth Galbraith entitled *The Age of Uncertainty,* the other by Milton Friedman and Rose Friedman, *Free To Choose.*[1] A survey of the discussions or writings on contemporary economic problems would indicate that the theme of the Galbraith series captured the ethos of the age: new problems, failures of traditional solutions, and new challenges and possibilities. Galbraith richly embroidered on the complexities of the age.

But Galbraithian complexity was reduced to clear simplicity by the Friedmans: most problems arise from government intervention in the economy, and the solution is its removal and a return to unbridled individual freedom.

If the ratings are any indication, simplicity won out over uncertainty, and that is in large degree the story of this chapter. For in the face of uncertainty and complexity, the public wanted simple answers: solutions that comprehend, explain and resolve with a few short and simple ideas. That is one of the lessons of the election of Ronald Reagan in 1980. His economic proposals combined a traditional program of Republican austerity—which was not popular because it always resulted in more unemployment—with a simple solution to low-growth, high-unemployment problems—the supply-side effects of tax cuts. Thus a simple, painless solution to stagflation was proposed: end inflation without lowering growth or employment. Despite its inherent contradictions, this simple program was effective in winning for Mr. Reagan eight years in the highest post in the country. In so doing the dominance of Keynesian orthodoxy was eliminated with one stroke.

The story of how this return to a theory of the past was engineered is the topic of this chapter in which we present the approach of the Conservative Economic Individualists (CEIs). The next chapter follows up with the story of how the CEIs fared as economic advisers to the Reagan administration during the 1980s.

THE CEI RESURGENCE

A useful starting point is to recall that in the 1960s the Keynesians had cornered the simplicity market: excessive unemployment could be combatted by an increase in government spending and/or a decrease in taxes; high inflation could be overcome by the opposite, a decrease in government spending and/or an increase in taxes. In the 1970s this simple logic lost credibility, for Keynesian solutions did not work in the face of both high inflation and high unemployment. All too often they lamented that the economy was not as simple as they had once thought and many resigned themselves to studying the various complexities they now perceived to pervade economic life.

When the intransigent 1970s struck, where were the classical and neo-classical economists? They also had a simple view of economic life that offered simple solutions to contemporary problems. They had contended that markets did, in fact, work well and for the government to maintain stability its policy actions should be quite simple—do nothing. This view had been largely discredited by the Great Depression; as economic counselors, the laissez-faire economists had been poorly prepared either to explain the genesis of the Depression or to propose avenues of escape other than cutting wages and toughing it out. Though attrition of laissez-faire economists during the thirties was high, belief in unregulated markets and market systems remained the sustaining vision of many economists, and there was never a successful assault on the basic microeconomic market analysis that was a central pillar of neoclassical economics. For the most part laissez-faire economists retreated to live in the obscurity of a few academic retreats and to reevaluate their theoretical and policy positions.

One such bastion later to take on substantial importance was the University of Chicago. Melvin Reder has described the developments that allowed Chicago economics to develop its laissez-faire orientation.[2] It is an interesting tale of personalities and almost chance events. The resurgence of free enterprise economics received a major impulse in 1963 when Milton Friedman, from the University of Chicago and later a Nobel Prize winner, and Anna Schwartz published *A Monetary History of the United States, 1867–1960*.[3] The central importance of the book was its interpretation of the Depression and other recessionary periods which placed the blame squarely on the shoulders of government and its control of the money supply. The depth of the Depression, they argued, was the direct and inevitable result of a drastic decline in the money supply from 1929 to 1933, resulting from mistaken government policy. The book was cogently argued and forcefully presented, and free market economists now had reason to claim that the economic system had actually been self-stabilizing all along. Only government errors had caused the catastrophe of the 1930s. Even though the Friedman-Schwartz claims were far from universally accepted, the vindication of pre-Keynesian, laissez-faire economics was now well underway.

Friedman soon had a broad group of followers and collaborators who not only adhered to his interpretation of macroeconomic phenomena, but also supported his doctrines of free enterprise, free choice, and individual liberty. Before long they became known as "monetarists," because of their emphasis on the money supply as the strongest and most reliable determinant of the level of prices and of economic activity. But this group of reincarnated classical economists espoused much more than just proper monetary control, so the monetarist label is misleading. Because they looked back to the pre-1930 economic ideas that opposed all subsequent change in the political economy, we should call them conservative. Because they advocated free unregulated enterprise, free markets, the sovereignty of the individual consumer, and individual choice as the measuring rod for all public policy, we find it appropriate to entitle them economic individualists as well. Thus we use as our description of the group, "Conservative Economic Individualists" (CEIs).

Throughout the 1960s when the economy was performing

exceptionally well, CEIs were definitely on the outside, acting as gadflies to point out difficulties with the Keynesian analysis. For the most part their points were technical, but they were maintaining and developing their own analysis in the universities and later in research institutes such as the American Enterprise Institute.

With the deterioration of the economy in the 1970s, the CEIs had their opportunity to become once again the representatives of conventional economic wisdom. During the 1970s, while the Keynesians were expending their energies trying to defend their economic policies, the CEIs remained in the opposition, claiming that no solution to the problems was possible until the Keynesians had been displaced and the CEIs had been restored to their proper role as advisers on economic policy.

With the election of Ronald Reagan as president, the 1980s promised the CEIs a chance to prove that their interpretation of the economy was correct and that the country should follow their advice. The new version of laissez-faire economics had been adjusted to the realities of the 1970s and had incorporated a number of new elements from the research programs that had been carried on in exile from the center stage of policy and in opposition to the Keynesians.

CEIs never believed that sustaining full employment by government actions was either possible or desirable. At the fundamental level they believed that the crisis of the 1970s was caused by too much government intervention in the economy. As Milton Friedman said, "We are suffering from inflation and recession produced by government attempts to promote full employment."[4] They reasoned as follows. Growth of government and inflation were the twin evils that threatened economic welfare and personal liberty. The establishment of full employment as a national priority had generated irresistible political pressures to achieve that goal, and the resultant policies set off the flames of inflation and created an increased need for government control. Moreover, the inflation could then proceed to trigger a recession. Inflation frustrated people's plans, destroyed their confidence, and created the type of uncertainties which lead both businesses and consumers to cut back on their spending plans.

In addition, CEIs argued that the ever-growing macromanagement functions and social security measures of the federal gov-

ernment had created a burgeoning bureaucracy and the politiciza-
tion of economic decisions which, in turn generated inefficiency,
a loss of incentive in the private sector, and a pandering to the
marginal voter by politicans with promises of ever more government programs to replace private activity. The only answer was a
sharp reduction of social welfare programs that adversely affect
personal incentives, a transformation of activist macromanagement into fixed rules, and the acceptance of the necessity of short-
term unemployment to cure inflation.

The CEI framework was turned into a salable political program by the addition of two new, or renewed, elements. The first
was a conservative treatment of poverty which was more coherent
than the traditional approach of the classical and neoclassical
economists to the question. Part of the argument simply blamed
the poor and looked for personality or attitudinal failures on their
part. But the more appealing aspect saw government as the culprit
in the continuation of poverty, in the creation of a culture of
poverty. According to the CEIs, the social welfare programs which
developed during the 1960s and 1970s—food stamps, medicaid,
and so on—had created a psychological dependence on the government and had sapped the incentives and energies of poor people.[5] Of course the same is true for the rich, whose incentives were
suppressed by high taxation. This rationale for reducing government programs had its roots in the classical tradition and was not
openly an attack on the basic needs of that portion of the population living in poverty.

The second new component was "supply-side economics." It
started again from the assumption that government programs and
taxation sap incentives to business, to savers, and to workers. Thus
a program of tax reductions could have very powerful effects in
stimulating the economy, increasing output, and increasing productive capacity. Inflation would fall with increased output. In the
process, of course, consumers would have more to spend as well.
This component of the program served to shift attention from the
oft-noted recessionary effects of efforts to fight inflation, and the
possibility of having the best of all worlds was the promise at the
end of the program. The mechanism was appropriately quite simple: less government activity and lower taxes.

While not all CEIs would accept these additions to the program, this was the form in which it was sold to and bought by the American public. The core of the CEI program remained a return to the free market, limited government activity, limited discretionary stabilization activity, and stimulation of individual enterprise. Politically CEIs had to live with the new components, and evaluations of CEI performance will have to include them.

Let us now examine the CEI program in greater detail.

CEI INTERPRETATIONS OF THE 1970s

CEIs believe a free market economy is self-stabilizing. If there are unavoidable disruptions (such as the OPEC oil price increases) that destabilize the economy, the market mechanism will enable the economy to adjust quickly and efficiently. According to the CEIs, the terms "boom" and "recession" would have little importance in national affairs if the economy were allowed to adjust on its own. Some take this one step further, even questioning whether the economy's poor performance in the 1970s warrants the commonly applied categorization of a crisis. Certainly CEIs agreed in the 1970s that there were a series of notable disruptions. The rise of OPEC, the failure of the Bretton Woods Agreement on exchange rates, the coincidence of high inflation and unemployment, the flight of business to Third World countries, and declining productivity, all were evidence of the deteriorating economic climate of the 1970s.

Nevertheless, many CEIs questioned the existence of a crisis on three grounds. First, they contended that the relevant statistics were structured so as frequently to overestimate the dimensions of problems. Second, many of the phenomena which appeared crisis-related may have been nothing more than transitional symptoms of an economy undergoing change. No economy is static, having always to adjust to new operational parameters (e.g., higher energy prices, new technological developments). Therefore the seeming difficulties may actually have represented a healthy and mature, but constantly changing economy. Third, when government intervention in the economy has been reduced, performance will begin returning to normalcy. Thus the economy was not in crisis, but government intervention kept an otherwise healthy economy from self-stabilization.

In the CEI view the futility of traditional government stabilization policy was more than evident during the 1970s. In desperation Richard Nixon imposed wage and price controls in 1971 in hopes of curbing inflation without the usual rise in unemployment. But when the unpopular controls were lifted in 1974, inflation soared as businesses and unions tried to recoup what they felt they had lost in the control period. Saddled with this high inflation, Gerald Ford declared inflation Public Enemy #1 and embarked on his "Whip Inflation Now" campaign. In order to bring down the double-digit inflation of 1974 to acceptable levels, Ford reduced the annual growth of the federal budget from 11 percent to 5.5 percent. Inflation declined to the 7 percent level, but at the same time unemployment shot up to over 8 percent. In 1976 the state of the economy became a major campaign issue for Carter and Ford, Carter exclaiming that an 8 percent unemployment rate was unconscionable, and Ford defending his policies of moderation in federal spending. After winning the election Carter immediately attacked unemployment. In 1977, the first year of the Carter presidency and the second year of a business expansion, the Carter administration raised federal spending by 5 percent (over and above inflation) and sustained a 25 billion dollar deficit. Also the Fed allowed the money supply to grow faster than it had during the Ford years. But with inflation at 7 percent and unemployment at 8 percent the government faced a Catch-22 situation; no combination of fiscal and monetary policy appeared capable of attaining acceptable levels of inflation and unemployment. Neither Ford nor Carter had good solutions, partly because they were innocent victims of their economic advisers and the advisers could come to no viable consensus. So while Carter's policies tended toward traditional Democratic positions and helped reduce unemployment to around 6 percent, inflation took off again and by the first quarter of 1980 had reached an annual rate of 18 percent.

The bewildering vacillation on stabilization policy in the last days of the Carter administration, as on many other questions, reflected uncertainty on which problem was the more serious, inflation or unemployment. There was nothing in the Keynesian tool-kit to combat them both at the same time. When in October 1979, the Fed opted to change its money supply growth target from interest rate maintenance to a steady growth rate of the money supply, interest rates skyrocketed to 20 percent, investment slowed (especially in the housing sector), and the long-awaited recession hit, causing unemployment to rise to 8 percent by June 1980. Meanwhile, realizing the grave consequences of their policy switch, Paul Volcker and Federal Reserve associates retracted and allowed the money supply to increase at a faster rate. By 1980 the government, according to traditional Keynesian economic wisdom, could do no right. Whichever way it turned, it only exacerbated one of the twin evils, while not greatly alleviating the other.

The accession of the Reagan administration brought a new consistency to economic policy, as both the monetary and fiscal authorities ostensibly were pursuing contractionary policies. This resulted in one of the shortest recoveries on record after the 1980 recession. By the second quarter of 1981, the economy slipped into recession again, a long recession which pushed unemployment rates to postwar highs, while bringing inflation far below its recent historical levels. But again it was an unsavory mix, even if policymakers were now ready to make their choice clear.

In the CEI view, the root cause of prolonged stagflation was government policy which prevented the economy from correcting itself. In addition, government meddling in the international sector had increased the problems of the domestic economy. They argued that international economic activity ought to enjoy the same freedom as that in the domestic economy. This meant the elimination of trade barriers such as tariffs and quotas, and the paramount importance of truly flexible exchange rates between national currencies. Instead, in 1980, the U.S. protected many domestic industries from foreign competition and intervened in exchange markets to maintain the value of the dollar. Although the Bretton Woods Agreement, which legitimized government intervention to maintain rigidly fixed exchange rates, had collapsed completely in 1973, the government continued to refuse to allow the dollar to float freely, intervening regularly in a technique known pejoratively as the "dirty float."

The CEIs thus responded to the problems of the 1970s in two

ways. First, they denied the existence of a crisis, arguing that whatever aberrations existed were necessary transitional features of a changing economy. The market economy is highly creative in adjusting to change, as the 1970s demonstrated. Some examples were: the dramatic changes in energy usage and the adjustment of the industrial structure of the economy to changing international competitive pressures. So rather than an era of crisis, the 1970s were a tribute to the creativity of the market. Certainly there were destructive elements, but they were far outweighed.

Second, they amended this assessment by berating the government as the cause of many of the phenomena of instability that were experienced during the 1970s. If the government had reduced its activist role back in 1970 when the thin Keynesian veneer of apparent activist successes began to peel away, uncovering the center of Keynesian ineptitude and faulty logic, then many of the problems in the 1970s would have rapidly subsided as markets worked to repair themselves.

CEIs went beyond criticism of policy to a technical description of the economy. The common element in their technical analysis was theoretical "proof" that government could play little or no positive role in aiding macroeconomic performance. Let us look at the main elements: the Phillips trade-off, the natural rate of unemployment, crowding-out, and rational expectations.

The Long-Run Phillips Curve

CEIs recognized that the key Keynesian dilemma was the coincidence of high inflation and high unemployment. They argued that their theoretical understanding of a free market economy provided a clear and simple explanation for this, as well as a solution.

Their reasoning is exemplified by the previously discussed Phillips Curve trade-off. In Milton Friedman's 1968 presidential address to the American Economic Association, even before the experience with stagflation in the 1970s, he outlined the CEI view that any reliance on the relationship between inflation and unemployment for creating policy was misleading. The reason is quite simple; as Friedman said, "there is always a temporary tradeoff between inflation and unemployment; there is no permanent tradeoff."[6] CEIs agree that government economic policy may succeed temporarily in reducing unemployment, but they hold that it would be unable to do so for an extended period of time. Policy can control inflation, and this should be its focus. Then unemployment will adjust to its "natural" market determined level. There is no trade-off.

To understand the dynamics of this argument consider the behavior of consumers, workers, and business managers in a hypothetical small country. Several industries have plants in the country and numerous small businesses exist that serve the needs of local consumers. Suppose that unemployment is 5 percent while inflation is zero. The government decides that 5 percent unemployment is too high; 4 percent would be better, and officials would even be willing to suffer a little permanent inflation if unemployment could be kept down to 4 percent. So the government decides to increase the money supply growth rate slightly. When the money supply growth rate increases, banks have more to loan out so they lower the interest rate on loans. With lower interest rates than before consumers are more likely to buy a new car, put an addition on the house, or take a long vacation. Spending goes up and the industries must produce more to meet the demand. The plants soon put up signs announcing that they are hiring. But to their surprise no more workers flock to their gate than before. As always, they experience a fairly steady proportion of their employees quitting to look for new jobs and they have just about the right flow of replacements. To boost output they must have more workers, so they increase wages to make the jobs more attractive. Thus fewer people quit to look for new jobs in other places and some people who were not in the labor force enter in response to the higher wage.

The industries adjust in another way, by raising prices. Demand is good, wages have increased, and there is every reason to take advantage of the buoyant economy. As prices in these core industries shoot up, it is not too long before other local businesses raise their prices too. The general price level edges upward and inflation has begun.

It is not too long before the workers who have been receiving higher money wages find they have gained nothing since higher prices mean they can purchase no more than before. Workers who were tempted into joining the labor force by the apparently higher wages now drop out again, regular employees begin to quit their jobs to look for better ones, and the unemployment rate inches back toward 5 percent. Policymakers are bewildered at their failure.

The implications for the unemployment-inflation trade-off are readily perceived. There are short-term changes in the unemployment rate only when workers are tricked into thinking their wages are higher or lower than they really are (in terms of purchasing power). If the politicians do nothing, then prices will once again stabilize, real wages will return to their market determined level, and unemployment will once again return to 5 percent. If, however, they persist in their efforts to keep unemployment below 5 percent, the money supply pedal will need another push. The same process will recur. Workers, however, will not remain foolish for very long. They soon realize that the increased wages offered by local employers will only offset the rising price level and before the employers even offer to raise wages, workers already demand it. If the price level has been rising about 2 percent per year, workers will automatically demand a 2 percent wage increase; and they will have no incentive to work more since the 2 percent increase just keeps them on a par with the rising prices. Unemployment will stay at 5 percent. If the government wishes to keep unemployment down they will have to get inflation moving even faster than 2 percent to fool the workers into working more.

Each time the government raises the money supply growth rate, unemployment will drop for a time, but gradually inflation will increase and unemployment will push upwards again. If eventually the inflation rate approaches, say 15 percent, then workers will automatically demand a 15 percent wage increase, and inflation will be built into the workings of the economy. Inflation will inch ever higher, but the base or natural unemployment rate will not change. The Phillips trade-off is thus not a viable guideline for policymakers. In our hypothetical country there is no long-run trade-off; as inflation went up unemployment at first fell but then returned to its beginning level.

Whenever government attempts to reduce the unemployment rate below this "natural rate," it will only succeed in raising the inflation rate in the long run. The same approximate rate of unemployment will prevail at practically any rate of inflation, and that inflation rate is set by monetary policy. CEIs argued that since Keynesian designed economic policy had continually sought to maintain unemployment below the natural rate, it should be no surprise that inflation had been so high.

So while Keynesians felt in a state of crisis, CEIs believed they understood the coexistence of high inflation and what was perceived to be high unemployment. The "long-run Phillips curve" explained not only the causes of stagflation but the reasons Keynesian stabilization policies were ineffective.

A central analytical element in this theory is the natural rate of unemployment.

The Natural Rate of Unemployment Hypothesis

The level of unemployment is determined in what economists call the labor market. The key consideration is the real wage rate. Negotiations between owners of labor, workers, and purchasers of labor, employers, result in a supply and a demand for labor that sets this real wage rate. More importantly, this negotiation in the market determines the amount of employment in the economy. This market-determined amount of employment, given certain characteristics of the labor force, also sets the rate of unemployment in the economy. Thus when CEIs speak of the natural rate of unemployment, they mean the rate that exists when the level of employment is determined in a competitive market.

What is that natural unemployment rate? A definition is problematic because the rate is not observable; so it becomes quite difficult to pin CEIs down. In the 1950s and 1960s a 4 percent rate of unemployment was considered "full employment" (the natural rate), meaning that at prevailing real wage rates, less than 4 percent of the labor force chose to remain unemployed. But in the 1970s that rate seemed all but illusory. Could it be that the "natural rate" had jumped to 6, 7, or 8 percent? This was the CEI implication. In the 1970s unemployment was appreciably below 6 percent in three years and dipped slightly below 5 percent only in 1973. Is it possible that 6 percent of the labor force chose to be out of work? Why would people openly choose not to work when jobs were available? To these questions the CEIs had a number of rejoinders.

First of all, our earlier illustration indicated that there are times when people choose to leave their present jobs and search for another. Since most jobs must be found during the hours of eight to five, workers often cannot look for a different job without quitting their present occupation. The time it takes them to find another job is a period of unemployment. In technical jargon such workers are referred to as *frictionally* unemployed, because they are between jobs. CEIs have argued that as more workers switch jobs, the economy benefits since workers will tend to move to jobs where they are more productive.

CEIs do recognize another type of unemployment which is structural in nature. Since the U.S. is a changing economy there are times when some jobs become obsolete and the workers trained in these skills can no longer sell their talents on the market. If they cannot adjust and learn new skills they might remain unemployed. This is called *structural* unemployment because the workers are willing to work, but they cannot find an employer in need of their abilities. CEIs, however, tend to downplay this source of unemployment, because there are always unskilled positions available, and if one is willing to take one of these jobs and to lower wage demands, one can obtain employment. Structural unemployment is a regrettable feature of a technologically dynamic and creative economy, but one that is substantially outweighed by the benefits.

For the CEI, these are the two types of unemployment, and the second is of doubtful importance. Generally speaking, if someone is out of work, the CEI believes it is because they make that choice. But if such frictional unemployment is the only kind of unemployment of any import, why would it change from 4 percent to 6 percent in a relatively short period of time? CEIs give two reasons. The first is the composition of the work force. CEIs are quick to cite the fact that the proportion of male workers 25 and older in the labor force fell from 60 percent in 1955 to 46 percent by 1975. The trend continued and by 1989 male workers over 20 years of age were less than 50 percent of the labor force. This indicates a rise in the proportion of both women and young workers who are characterized by a much less stable work pattern than are older males. Male workers are generally family breadwinners and the security of a long-term job is a desired asset. According to CEIs, the absence of the same familial financial burden in younger and female workers permits more freedom to change jobs. So the proportion of people between jobs (of their own volition, remember) has risen over the years as the labor force composition has changed; and therefore the natural rate of unemployment has naturally risen.

Policymakers, therefore, ought no longer view 4 percent as some magic target level of unemployment that signifies all is well with the economy (4 percent is, in fact, the unemployment rate that the Full Employment and Balanced Growth Act of 1978 [Humphrey-Hawkins] targeted as its measure of "full employment"). How, then, does the government know what unemployment rate should be the target? It doesn't, and shouldn't! It should eliminate interventionist policies and let the market work. Whatever unemployment rate results will be the natural rate, the rate which can be considered the sum total of the free choices of workers themselves.

The second reason more people choose to be unemployed is a direct result of government intervention. Before the government intervened, the unemployed received no wages for the simple reason that they performed no work. However, with high unemployment benefits which in some cases could last up to 52 weeks, it pays not to work. When unemployment is "subsidized" in this way workers can afford to be much more choosy in accepting new jobs than they had been previously. CEIs claim that workers will therefore remain out of work when jobs are available. Again, the increase in workers who choose to remain unemployed is perfectly predictable. It is a rational response by the economic decision-maker to changes in the incentive patterns generated by government designed structural rearrangements of the competitive labor market.

Another government policy designed to assist the poor has also been counterproductive by increasing unemployment. Minimum wage legislation that raises the bottom wage above what many employers can afford to pay has swelled the ranks of the jobless. Instead of hiring workers, more employers mechanize because it becomes cheaper to do so. Many teenagers and women who would ordinarily be willing to work for less than the minimum wage are therefore left with nothing when, without the minimum wage laws, there would be jobs available for them. So the rise in unemployment rates in the 1970s was the result of natural market forces and misguided public policies.

The Crowding-Out Hypothesis and Monetary Policy

The CEIs also argue that fiscal policy is ineffective as a stabilization tool. Deficit spending for the purpose of stimulating the economy, they say, is nothing but a hoax. All deficits, of course, must be financed somehow. Suppose, for example, that the deficit was financed by printing new money. In this event the same sort of process as that described above occurs. Spending increases (some or all of which will be on the government project), inflation rises, and soon workers demand inflation-compensating wage hikes. The economy quickly is back to where it started, but with higher inflation and greater government involvement. The same occurs if the government deficit is financed through borrowing on the open market or through the selling of bonds. In this case the government demand for loans increases the interest rate and effectively reduces the amount of financing available to private businesses. As government activity grows, private sector business declines, since borrowed funds are more difficult to obtain with the government as a competitor.[7] This is popularly known as the "crowding-out" hypothesis: government crowds business out of the financial markets thus reducing private investment, which in turn reduces productivity and economic growth. So an activist fiscal policy can only be detrimental. The strident concern with crowding out has become more muted since 1981 and the historic Reagan administration deficits. Politics may have determined this silence, or the ample supply of international financial resources to the U.S. may have made the argument even less tenable.

Crowding-out still assigns an important role for monetary policy, though different from its role in Keynesian theory. CEIs claim that the Fed can control the money supply, in the absence of correctable technical mistakes by the Fed. In addition, the Fed does not need to create the money that the federal executive's programs require; it can set the money supply according to its view of the economy's needs.

The remaining problem with monetary policy is that its effect is subject to lags in the same way as fiscal policy; and so discretionary monetary policy should be avoided. Its place should be taken by a "monetary rule," a Fed-specified rate of growth of the money supply decided by a technical analysis of the economy. The rate should be keyed to the growth in productivity in the economy and the increase in the need for money for transactions in a growing economy.

This is indeed the policy which the Fed adopted in 1979, thereby rejecting any efforts to set interest rate targets. In subsequent years, this policy raised a series of additional problems, not the least of which was the radically higher interest rate structure which resulted; and the Fed became much more flexible in light of the many difficulties its monetary rule entailed. But CEIs continue to believe that such a policy would operate well, the Fed would not destabilize the economy, and the rate of inflation would be determined by the growth of the money supply.

The Rational Expectations Hypothesis

By the late 1970s an even more rigid variant of the "stabilization policy is ineffective" position had emerged: the Theory of Rational Expectations. Its outline is as follows. Since businesses and unions are getting larger and are increasingly hiring highly educated personnel capable of anticipating, analyzing, and predicting government actions, there is little reason to believe that any significant group will be fooled about how the economy will perform. Unions and businesses rapidly recognize when a government policy is inflationary, e.g., an increase in money supply growth, and they adjust their wage and price decisions accordingly. The net result is that no one will be tricked, and fiscal and monetary policy will be ineffective in bringing about even temporary increases in employment above the natural rate.

Again it is difficult to test rational expectationist claims, especially when they concede the possibility of short-run inflation because of some unanticipated outside shock to the economy. However, the hypothesis is less credible in light of experience in the early 1980s when unemployment increased rapidly by over 2 percentage points and inflation fell dramatically. Unless one is willing to claim there were rapid changes in the natural rate of unemployment, the evidence on the short-run trade-off seems unassailable. Nevertheless, this analysis may become more relevant as each sector in the economy is concentrated in fewer hands and as more sophisticated methods of predicting the future economic climate are developed.

Conclusion

The CEI position, beneath the technical claims, is quite simple. The problems of the 1970s were overblown. If competitive markets had been allowed to function properly, there would have been minor problems, but nothing of lasting significance. Those who trumpet supposed indicators of economic malady and who lament the inadequacy of the economic system all too often prescribe patchwork panaceas that only create sweeping inefficiencies; even worse they are often successful in persuading befuddled policymakers to enact their ill-conceived proposals.

Hence, for CEIs, the economic problems of inflation, unemployment, low capacity utilization, and low productivity growth are caused directly by government policy, or are developments reflecting natural tendencies of economic change.

From the textbook point of view, the CEIs seem almost flawless, once one accepts their initial assumptions about the behavior of people (i.e., self-interest is the drive and motivation behind every economic action) and the performance of markets. Their analysis had been built up as a critique of Keynesian economics, and both its internal logic and the problems the Keynesians faced in the 1970s made it appealing. However, though their textbook analysis seems sound, it is also undeniable that reality deviates from their claims in many ways. The competitive market model of the economy is only a crude approximation of real world markets. And when actually put into operation, few of their technical claims seemed correct. Technical problems in controlling money continue, and the monetary rule had to be abandoned. Stability of the economy, and particularly of individual markets and in the international economy, has been no greater in the 1980s under CEI policies as implemented by the Reagan administration. Crowding out has not lived up to the dire predictions, even in the face of massive federal budget deficits. And only a very flexible

interpretation of the natural rate of unemployment could find its
presence in the behavior of unemployment in the 1980s.

Nevertheless, there is consistency and a certain strength in
CEI analysis; and given their assumptions, it is easy to be per-
suaded to support some of their policies. Certainly the theory as
politically packaged in the 1980 elections appealed to many
Americans looking for simplicity in the face of uncertainty. Their
approach to the other economic problems fit the same mold.

THE BROADER CEI CONTEXT

The focus has been on stabilization policy to this point, but
the CEI position is much broader than those technical issues. It
cannot be repeated too often that the heart of the CEI position is
that a market economy generally operates optimally, government
is limited in its ability to improve the economy, and most of our
economic problems are caused by inappropriate government intervention.

We have covered this argument in detail in the case of macroeconomic policy. CEIs have a similar approach to the three other
problems which usually are the basis for government activity: monopoly, externalities, and unequal opportunity. The failure to deal
with these four problem areas of a free market economy caused
the eclipse of laissez-faire economics for fifty years and the ascen-
dancy of Keynesianism.

The Other Economic "Problems"

As might be expected, CEI analysis calls into question the
importance of these problems. The CEI worldview sees economic
reality as the outcome of a process of voluntary exchange in markets by rational, atomistic agents acting as buyers and sellers. The
resulting market supply and demand determines the prices of
goods and services as well as of capital, labor, and natural resources. The prices signal producers what consumers want and
what is the lowest cost means of production. As a result, consumers
get what they want at the best possible prices and input suppliers
receive what the inputs are worth in production. This theoretical

world of the CEIs by its very nature is one in which externalities are of minimal importance, power is widely diffused, countering any tendency to monopoly, and personal inequalities reflect whether people take advantage of their opportunities, or not.

Monopoly. If monopoly power exists, it is not institutional or endemic to modern industrial society. Existing monopoly power is largely traceable to government interference in the economic system. Import tariffs and quotas can be used to protect areas of monopoly power and to allow prices to be higher than the market would determine. Licensing of doctors, attorneys, and accountants prevents competition and consumer sovereignty from setting the amounts and prices of these services. Regulation of industries is often simply a means of providing a barrier to the entry of competitors. Even in the large utilities such as electricity generation, where government regulation was seen as necessary because scale economies would allow one firm to drive out all others, new technologies and the exhaustion of economies of scale mean that competition can and should rule.

Since the problem is simple, the solution is as well—remove government interference and monopoly will disappear.

Externalities. External costs are minimized by CEIs who label them "neighborhood" effects. They also make the theoretical claim that market forces provide an incentive for most externalities to be corrected through private negotiations among the affected parties, thus making any policy steps unnecessary. For example, those who breathe the air have an incentive to pay the firm not to pollute. The only acceptable policy is to create markets which internalize the externality, e.g., an auction for rights to pollute up to a certain agreed upon level. The firm would have to weigh the costs of cleaning up against the cost of the license to pollute.

Unequal Opportunity. CEIs have developed elaborate arguments to demonstrate that poverty is the result, not of unequal opportunity, but of a combination of poor choices by individuals and misguided attempts by government to help, which make the situation worse by creating dependency and killing incentives to work. The Horatio Alger stories of the immigrant or poor person who made good are true and are certainly one of the inspiring successes of the American system, but they overlook the many sources of an "unequal playing field" in the U.S., as well as the real successes of a number of government programs in levelling that field in some degree. As Deborah Espy, assistant district attorney of Atlanta, said: "The Kennedy-Johnson era lifted a whole generation of black students out of abject poverty because there were equal-opportunity grants for education. I became the first in my family to attend college."

Government Failure. An underlying thread in the CEI response to these problems is that government attempts to correct these alleged problems necessarily fail and in the process create new problems, particularly in the area of incentives. The catalog of examples is long indeed: occupational health and safety regulations increase production costs, reduce productivity, and do little to improve health and safety; environmental standards and conservation measures increase costs, lower productivity, and eliminate jobs; consumer protection regulations increase costs and violate individual freedom of choice; minimum wage laws create unemployment among the unskilled; social welfare measures undermine individual self-reliance and the incentive to work; public education restricts free choice and relegates the poor to inferior education; the social security system takes away freedom of choice and concentrates resources in government hands. Furthermore, the large government bureaucracy necessary to run these programs is costly, unproductive, full of waste and inefficiency, and generates burdensome regulations and paper work for private industry. Finally, these programs and the resulting bureaucracy require high taxes which discourage productive investment in the private sector. That, in turn, lowers the growth of productivity and economic output. Government fails when public policy promotes economic inefficiency.

There are several reasons CEIs claim these results are to be expected. First, politicians frequently try to hide proposals' costs to the general public while promoting the benefits to those who stand to gain; and it is usually difficult for voters to recognize the impact of policies on their interests. Second, when the benefits of a policy are reaped in the short run and the costs incurred only in the long run, there is a "short-sighted" incentive to vote for the policy. Third, managers in public agencies usually are unable to benefit personally from improving the efficiency of their units and there is no profit or loss constraint to monitor their behavior.

So in CEI eyes, the problems are either non-problems or are governmentally induced.

The Underlying Philosophy

One of the strong points of CEI analysis is the internal consistency of its logic. This consistency is most clear with the libertarian strain of the CEIs, which traces directly back to the classical economists of the eighteenth and nineteenth centuries. Classical liberalism (of Smith and Mill) assumed that the chief threat to individual liberty was government and the surest road to progress along with the best protection of liberty was reliance on individual initiative within the context of a free market economy.

Modern liberalism (the New Deal-Keynesian consensus) sees the chief threats to individual liberty as large private power centers—particularly big business—and the poverty and lack of opportunity which make liberty empty of meaning. Thus government must curb that private power and promote prosperity and opportunity.

Modern conservatives still see the state as the chief enemy of individual liberty. But the threat to liberty from the power of large corporations does not arouse conservative concern. And eight years in power in Washington pointed to a number of practical differences among conservatives. The level of "sleaze" under the conservative administration was notable. It grew from the disdain for government and for the ethics of "public service." It was clearly a small step to translate this disdain into a willingness to use government for one's own personal gain, justified often by how much one could have earned in the private sector. Well over one hundred high employees of the Reagan administration quit under a cloud or were charged for such behavior. A second split in conservative ranks came on the freedom—or rights—of government employees. The administration was quite willing to require widespread use of lie-detectors for government employees and had few doubts about mandating drug testing for workers in the transportation sector, including over-the-road truck drivers. The libertarian tradition became subservient to the conservative social agenda.

The more consistent modern libertarian wing shares with classical liberalism the distrust of governmental power, but would push the logic much further than the typical conservative. For example, Milton Friedman opposes all state licensing—whether of physicians, lawyers, or whatever—as inefficient and an infringement on individual liberty. He believes that if individuals are left to look after themselves in all spheres of life, the best of all possible worlds will ensue. No one can dictate what individual needs and wants are, and no one should. A natural social harmony exists when individuals are permitted to pursue their own ends.

In terms of the goals of the economy specified earlier, libertarians place primary emphasis on the third—freedom. And freedom would rank far higher than most other goals. It should include consumer sovereignty for certain, and at a theoretical level should also include citizen sovereignty and worker sovereignty. At a practical level, however, there may be problems with the latter two. Voters may choose means of protecting themselves and may actually vote to interfere with markets and competition, and they may be able to sway politicians. This may require some constraint in the form of limiting what is permissible for government to do, even if a majority want it. Also, many efforts toward worker sovereignty—worker management, worker ownership, job enrichment—are seen as inefficient. The hierarchical corporate structure is thought highly efficient in harnessing productive enterprises to their proper task, profit maximization.

Much of the appeal of the CEI philosophy, especially its libertarian strain, is that, in addition to the prominence given to freedom, there is complementarity between it and the other goals. The invisible hand of the market system will take individual choices and meld them together into an efficient economic system which will deliver the maximum amount of goods for the resources available. And self-esteem comes from operating as a rational, independent individual. Earning your own way is the surest road to self-esteem.

Society functions well only because the self-interest of each individual is benefitted thereby. No person has a moral obligation to his or her neighbor other than that agreed to in a mutual contract. Since individuals are sovereign, and since any decision to coexist with others is based on individual gain, the CEI accepts limits on individual decision-making only where it interferes with another person's rights. However, these interdependencies are seen as exceptions. Consequently the philosophic objection to government intervention in the economy is that it is an affront to natural human rights. CEIs oppose the growth of government bureaucracy; and they are concerned when economic decisions become politicized, and the individual is hindered in the exercise of his or her fundamental right to make personal economic decisions.*

Because of their focus on individual liberty and their faith in the free market, CEIs do not feel the need to discuss equity at any length. They argue that equity is a function of the process, not of the outcomes of an economic system. If the process is fair, then the system is fair regardless of outcomes.[8] In a decentralized competitive market system, each person earns in accordance with what they contribute to production. Hence, effort, ambition, and innate skills are rewarded; laziness, foolishness, and stupidity are not.

Conclusion

The classical liberal tradition which CEIs represent, at least in part, places ultimate importance on the freedom of the individual to determine his or her own fate. Their policy stance is founded on the belief that the theoretical model of competition can be incorporated in policy and that a laissez-faire market economy will maximize both individual freedom and economic welfare. Milton Friedman, in his usual trenchant manner, provides a short summary of the CEI position:

> The central planners want planning by them for us. They want the government—by which they really mean themselves—to decide "social priorities" (i.e., tell us what is good for us); "rationalize production" (i.e., tell us where and how we should work); assure "equitable distribution" (i.e., take from some of us to give to others of us).

---

*The libertarian wing has effectively been forced into research institutes such as the Cato Institute and the Fraser Institute in Canada as the "conservative social agenda" in areas such as drugs, abortion, and sex education was adopted by the Reagan administration. George Bush's willingness to consider limits on imports of automatic weapons in the interest of fighting drugs shows that libertarians will remain on the sidelines.

Such planning, from the top down, is inefficient because it makes it impossible to use the detailed knowledge shared among millions of individuals. It undermines freedom because it requires people to obey orders rather than pursue their own interests. I am for planning, too, but planning by each of us separately in light of our individual, though shared, values, coordinated by voluntary exchange in free markets. Such planning, from the bottom up, enlists the interests of each in promoting the well-being of all. Government has its role—to provide a stable legal and monetary framework, enforce contracts and adjudicate disputes and protect us from coercion by our fellow citizens.[9]

Adam Smith could not have said it better. Two hundred years of change in the economic world are irrelevant to the economic theory of the CEIs. No Rockefellers, no multinational corporations, no imperialism, no environmental destruction, just many small buyers and sellers engaging in production and exchange, maximizing their freedom and economic welfare. If we only could get government to tend to its proper business, all would be well. This vision of the world may be beautiful, but it is a vision, and a vision which we feel to be completely at odds with the realities we must operate in.

CEI PROPOSALS FOR PRODUCTIVE REFORM

The CEIs underlying philosophy and critique of the Keynesians signal the type of policy reforms the CEIs proposed in the late 1970s. A synopsis of their reform program emerged in the refrain "get the government out of business." Since CEIs view the economy as governed by certain natural laws which are, for all practical purposes, immutable, the government has no business fiddling with them, and can do nothing but harm. CEIs claim that without government intervention, the economy would stay very close to a self-determined natural rate of unemployment, would function without the problem of inflation, and would adjust quickly to any unanticipated shocks. As a result, policies emanating from economists of the CEI tradition were, at least in some sense, anti-policies; for they sought to remove instead of install.

Limiting the Role of Government

CEI proposals to limit the role of the government in the economy logically followed from their criticisms of Keynesian policy. First, they called for a general reduction in government expenditures to reduce the size of government, to reduce its impact on the economy, and to allow greater room for private sector activity. Wherever possible, necessary public functions should be transferred to lower levels of government.

Second, they urged cuts in social welfare expenditures which, in their view, reduce individuals' incentive to work and are a major source of waste and fraud in government.

Third, they proposed that government programs and legislation which contravene the workings of the free market be repealed. Examples were minimum wage laws, import tariffs and quotas, rent controls, farm price supports, and subsidies to the ship building industry.

Fourth, they called for deregulation—i.e., the elimination of regulations on business activity that increase the cost of production and lower productivity. Examples were occupational health and safety laws, consumer protection regulations, control of airlines and trucking, and environmental protection requirements.

Finally, they proposed a general tax cut to pass on to the taxpayers the savings from the above proposals. Presumably, the size of the tax cut was constrained by the need to maintain a balanced federal budget.

Stabilization Policy

On the key question of stabilization, any arbitrarily chosen target goal of full employment had to be abandoned. The government has very little influence on the unemployment rate, and a target simply justifies ever-increasing government expenditures and consequent inflationary pressures. The government was no longer, therefore, to be seen as the front line defense against recession; and the size of government expenditures had to be strictly limited so that the private sector could operate freely in attaining individuals' goals. The government should operate with a balanced budget in order to avoid crowding out private expenditures.

While fiscal policy was to be eliminated, monetary policy was the key to stability. Since monetary shocks had been behind every major recession and expansion in the U.S., CEIs believed that economic stability required stable growth of the money supply. Activist monetary policy could not realistically hope to counter recessionary or inflationary tendencies; and in fact, anything other than steady money growth would cause instability rather than cure it. Monetary policy should therefore never be used to regulate economic activity, but should pursue a steady rate of money expansion related to the normal rate of economic growth. In this way individual decision-makers would not spend resources anticipating Federal Reserve actions, but would know exactly what to expect from the monetary authorities; their rational expectations would be fulfilled.

The final CEI stabilization policy called attention to the need for a stable international monetary structure, brought about by monetary rules in all of the countries of the world.

CEIs claimed that these policies would lead to a sharp expansion in economic growth which, when combined with a constant rate of monetary growth, would eliminate inflation over time and reduce unemployment to its "natural" level. At the same time freedom of the individual would be preserved by reducing government intervention and instead relying on the private sector.

These were radical proposals which would hurt some vested interests, would cause a number of substantial short-run problems, and whose long-run success was far from agreed upon by any but the true believers. Their effect in previous periods of implementation had been nowhere near so favorable, with recession the usual result. This experience made their enactment doubtful, but the problems of the 1970s and the election of 1980 opened the door—but only after traditional CEI analysis was packaged with a new panacea.

The New Component: Supply-side Economics

Most of the above policies are vintage Adam Smith, but something new and salable was added with "supply-side economics." In addition to cutting government expenditures and deregulating the economy, supply-siders wanted massive tax cuts (even if they caused short-term budget deficits) to provide incentives for new saving and investment which would increase productivity and aggregate supply in the long-run. This would create jobs and lessen inflationary pressures, thus curing the dual problems of the 1970s.

Supply-side economics had an ambitious version and a more modest one. The first argued that a reduction in tax rates (not offset by an equivalent reduction in government expenditures) would increase real output enough to increase actual tax revenues even with the lowered rates. It would do so by operating on the supply side of the economy.

Keynesians had made a similar argument based on the demand side. If there were unemployed resources in the economy, a tax cut would stimulate demand, putting the idle resources back to work and, thus, increasing real output and tax revenues. Supply-siders, in contrast, started with the assumption that there are no unemployed resources, but more resources would be offered for sale or hire if the real rate of return were higher. A tax-rate cut would increase the after-tax rate of return to productive resources, thereby increasing their supply. Over a short period of time this would increase real output and thus tax revenues.

There were two key assumptions, both based on empirical claims:

1. That a tax cut would provide an effective incentive for people to save and invest more in productive plant or equipment and to supply more of their labor.
2. That the magnitude of the effect would be sufficient to increase tax revenues.

The assumptions were very dubious. There was little empirical evidence one way or the other. Moreover, increases in output of the size necessary to generate the required increases in tax revenues were most improbable.

The modest version of supply-side economics was more careful in claiming only that a cut in tax rates would increase real output, though tax revenues would decrease. Even this modest version was not obviously true. Again it depended on the magnitudes of the effects. As Professor Herbert Stein, a non supply-side CEI, wrote: " ... if the increase in private sector saving is less than the decrease in public sector saving (the increase in the budget deficit resulting from the tax cut) private investment will be crowded out and there is no reason for counting on an increase in the long-run growth rate."[10]

An extreme version of supply-side economics, popular within the Reagan administration in the early 1980s, maintained that inflation could be stopped without unemployment by utilizing tax rate cuts to increase aggregate supply. They argued that since inflation was simply the excess of aggregate demand over aggregate supply, there was no need to use Keynesian demand constriction, creating a recession, when supply could painlessly be increased. This version was called "voodoo" economics in 1980 by George Bush because of the magnitude of the effects required. In the 1988 election Bush embraced that economics and won the presidency.

Herbert Stein's 1980 view of supply-side economics provides the proper dose of skepticism: "Supply-side economics may yet prove to be the irritant which, like the grain of sand in the oyster shell, produces a pearl of new economic wisdom. But up to this point the pearl has not appeared."[11]

CONCLUSION

Our evaluation of the whole CEI program, as implemented in the Reagan administration during the 1980s, is in the next chapter. The CEIs had long enjoyed the luxury of being the critics and had developed a formidable intellectual apparatus in that task. Their underlying philosophy carried a basic appeal to Americans. When they took the reins of power in 1981, they had to take responsibility both for their technical claims on how the economy functions and for the results of their policies in dealing with the basic economic problems of the country. They went from spectators directly to the firing line.

5. The Reagan Years: CEIs and the Haunted Prosperity of the 1980s

CEIs were in an enviable position as the 1970s closed, since they were critics at a time when the economy was clearly in trouble. Combined with the simplicity and apparent coherence of their theory, this made them an appealing alternative to the struggling Keynesians. However, there were few *scientific* or empirical reasons to expect their proposals to fare better than the Keynesians'.[1]

It is particularly difficult to verify or falsify the constituent propositions of the CEIs' laissez-faire theory. Its survival and attractiveness derive in part from its shifts between interesting empirical propositions and true, though empty, tautologies. For example, they start from the *truism* that people seek their economic advantage[2] and then deduce the *empirical proposition* that productive investment and work effort are reduced by taxes and other government measures that reduce the economic rate of return. However, when confronted with evidence that investment rates over the period 1948–1980 *actually* were stable or even increased slightly in the face of escalating tax rates and government regulations, they retreat to a comparison of *potential* effects: in the long run if tax rates and other burdens were increased enough, eventually productive investment and work effort would fall. Thus, an apparent empirical falsification can always be sidestepped by recourse to a long-run, abstract potentiality. The ability to avoid falsification certainly accounts for some of laissez-faire theory's renewed vitality at the end of the 1970s.[3]

Another central element in its appeal was the implicit social philosophy and its policy prescriptions for the "good society": atomistic individualism, coordinated by the market, and resulting in the common good through the operation of the invisible hand. Despite its obvious appeal at the end of the turbulent seventies, this social philosophy seems particularly inappropriate for solving today's socioeconomic problems. The modern economy is characterized by interdependence among its economic actors, not independence. Externalities are the rule, not the exception. Firms are not simply price takers; they are dependent upon each other's price and quantity decisions. Power is necessary to market new products, attain government favors, and compete internationally. General Motors, ITT, and IBM, not the corner newspaper dealer, typify the "representative firm" of today. The Japanese understand this, and their economic ascendency is largely attributable to policies which take this reality into account, policies quite different from those suggested in the CEI laissez-faire approach.[4]

The perfectly competitive model of the CEIs has little to say in the face of today's urgent socioeconomic problems, other than to exhort us to believe that the problems will all evaporate if we simply return to laissez-faire government policy. Technological change will not undermine competition; competition will check any tendencies toward concentration of economic power; external diseconomies will transform themselves into minor "neighborhood" effects; and job dissatisfaction will disappear because workers will be able to equate the disutility of work with the utility of income. The market, unfettered by government control, will provide a stable and growing prosperity for all.

When Ronald Reagan was elected president in 1980, the CEIs had the opportunity, and the responsibility, to reshape the structure of the American political economy built up over the past fifty years. The success of their policies would provide a test of the laissez-faire approach which was so appealing in theory.

THE REAGAN-CEI PROGRAM

The CEI economic program represented a radical change from the anemic Keynesianism of the 1970s, and it is a tribute to the political abilities of Ronald Reagan and his first-term advisers that the policies suggested by the theory were for the most part implemented.

At the heart of CEI thought was the idea that New Deal–
Keynesian policies had undermined the creativeness of the market
economy by blunting incentives through high taxation, over-regu-
lation, and excessively generous social welfare programs. They
believed that by reducing these government activities and restor-
ing incentives, the basis for future economic growth would be
established. Therefore, CEIs had proposed reducing the role of
government in the economy.

Under the Reagan administration, the growth of non-de-
fense expenditures was slowed and the possibilities of transferring
some government programs to the private sector became part of
the debate. The overall effect on government expenditures was
lessened because of the unprecedented increase in peacetime military expenditures. Social welfare expenditures were reduced and
entire programs cut, though programs for the elderly were a major exception because of their political power. Government intervention in markets was limited: because of inflation the minimum
wage became increasingly irrelevant to the actual labor market;
many trade restrictions were resisted or removed; and a number
of subsidies were removed, though farm subsidies were excepted
because of political opposition generated by the farm crisis of
1984–85. In addition, the regulation of business was reduced, except in areas of defense where draconian controls on technology
were attempted. The initial crude attempts at deregulation such
as the Burford-Lavelle debacle at the Environmental Protection
Agency were supplanted by more sophisticated non-enforcement
of provisions and efforts to change regulation.

Finally, the tax cuts central to the supply-side component of
the CEI program were enacted through the dramatic 1982 tax cut
and the 1987 Tax Reform. The first provided a reduction in the
total taxes paid, especially by the wealthy, and the second a reduction in the marginal tax rates, again especially those of the wealthy,
though many of the working poor were also removed from the tax
rolls. The theoretical incentives to saving, work effort, and investment had now been incorporated into the tax code.

In the area of stabilization policy, fiscal policy became moot,
just as CEIs had proposed. All expenditure and tax proposals
were made without specific reference to their effects on stabilization of the economy. Monetary policy in the initial years followed

the ideas of Milton Friedman and concentrated on the growth of the money supply rather than on interest rates, though the unsatisfactory experience reversed the approach in later years of the administration.

Given the success of the Reagan administration in putting in place the CEI program, has the promise been realized? Our answer is No. Though there have been some successes, most notably a lower inflation rate, the program has not lived up to its promises to solve the problems of the 1970s and to lay the ground for future economic growth. We will examine these claims in turn. The conclusion is that "freeing-up" the economy may have liberated capitalism's creative tendencies, but they have been too anemic to solve the country's problems.

In addition, and perhaps of greater importance, CEI policies have generated a series of new problems and tensions in the society that are far more grave than those of the 1970s. Any prosperity has been haunted by these suppressed issues. Most importantly, the CEI-Reagan policies resulted in reinforcing capitalism's destructive and unequal developmental tendencies rather than mitigating them. Large tax cuts, particularly to higher income groups, reductions in social expenditures, increases in military expenditures, the removal of government regulation of business, and the unified attack on labor have led to declining real wages, increases in income inequality, deterioration of social infrastructure, and the creation of a social deficit that the country will have to confront in future years. Finally the prosperity has floated on a swelling sea of debt, created by the federal budget deficit and by the deficit in the balance of payments. The prosperity of the Latin American countries in the 1970s was similarly debt-led; their subsequent instability may be an indicator of things to come.

Let us first examine the Reagan-CEI record in solving the economic problems of the 1970s and laying the basis for renewed economic growth. Then we can turn to the Reagan-CEI legacy of suppressed and newly created problems.

THE REAGAN-CEI RECORD

In its simplest form, the Reagan-CEI program promised to solve the problems of the 1970s. Inflation was too rapid and unemployment too high; economic growth was low and productivity had stagnated. Finally there was an economic malaise in the land, the American dream was not being fulfilled. Did the Reagan-CEI program live up to its promises?

Inflation

· The major economic success of the Reagan era was the conquest of inflation. The average annual rate of increase in the Consumer Price Index was reduced from 9.3 percent during the period 1973–80 to 4.7 percent during the period 1981–88.[5] The fall was even more dramatic when single years are compared. In 1980, President Carter's last year in office, the rate of inflation was 13.5 percent. By 1983 that had been reduced to 3.2 percent. However, it is only fair to the Keynesians to point out that the inflation rate during the period 1960–73, before the supply shocks, was 3.1 percent.

In addition, there are a number of qualifications which should be offered before the lower inflation is taken as a pure success. First, inflation is detrimental when it affects the real economy, the production and availability of goods and services. CEIs claim that inflation causes inefficiencies as people hedge to protect themselves from its effects and because it shifts income from creditors to debtors. They also fear that inflation is self-perpetuating through its impact on expectations of future price increases. Nonetheless, other countries have functioned quite well with rates of inflation higher than the U.S. rate. Indeed, in the 1962–1988 period, of the seven major industrial powers, only Germany has had lower inflation than the U.S., implying that higher inflation rates might not be an economy's worst problem.

More importantly, the process of stopping inflation often has important effects on the rest of the economy. William Greider has made a convincing case that the pressure to slow inflation came from the relatively few, but quite wealthy, holders of financial assets.[6] Only 10 percent of the families hold 86 percent of the net financial wealth of families and the control of institutional assets is similarly concentrated. Many of these wealth-holders had seen inflation erode the real value of their assets, and inflation had increased the uncertainty and risk for others. They were the major beneficiaries of the lower inflation; the administration's removal of financial regulations furthered their gains.

Secondly, inflation was whipped by the old-time remedy of a recession.[7] The Reagan administration cooperated with the Federal Reserve Board's tight money policy begun in October 1979 and this resulted in the deepest recession and the highest level of unemployment since the Great Depression of the 1930s. Unemployment peaked at 10.3 percent during January and February 1983 and averaged 9.5 percent for both 1982 and 1983. For the period 1981–87 the average was 7.4 percent, compared to 6.7 percent for 1974–80 and 4.9 percent for 1960–73. In 1987, after four years of recovery, the unemployment rate was still 6.1 percent, though it dropped to the 5 percent range in 1989.

Furthermore, the effect of the Reagan deflation is understated in these numbers. It played a role in throwing a large majority of the world's economies into deep recessions which in many cases continue today. Some Latin American countries saw GNP decline by over 20 percent between 1982 and 1986 as their export prices plummetted and their debt burden continued unabated. World growth slowed markedly (table 1) especially in the Third World, and only the countries with an already developed manufactured export capacity, such as Korea or Taiwan, or the protectionist countries such as China and India were able to resist these blows.

TABLE 1

Growth of Gross Domestic Product
(Annual Average Percent)

	1965–80	1980–86
Low-Income Countries (except China and India)	3.1	2.9
China and India	5.3	8.6
Middle Income Countries	6.6	2.3
All Developing Countries	6.1	3.8
Industrial Market Countries	3.6	2.5

Source: IBRD(World Bank), *World Development Report, 1988,* Table 2

So stable prices were purchased at a very high cost in the U.S. and in the world, and with benefit primarily to a narrow segment of U.S. wealth-holders. The high cost of reducing inflation should temper our enthusiasm for this particular accomplishment. The quickening of inflation since 1987 should also be a sobering influence.

Unemployment and the Labor Market

The record on solving the unemployment problem has been poor. While the very high unemployment of the mid-1980s is in some degree counterbalanced by the fall in unemployment below 6 percent by the end of the Reagan era and by the 12 million person increase in total employment over the period, there is less to these claims than may first appear.

The particular character of the unemployment resulting from the 1981–83 recession has not only held down wage inflation; but, combined with reductions in social welfare and unemployment benefit programs, has produced the "new poor"—destitute, sometimes homeless, former workers and their families. In the 1981–83 recession, permanent job loss as a percent of total layoffs was over 53 percent compared to 36 percent in the three previous recessions (1969–70, 1973–75, 1979–80). In addition, those permanently unemployed from their previous positions stayed jobless for longer periods of time before finding new work. By 1983 nearly 3 million workers, which was 25 percent of all unemployed, were counted as "long-term unemployed," having been jobless for more than six months. Over 1.5 million had been out of work for more than a year, which was thirty times the comparable figure in the 1969–70 recession. They also received less support as unemployment insurance coverage was lowered and its value eroded through inflation; and other programs such as Trade Adjustment Assistance were scrapped.

Direct attacks on labor reinforced the recession's effectiveness in deflating wage demands. President Reagan fired the striking air traffic controllers and destroyed their union, PATCO, letting business know that the federal government would not interfere with union-busting tactics used to control wage costs; and the National Labor Relations Board greatly strengthened the bargaining power of employers by its decisions.[8] In the ensuing years business adopted a policy of wage reductions, plant relocations, strategic bankruptcy filings, and replacement of union labor with non-union labor, often claiming that this was the only way to meet the challenges of our declining competitiveness in the world economy.

As a result, wage differentials between high- and low-paid jobs have increased; there is (controversial) evidence that 60 percent of the new jobs created pay less than $7000 per year, and the use of contingent workers, temporaries, on-call or contracted-out workers has increased rapidly to 25 percent of the work force. This has led to a substantial increase in involuntary, part-time workers, from 3.8 percent of those working in 1979 to 4.9 percent in 1988.[9]

The unemployment problem has not been solved in any meaningful sense; and in addition, the unemployment costs entailed in the effort to stop inflation must be taken into account in any evaluation of the program.

Economic Growth and Productivity

A central promise of CEI advisers to the Reagan administration was that reducing government interference in the economy would increase efficiency and productivity, which in turn would result in accelerated economic growth. The actual record shows that from 1981 through 1988 the average annual increase in GNP was 2.7 percent, compared to 3.9 percent during the Keynesian "hey-day" of 1960–73 and 2.2 percent during their darkest days of 1974–80. This is hardly an exceptional performance.

A major factor in this lethargic performance has been that productivity gains fell far short of CEI expectations. The average annual increase in output per hour in the business sector was less than 1.5 percent from 1981 through 1987. This is substantially better than the 0.5 percent rate of 1974–80 but far short of the 2.7 percent achieved during 1960–73.

Under-utilization of manufacturing capacity and the lagging investment rate have contributed to slow productivity growth. From 1981 through 1987, capacity utilization in manufacturing averaged only 78.4 percent, compared to 80.3 percent during

1974–80 and 84.0 percent during 1960–73. During 1988, after
five years of recovery, we had finally reached 84.0 percent of
capacity. Thus we have been wasting significant amounts of our
productive capacity as the price of holding down cost inflation.
Of greater importance in the long run is the stagnation of non-
residential fixed investment, the new plant and equipment which
fuel future growth. From 1981–87 this investment increased an
anemic 12 percent, far lower than the 1973–80 increase of 19.5
percent, though the pace had picked up in 1987 and 1988. So not
only was actual growth low, but little basis for future growth was
laid. The creative dynamo of capitalism was certainly not ener-
gized by the Reagan revolution.

Poverty and Income Distribution

On the other hand, the destructive tendency toward uneven
development is much clearer. The Reagan years have witnessed
an increase in every overall measure of poverty and a widening
of the gap between rich and poor. The number of persons living
below the official poverty line increased from 26.1 million in 1979
to 32.5 million in 1987, an increase from 11.7 percent to 13.5
percent of the population. By comparison the rate fell from 19.5
percent in 1963 to 11.1 percent in 1973 and remained relatively
stable through the economic problems of 1973–80. Poverty wors-
ens only with the enactment of CEI policies under the Reagan
administration.

At the same time poverty was increasing and income distribution was becoming more unequal, the Reagan administration was
cutting aid to the poor. Cuts from the Food Stamp Program between 1982 and 1985 totaled $6.8 billion, taking more than a
million recipients off the rolls and reducing benefits for 20 million
others at a time of high unemployment and increasing poverty.
From 1982 to 1985, $5 billion was cut from the four basic child
nutrition programs: school lunch, school breakfast, child care
food, and summer food programs. From 1981 to 1985 the Social
Security Administration (SSA) dropped 419,300 disabled persons
from the rolls. After long administration and court proceedings,
more than 200,000 were reinstated and SSA actions were found
to be illegal. In addition, in the face of growing unemployment,

the response of the federal government was to cut back on unemployment benefit programs. In 1980, 50 percent of the unemployed were covered by unemployment insurance; by 1988 less than 33 percent were covered. The effect on payments to the unemployed was dramatic. In the 1982 recession, fewer than half of the unemployed received benefits and in 1983 fewer than a third did. By contrast in the last year of the 1973–75 recession, more than three-fourths of the unemployed received benefits.

One summary measure of this tendency to uneven development under Reagan administration policies is the distribution of income. In 1986, the richest 20 percent of American families received 43.7 percent of national family income—the highest percentage ever recorded. The richest 5 percent of families received 16.7 percent of all national family income. The poorest 20 percent of families received only 4.6 percent of family income—the lowest share since 1954. The middle 20 percent of families received 16.8 percent—the lowest share ever recorded.[10]

Stability

The Depression was a millstone around the CEI neck; Milton Friedman's success in plausibly shifting part of the blame to the government was an important factor in their rehabilitation. The question still remains whether a free market economy has an inherent tendency to instability. The recession during the early years of the Reagan administration appeared to provide a clear yes answer; however, the slow and steady recovery since 1983 makes that answer less certain. Nonetheless there are valid concerns about the stability of an economy made over in their image.

While there have been no macroeconomic gyrations since 1983, specific markets have been wildly erratic. The best example is the stock market whose decline of 508 points on October 19, 1987, was sobering and led to a series of steps to limit the operation of this market when it shows signs of instability. Foreign exchange markets have also been extremely volatile, with the dollar rising to exchange for 260 yen in 1985 and then plummetting to be worth 123 yen in 1988. These fluctuations put U.S. producers of goods traded internationally on a roller coaster ride that was of benefit neither to them nor to the economy.

Business failures climbed to 120 per 10,000 in 1986, far higher than the postwar recession average of 49. And bank failures rose over the entire period from 10 per year in 1981 to 180 in 1987 and to a record 221 in 1988, putting severe pressure on the insurance pools whose role is to avoid financial panic. And of course the bailout of the Savings and Loan industry which is likely to cost over $140 billion is in large measure a result of allowing S&Ls to "compete" in the free financial markets while government regulation took on a spectator's role.

In addition, much of the recovery from the recession has been fueled by large government deficits and facilitated by the impressive trade deficit; had the rest of the world been less accommodating to the U.S., the likelihood of instability would have been greatly heightened. And the time may well be coming when international constraints will again force the U.S. to undertake contractionary domestic economic policy. In the meantime, the main implication of the improved performance in recent years is not support for the CEI-Reagan theory; rather the basis of much of it has been traditional (Keynesian) demand stimulation through budget deficits, with resultant improvement in employment and capacity utilization. So the "success" of the Reagan program in lowering inflation can be plausibly attributed to its ability to engender, and withstand, the deepest recession of the postwar period. And the recovery from the recession can also be attributed to traditional demand stimulation; the Reagan "success" was its ability to raise the government deficit to unprecedented levels in order to fuel the recovery.

So the Reagan record is far from the success that its proponents hoped for. Lower inflation and recent modest growth cannot be clearly attributed to diminished government activity and the unleashing of the market. And the costs of any success have been substantial. Poverty has worsened and the benefits of growth have been very unevenly distributed. Given the weak response of business investment and productivity to CEI policies, there is little evidence that capitalism's creative powers will be adequate to the task of solving the problems of the 1970s, nor the new problems which have been created in the 1980s. The opposite may indeed be the case.

THE REAGAN-CEI LEGACY: A HAUNTED PROSPERITY

The Reagan economic recovery since 1983 has covered up a number of problems which will come back to haunt us in future years: (1) record federal budget deficits; (2) record trade deficits; (3) an unprecedented increase in consumption expenditures and decline in savings; (4) a tragic deferral of infrastructure maintenance; (5) deindustrialization of the U.S. economy with consequent growth of a two-tiered wage system; and 6) growth of an "underclass" of poor trapped inside the lowest wage sectors of the economy or pushed outside the economy, freqently hungry and homeless.

The Twin Deficits

The most dangerous legacy for the economic counselors of the Bush administration is the twin deficits, the massive federal budget deficit and the trade deficit. Table 2 illustrates the challenge they will face.

At the outset of the Reagan administration, the federal debt was $914 billion; by 1988 it had risen to $2.6 trillion. At the start of the Reagan administration, the U.S. had a surplus in its trade

TABLE 2

Growth of Federal Budget and Trade Deficits

Year	Federal Deficit ($B)	Trade Surplus ($B)
1980	−73.8	32.1
1981	−78.9	33.9
1982	−127.9	26.3
1983	−207.8	−6.1
1984	−185.3	−58.9
1985	−212.3	−78.0
1986	−221.2	−104.4
1987	−149.7	−123.0
1988	−155.1	−111.1
1989 (EST.)	−161.5	

Source: *Economic Report of the President, 1989*, Tables B 76 and B 1.

in goods and services. By its end the magnitude of the deficit was almost inconceivable.

The increase in the federal budget deficit was the direct result of the 1982 income tax reductions coupled with the Reagan peacetime defense buildup.

Recall that in the late 1970s some CEIs argued that the supply-side effects of a tax cut would so stimulate the economy that tax revenues would fall little if any. At the time there was very little empirical evidence that these CEI policies would work.* One economic model had been touted in the literature as showing the beneficial effects of a CEI, supply-side program on saving, work effort, and investment. An earlier version was scrapped by its sponsor and there was little information to indicate successful implementation of the new version.[11] Indeed, supply-side CEIs had difficulty in formulating a macro-model. David Stockman of the Office of Management and Budget found that when his expenditure and taxation plans were fed into the Congressional Budget Office model, the results were unacceptable (budget deficits of $70 and $80 billion). Stockman turned to an economic model developed at the Claremont Economics Institute but that did not suit his needs. Finally, he teamed up with aide Lawrence Kudlow to construct what was described as "a framework for constructing general economic 'scenarios'."[12] The various assumptions in the "framework" apparently produced what Stockman had been after—the conclusion that implementation of the Reagan program would lead to growth of 4 percent per year and, by 1983, a balanced budget with inflation of 5 percent. Including these claims as assumptions, however, was far from providing evidence, and the economy paid the price for such sleight-of-hand.

George Bush had aptly termed the program "voodoo economics"—in addition to its economics, it embodied a concealed political agenda. Stockman quickly recognized that the economics was flawed. For public consumption he touted the economic models cited above; privately he admitted that "to balance the budget we would need huge spending cuts too—more than $100 billion

---

*However it made a great political gambit: we could have our cake and eat it too. Cut tax rates and tax revenues would not decline.

per year. The fabled feedback of the Laffer curve (lowered tax rates produce more tax revenues) had thus slid into the grave of fiscal mythology 40 days after the supply side banner had been hoisted up at the G.O.P. Convention."[13] Stockman's solution was to create a fiscal crisis. The resulting deficits would force Congress to "turn against their own handiwork—the bloated budget of the American welfare state. Why would they do this? Because they had to! In the final analysis, I had made fiscal necessity the mother of political invention."

Congress did cut social welfare programs, as noted above. However, defense had to grow rapidly, social security was political dynamite, and interest on the public debt was uncontrollable. The result was continuing fiscal deficits that kept real interest rates high and contributed to the overvaluation of the dollar on the international economy through 1985 with resultant enormous trade deficits. The later fall in the dollar has not solved the trade deficits because the markets lost have been extremely difficult to reclaim.

In addition, it has become political suicide to attempt to lower the deficit through raising taxes or reducing politically popular programs such as social security. "Read my lips," said George Bush enroute to winning the presidency in 1988. As a result fiscal flexibility has been lost, and future adjustment of fiscal policy to new economic conditions will be quite difficult if not impossible.

The U.S. balance of trade in goods and services deteriorated from a surplus of $9.5 billion in 1980 to a deficit of $140.5 billion in 1987. The trade deficit worsened because imports exploded while exports rose barely above the 1980 level. Manufactured imports accounted for 54 percent of all imported goods in 1980, but by 1987 had expanded to 77 percent. The situation was aggravated by the slow rate of recovery in other industrial countries which held back expansion of their demand for U.S. exports. And Third World countries, especially in Latin America, were forced to restrict imports and to run large surpluses, simply to generate the foreign exchange necessary to maintain payments on their international debt. This uneven world recovery was the final factor leading to the record-breaking trade deficits in the 1980s.

Heavy borrowing from abroad has been necessary to cover the trade deficit. This has transformed the U.S. from the world's largest creditor in 1982 to the largest debtor nation in the world, with a net asset balance of -$368 billion in 1987. This will represent an additional drain over time with some estimating that payments of interest on this debt soon may reach over $50 billion a year. In the first quarter of 1988, for the first time in the postwar period, the U.S. had a deficit on its investment income. President Reagan dismissed these problems in the terms a University of Chicago economist had dismissed the Latin American deficits: "Thank God for the deficits, since they show that foreign lenders have faith in the economy." The faith of foreign lenders is a very frail reed to support an economy, as the Latin Americans have discovered.

The result of these twin deficits is a distorted and fragile economy. After promising to reduce the size of budget deficits, CEIs have presided over unprecedented increases. Fiscal deficits averaged 1.7 percent of GNP from 1970 to 1979 but increased to an average of 4.0 percent between 1980 and 1987.[14] Interest payments on the national debt of $159 billion in 1988 far exceeded the expected gain in private savings generated by the 1981 tax cut. Keynesian theory suggested that budget deficits could offset the cyclical behavior of the economy, and that the budget should be balanced over the cycle, with surpluses in boom years offsetting deficits in downturns. This is no longer possible; any prosperity in the economy is dependent on deficits, much as a drug user's euphoria depends on an infusion of the drug. Remove either and a crash is likely.

CEIs also promised increased international competitiveness through improved efficiency and productivity; yet their policies generated massive trade deficits. "Today, despite ... extraordinary luck on the energy front, we have managed to twist the global economy into the most lopsided imbalance between saving (foreign) and spending (American) ever witnessed in the industrialized era."[15]

Consumption, Saving, and Investment

The Reagan-CEI recovery has been powered by consumption spending, not by the promised increase in saving and investment that were supposed to result from the 1982 tax cut. "Far from being an investment boom, we have been on a consumer binge financed by liquidating our assets abroad, by gorging on a huge flow of imports, and by depressing national saving and investment to the lowest level since the 1930s."[16] Net private saving (personal plus business saving minus depreciation on capital equipment) was only 4.7 percent of GNP in 1988, after five years of recovery, though it did begin to recover in 1989 to 5.8 percent as economic uncertainty increased. Even this was well below the long-run average of 8 to 9 percent. Over one-half of this saving was absorbed by government deficits (dissaving). As a result the net national saving rate was less than 2.0 percent, the lowest since the 1930s. CEI policies also have generated the weakest net investment performance since the 1930s, averaging 4.8 percent of GNP over the period 1981 to 1988. And this was possible only because of the huge inflow of foreign saving. Contrast this with the Japanese saving rate of 18.0 percent or its investment share of GNP which reaches 33 percent, and the implications become clearer.

Peter Peterson sums up the Reagan-CEI era in these terms: "This is, quite simply, the dirty little secret of Reaganomics: behind the pleasurable observation that real U.S. consumption per worker has risen by $3,100 over the current decade lies the unpleasant reality that only $950 of this extra annual consumption has been paid for by the growth in what each of us produces; the other $2,150 has been funded by cuts in domestic investment and by a widening river of foreign debt. . . . This is how we have managed to create a make-believe 1960s—a decade of 'feeling good' and 'having it all'—without the bother of producing a real one."[17]

Deterioration of Infrastructure

The laissez-faire philosophy underlying CEI policies with its explicit attack on government undermined all government activity, often with unfortunate effect. For example, little attention was given to the need to maintain the public infrastructure of highways and streets, sewers, bridges, subways, and parks. Making government smaller was the concern, and the result was a deferral of maintenance that has been estimated to cost $100 billion.

The key factor has been the decreasing federal support for local infrastructure investment. Federal grants in aid now account for 20 percent of local government receipts, down from 30 percent in the late 1970s.[18] Over one-half of public works investment is done by local governments, and traditionally over one-half of that is financed by federal grants. Every budget proposal of the Reagan administration has been for further cuts, implying continued deterioration in much of the country's basic infrastructure.[19]

Deindustrialization

One point of current debate is whether the CEI policies have led to deindustrialization of the U.S. economy. Unfortunately there is no agreed-upon meaning of the term. In terms of share of GNP, manufacturing output has remained stable since the 1970s at about 22 percent of total production. However, there have been substantial changes within the manufacturing sector—the smoke-stack industries have declined while the high-tech industries have increased. In terms of employment, however, there has been a marked decline of manufacturing from 1979 through January 1988 as table 3 illustrates.

Certainly one factor has been foreign competition, exacerbated by the overvalued dollar. Between 1980 and 1987 manufactured imports grew rapidly—from $139 to $325 billion—while

TABLE 3

Job Creation in the 1980s and Existing Wage Structure

Sector	Job Loss/Gain	Average Hourly Wage (January 1988)
Manufacturing	−1,620,000	$10.09
Mining	−212,000	12.61
Transportation and Utilities	361,000	12.10
Construction	703,000	12.90
Government	1,374,000	—
Finance, Insur & Real Estate	1,702,000	8.92
Wholesale and Retail Trade	4,450,000	7.10
Services	7,736,000	8.80

Source: U.S. Bureau of Labor Statistics, various publications.

manufactured exports grew slowly—$156 to $172 billion. The result was a change from a $17 billion export surplus of manufactured goods in 1980 to a $153 billion deficit.

This apparent contradiction between the share of manufactured output and the behavior of employment and wages is consistent with the "hollowing out" thesis that U.S. firms are moving their production to Asia in order to compete with the Japanese, and in the process U.S. workers are gradually losing certain critical skills. The longer run problem is that U.S. technological dominance is also slipping; one study found that Japan now dominates the U.S. in twenty-five of thirty-four critical new technologies.[20]

A related result of deindustrialization is that a two-tiered wage system is appearing in the economy as a result of CEI policies and failure to deal actively with the changing international economy. Table 3 shows that a substantial number of new jobs have been created during the past decade. However, there are reasons to be concerned that the quality of new jobs has declined[21] resulting in a polarization of job quality—pay, stability, future, benefits, etc. For example, the rapid growth of employment in the U.S. relative to other countries has been the result of much lower productivity growth which, in turn, limits the standard of living. Also, the rapidly growing involuntary part-time jobs usually have lower pay, fewer benefits, and less security. This has certainly been a contributor to increased income inequality during the 1980s.

Finally, as table 3 shows, the new employment has been largely in lower wage sectors of the economy. This reflects the hollowing out of U.S. industry, the decline of the old export and import-competing industries, forced by the changing international division of labor characteristic of capitalist development. In addition, firms within the manufacturing, service, and trade sectors have changed their labor demand in response to the resulting competitive environment. The number of small low-wage firms and subcontractors has increased and the traditional large high-wage firms have resorted to using pools of low-wage labor through such schemes as wage rollbacks, two-tier wage structures for existing and new workers, and increased use of part-time and temporary workers.

These changes have generated increasing income inequality, and labor's share of personal income has fallen by 1 percent since

1980 while the share of payments to owners of assets has increased from 23.1 percent to 25.7 percent, a dramatic change in such a short period of time.[22]

Changes in the employment structure of the economy have created a situation where the poor have become more numerous and poorer. Commentators talk about the "New Poor" and the "Underclass," our next example of the Reagan-CEI legacy of the 1980s.

The New American Poor

The 1980s witnessed the growth of an "underclass" of poor trapped in the lowest wage sectors of the economy or outside the the economy altogether, frequently hungry and homeless.

Hunger and homelessness are only two factors in a cruel equation of poverty where there is never enough income to cover needed amounts of food, housing, clothing, heat, light, transportation, and health care. Thus a threatened heat shutoff or medical crisis may mean less food bought, a skipped rent payment, or deferred medical treatment. People are hungry and homeless because they are too poor, incapacitated, or otherwise unequipped to provide themselves with sufficient food or housing.

The poverty rate in 1988 was far higher than at any point between 1969 and 1979. In addition, while the official federal poverty line measures the amount needed to survive, over 40 percent of those below the line had incomes less than half that amount. Of the 21.3 million people over 15 years of age in poverty in 1986, 8.8 million had worked during the year, and 5.2 million had worked full time. The National League of Cities 1988 study, "Poverty in the Cities," found poverty to be more persistent, more concentrated, and those in poverty more isolated from traditional avenues of escape.

Certainly there are individuals or families who take advantage of the existing social welfare programs and who exert as little effort as possible. However, one cannot deal with this reality by blaming the poor through examples of "welfare queens" or by hypothetical "Harold and Phyllis" cases[23] which show the disincentives poverty programs give to self-help efforts.

This argument can be turned back upon the Reagan-CEI

theorists. There is evidence that the adulation of individualism and self-interest has encouraged forms of behavior—such as low saving and conspicuous consumption among the wealthy and consumption of anti-social goods such as drugs among the poor—that are quite inconsistent with the economic improvement promised by CEI policies. The creation of an "enterprise culture," as it is termed in Thatcher England, may in many ways be self-defeating.

In addition the government program cuts may be very short-sighted, for poorer prenatal care oftens results in higher hospital expenses for underweight babies, less immunization results in higher medical costs later, less preschool education may result in greater education, welfare, or prison costs, and less remedial education may result in higher expenses as students repeat grades.

Social forces such as deindustrialization and the shift in public policy from an emphasis on full employment to fighting inflation are the root causes of the growing poverty. The counter-forces—jobs with a living wage, adequate public assistance, low-cost housing, medical care—are becoming ever more deficient.

Hunger. There is no universal definition of hunger but the medical community commonly defines it as the involuntary shortage of enough nutritious food to maintain body growth and good health. By this definition, "12 million children and 8 million adults, or about 9 percent of the population [are hungry]. A few of those people might be going hungry because of ignorance or indifference, but for most of the group the reasons are an economy that leaves many families below the poverty level and a social-welfare system that gives them insufficient help."[24]

Extensive hunger in the U.S. was identified thirty years ago. This finding stimulated government programs during the 1960s and 1970s that virtually eliminated the problem. The food stamp program was expanded to serve 20 million people. Programs were instituted to reach and feed the isolated elderly. School lunch and breakfast programs were increased. A supplemental program was established to supply food and nutritional advice to poor pregnant women and mothers, and food to their infants.

Then in 1981–82 came the deepest recession, with the highest levels of unemployment, since the 1930s. In 1981 the Reagan administration began reducing and modifying those food programs. By 1982 signs of hunger were widespread. Between 1982

and 1987 there were more than thirty national and regional studies on hunger, and more than forty state and local studies. All of
them agreed that hunger was a widespread and growing problem.

It is sometimes charged that the real cause of hunger is that
the poor spend food money on drugs and are nutritionally ignorant. In some degree it is true that drug usage reduces the funds
available for food and drug usage is one of the most serious problems facing the nation. But this is a small part of the hunger
problem.

There are two critiques with the second claim. First, hunger
declined through the 1960s and 1970s and then increased during
the 1980s. Does that mean that the poor were becoming less ignorant earlier and more ignorant later? That is clearly silly. Second,
there is evidence that the poor are no more ignorant of nutrition
than anybody else. Two national studies, one prepared by the
USDA itself, reported that Food Stamp recipients compared to
others spent the same percentage of their income on the major
food groups but bought less expensive items, less snack foods and
more dry beans and peas.[25]

The simple fact is that hunger is correlated with income. The
poor, because they are poor, are likely to have too little income to
support a nutritionally adequate diet. This results in reductions
in both mental and physical functions and even death. Infant mortality rates are closely correlated with income levels. For example
the Children's Defense Fund reported that the "non-white infant
mortality in our nation's capital exceeds that in Cuba and Ja-
maica."[26] In Memphis, the rate among non-white families living
in high poverty neighborhoods is higher than in Iran.

Widespread hunger has not only persisted through the years
of recovery since 1982, but has actually spread to new classes of
the population. It is worthwhile to quote a recent report:

> The increasing numbers of blue collar families appearing in
> bread lines come from the traditional bedrock of the economy,
> people whose labors produced national prosperity . . .
> . . . The bankrupt farm family that swallowed its pride to ap-
> ply for Food Stamp assistance learns that it is not considered worthy
> of help. The household has no income, but governmental regula-
> tions say that their farm machinery disqualifies them for help. To

receive assistance they must first discard this means of future productivity . . .

. . . The hotel maid works six days a week to support her family, but learns that her children can no longer get school meals. The household faces further economic stress and nutritional risk as a result . . .

. . . The medically uninsured miner cannot afford to feed his children properly due to the expenses of his wife's surgery, a dilemma with which most parents could empathize but none could solve . . . [27]

Since there is a clear correlation between hunger and poverty, those factors which increase poverty increase hunger: the holes in the U.S. safety net, the persistent unemployment and underemployment in the economy of the 1980s, and the cutbacks in government programs designed to deal directly with hunger.

Finally it must be remembered that the various items in a household's budget are related. Thus as housing costs go up there is less available for food. Too often the poor have been faced with the choice of going hungry or becoming homeless.

The New Homeless. Attempts to count the number of homeless face many difficulties. The available evidence comes from local studies and testimony of shelter and soup kitchen workers. In November 1983, HHS reported, on the basis of estimates provided by advocacy groups, that as many as two million people may have been homeless nationwide. Six months later, HUD issued a report which asserted that the "most reliable" range for the total number of homeless on a given night in the winter of 1983–84 fell between 250,000 and 350,000. Jonathan Kozol estimates the total at 2 to 3 million for 1987. A 1987 study of housing prepared for Congress by Professor Phillip Clay of M.I.T. projects the possibility of nearly 19 million homeless by 2003. It is clear that the problem is not solving itself. In 1978, 900 families were housed in formal shelters in New York on any given night; by 1984, the number was 2,900; by the spring of 1985, it was 4,000; and by the spring of 1987, it was 5,000.[28]

If estimates of the number of actual homeless—those living in the streets, squatting in abandoned buildings, or staying at shelters—are unreliable, figures on the almost homeless are impossible to obtain. They live in the boiler rooms, basements, and roofs of apartment buildings, in the abandoned shacks that "house" the rural homeless, in the urban flophouses that have become permanent housing by default, or they double up with relatives and friends, who themselves may therefore risk eviction for violation of their leases. Jonathan Kozol estimates that there are more than 3 million families living doubled up.

Studies of homelessness usually cite four main reasons for its explosive growth: rising average rates of unemployment, a critical shortage of low-cost housing, deinstitutionalization of patients from psychiatric hospitals, and changes in the disability program that removed one half million people from the rolls and made it more difficult for new applicants to enroll. However, these only describe the problem; they in turn need to be explained since all of these factors have been present at various times in the postwar era but did not result in massive homelessness. Closer examination of the trends in the economy, demography, and relevant public policy shows how they have converged to create widespread homelessness in the 1980s. It will also show that while the trends began in the 1970s, the economic policies of the 1980s reinforced the trends, doing nothing to counter them.

The slight increase in the inequality of income distribution and the deterioration in economic conditions for the very poor, combined with related trends in the private housing market, had two critical results during the 1970s: (1) they provided the impetus for housing abandonment and gentrification; (2) they pushed many households to the point where they could no longer afford their housing.

An important cause of the growing scarcity in low-cost housing has been a changed housing market. In the private market investment capital was directed to more profitable alternatives and there was a growing incidence of abandonment and gentrification; shelter costs rose steadily, especially for land, fuel, and interest; government subsidies for new construction, renovation, and rents eroded, while generous tax breaks for the conversion of low-rent housing to high-rent apartments or condominiums were offered. These have all added to the scarcity of low-cost housing.

There was substantial new housing construction during the

1970s. However, it was heavily weighted toward relatively large and expensive units. At the same time, construction of low-cost housing of any sort virtually came to a halt. Overall, improvements in substandard housing halted, and over the decade, there was no change in the percent of units with structural defects.

The proportion of housing units occupied by owners, not renters, changed little during the 1970s. However, there was a real shift in the relative economic condition of the two groups.[29] In 1970 the median income of renters was 65 percent of owners; by 1979 it had declined to 55 percent. In 1970 less than 50 percent of renter households were made up of single men or female-headed families. In 1980 they accounted for 67 percent of renter households. During the 1970s rents rose more slowly than the CPI but more rapidly than tenant incomes—nearly double the rate, according to some estimates. The result was a large increase for all renters in the proportion of income going to rent. It increased from a median of 20 percent in 1970 to 27 percent in 1980.

For the very poor the changes were disastrous. In 1980, half of the 2.7 million renter households with incomes below $3,000 spent more than 72 percent of their incomes on rent, compared to 34 percent in 1970. In 1980, these households had only $71 per month remaining for all other needs. The National Low Income Housing Coalition has calculated the level of severe housing distress: in 1980, 7 million households paid more than 50 percent of their incomes for housing costs. Almost 70 percent were renters and their median household incomes were $4,000–5,000 a year. Another 6 million households paid between one-third and one-half of their incomes on housing. Of these, 60 percent were renters with a median income of $7,400. Low-income households paying more than 50 percent of their income in rent cannot afford other necessities—food, utilities, etc. Very high rent-income ratios are but one factor pushing households toward the edge of homelessness.

Over the past two decades some 2.5 million people have been displaced from their homes each year. In addition, about one-half million low-rent units are eliminated each year as a result of conversion, arson, abandonment, inflation, and demolition. Until the late 1970s these displaced families filtered down the housing market to even lower cost units. But many have now been pushed out of the housing market altogether, because of the growing shortage of low-cost units.

According to Hopper and Hamberg, "the polarization of income distribution and the relative deterioration of the economic situation of the poor, especially the dependent poor, have been important factors in creating the conditions for both abandonment and gentrification. . . . in the 1970s landlords and financial institutions gave up on the "bottom" of the market—both the buildings and the people. . . . Thus, while there is a growing surplus of people and buildings at the bottom, rents and incomes do not match up. Hence, abandonment—often of sound housing— and homelessness."[30]

The steady disappearance of rooming houses and "single-room-occupancy" hotels (SROs) has been an important factor in precipitating the crisis of homelessness. They were important sources of housing for the elderly, young working adults, the unemployed, and the recently deinstitutionalized. During the 1970s the number of single person households increased to record levels while SROs decreased steadily. This housing was drastically reduced, first by urban renewal and highway construction in downtown areas, and second by abandonment and gentrification. Between 1970 and 1982, 1,116,000 SRO units, almost half of the total national stock, were eliminated. New York lost 110,000 units, 87 percent of its total low-rent SROs, because of rent inflation, conversion, and demolition.

The policy of deinstitutionalizing patients from mental hospitals began in the mid-1950s but was speeded up in the 1960s with the passage of the Community Mental Health Act (1963). The population in mental hospitals declined from 559,000 in 1956 to 133,550 in 1980. Unfortunately, the network of appropriate housing and support services for them was never adequately funded. Most people were transferred from mental institutions to nursing homes, returned to families, or were settled in a variety of housing arrangements such as board-and-care facilities, adult homes, or SROs. Most former patients were not immediately homeless. They did have housing, however inadequate, after leaving the hospitals. But this changed over time. Many landlords evicted them on excuses, such as a late check, to obtain more desirable tenants. Many of the former patients were simply unable to cope with their finances and other difficulties without social service support. Finding replacement housing became ever more difficult in the face of the declining stock of low-cost housing, particularly of SROs.

Deinstitutionalization was accompanied in the 1970s by tightened admission standards, which became an even more serious problem. People who would have been admitted in an earlier era and then helped to return to society were now being turned away, usually without any other recourse or refuge. It is important to remember that the problem of homelessness among the mentally ill did not arise until the late 1970s well after most of the deinstitutionalizations had taken place.

By the end of the 1970s a large number of poor households were on the edge of homelessness but were, in fact, hanging on. The recessions of 1979–1982 brought unusually high and persistent unemployment rates and high real and nominal interest rates. These effects combined with the Reagan administration's budget cuts in social services and regressive tax policies pushed many households over the edge into homelessness. As Hopper and Hamberg point out, "The fact that homelessness, instead of receding with the 1983 economic upturn, continued to rise, is an indication not only of the impact of the cuts in social spending, but also of the unevenness of the recovery and of the deep structural roots of the problem."[31]

Regressive tax policies and cutbacks in social welfare spending intensified the economy's structural tendencies toward income polarization and increasing poverty. In addition, the Reagan administration's housing policies deepened the crisis. In fiscal year 1981, President Carter requested $33.5 billion for housing programs and Congress appropriated $30.8 billion. For fiscal year 1987, President Reagan requested only $2.3 billion and Congress appropriated $7.8 billion, a 75 percent reduction in housing aid.

The particular character of the unemployment resulting from the 1981–82 recession, combined with reductions in social welfare and unemployment benefit programs, produced the "new poor"—destitute, sometimes homeless, former workers and their families. In the face of this greater need the response of the federal government was to cut back on unemployment benefit programs.

The real value of AFDC benefits eroded through the late 1970s and through the 1980s. In real terms, welfare benefits have decreased 35 percent since 1970. As the result of 1981 regulations, 50 percent of the nearly half million working families receiving AFDC lost eligibility and another 40 percent had their benefits reduced. Nearly 40 percent lost health and medical benefits.

Between 1981 and 1983 the Social Security Administration terminated almost one-half million persons from disability benefits. "Studies of those whose benefits were terminated show that most often the loss of benefits is due to the impaired ability of the recipient to challenge the ruling, and not to a legitimate weeding from the ranks of those who have recovered."[32] Approximately half of those who were capable of carrying through an appeal were reinstated. The mentally disabled, who made up 11 percent of those receiving disability payments, made up nearly a third of the terminated cases.

Hunger and homelessness in America of the 1980s are the result of long-term forces in the economy combined with short-sighted government policies. Public policy in the 1980s is well labeled the "mean season." Two examples epitomize the attitude of the Reagan administration.

Previously, as part of the Food Stamp Outreach program, there were signs in grocery stores explaining the availability of food stamps and a toll-free number where one could obtain information on eligibility and benefits. In 1981 outreach was eliminated and the store signs were changed to urge the use of a new toll-free number to report fraud and abuse. Also in 1981, the Reagan administration cancelled the White House Conference on Children—the first time since 1909 that this once every decade conference was not held.

An "Enterprise Culture"

A major goal of Reagan-CEI policies was to "get America moving again" by creating incentives for people to save, invest, and work. Extolling and rewarding self-interest would create what the Thatcher-CEI government in Great Britain calls "the enterprise culture." However, the legacy of this attempt is not what was expected. There is clear evidence that it has encouraged individualistic and self-interested behavior. The invisible hand required to meld self-aggrandizement into a process which improves all elements of society seems to have fallen asleep. Indeed, by moving to the background the constraints on individual behavior—moral canons, communitarian demands—this set of policies has encouraged behaviors which are very costly to society.

We already have seen that saving and investment declined rather than increased during the 1980s. The promotion of self-interest led to an unprecedented boom in consumption and debt. Enterprise became epitomized by Wall Street stock brokers and merger specialists and the goal of newly minted Harvard MBAs was to make $1 million per year before their thirtieth birthday.

The philosophy of limited government and low taxes led people to value private consumption and undervalue public goods. As a result popular support collapsed for social welfare, public infrastructure such as schools, sewers, and public transportation, and for communal values generally.

At the bottom of the socioeconomic scale, this philosophy of self-interest led to attempts to imitate the consumption habits of the better-off. Again, saving and hard work were not the path chosen. Getting today whatever one could get became the rule. Many, not able to obtain their desired life-style, turned to drugs as a substitute. They could feel like a million dollars, even if only for a moment. This often led to anti-social behavior, and social policy was forced to use punitive methods to protect itself. As a result, Thatcher's England has the highest rate of incarceration in Europe, 98.2 per 100,000 population compared with France's rate of 92.0.[33] And the jails in every state of the United States bulge, often forcing early release programs in order to cope with overcrowding. The prison population in the country has swollen from slightly over 300,000 in 1980 to over 500,000 in 1986.[34]

When communal ties are denigrated and when individual effort often leads only to a minimum wage job, it is not surprising that many spurn such jobs for whatever immediate gratification is possible, even if society disapproves.

The legacy of this enterprise culture is an upper-class bent upon immediate gains and conspicuous consumption and an underclass frequently hungry, homeless, and incapacitated by drug dependency. The lack of fellowship among the better-off and the lack of self-esteem among the worse-off bode ill for the future of the American economy and polity.

CONCLUSION

In the 1970s CEIs inspired a healthy critique of Keynesian policies. Since the 1930s the CEIs had played the role of a gadfly. Most economists believed that they were unlikely to obtain the reins of power again. That prediction was wrong. Continued high inflation created a wave of support for anyone who expounded answers different from those in power. Since the CEIs based their economics on values that spoke to the core of many patriotic Americans, and since the CEI explanations and solutions were relatively simple, increasing numbers of the dissatisfied public turned to them in search of an America they thought had once existed. In a time of national crisis one is easily swayed by nostalgic pleas to "make America great again."

President Reagan voiced practically all the CEI criticisms and proposals (he had favored a return to the gold standard which CEIs do not unanimously support). We have tried to show in this chapter that those proposals enacted into policies have been successful only in reducing inflation and have failed in terms of accelerating economic growth, increasing productivity, increasing saving and investment, generating stability, lowering poverty, and making the economy more competitive internationally.

The end result of those CEI policies has been an economy crippled by huge budget and trade deficits, a tragic deferral of infrastructure maintenance, deindustrialization with a consequent growth of a two-tiered wage system, the morally and economically indefensible growth of an underclass, and the creation of a corrupt enterprise culture that may turn out to be the biggest impediment of all to a renewal of the economy. The unclear call for a "kinder, gentler society" voiced by George Bush shows some realization of this reality. However, the timid moves toward dealing with any of the issues indicate that little change from the Reagan-CEI policies is likely.

In spite of these poor results, concerned economists cannot sit back idly and say, "I told you so." The Keynesian response, as articulated by Walter Heller, Chairman of the Council of Economic Advisers under Presidents Kennedy and Johnson, is also inadequate: " ... Keynesians have regrouped, built Milton Friedman's natural rate of unemployment into their models, developed a credible theory of wage-price rigidities, and seem to be regaining the intellectual and policy-oriented high ground in economics."[35] However, improved models will not enable Keynesians to solve the impasse reached in the 1970s by the New Deal–Keynesian consensus. The crisis of uneven development still awaits solution, and the promised dynamo of loosely fettered capitalism has been found wanting.

So we must continue to study, analyze, create, and speculate on new and possible approaches to all of the current problems. The crisis has not gone away under the Reagan presidency and its program of "anti-policies." George Bush is providing no new and bold directions. And it is doubtful that a Keynesian successor would do much better. Therefore we must be ready to respond with new ideas to the problems of uneven development that continually arise in the ever-changing economic environment of a capitalist country.

This is the task of the remaining chapters. Chapter 6 outlines the attempts to explain our present crisis through the use of long-run cyclical analysis. Chapter 7 evaluates the Marxian argument that the inherent contradictions of a market economy keep us in perpetual crisis and that the only solution is a socialist transformation of the economy.

In the remaining chapters of the second part of the book we attempt to present an alternative analysis of what is causing the crisis in the U.S. economy and what can be done about it. This requires a reconsideration of its institutional structure.

PART TWO

Two Challenging Critiques

6. Cycle Theories: Watch and Hope

All of the theoretical structures covered in previous chapters share a belief that steps can be taken to improve the functioning of the economy. Government should do more—or government should do less. There are clear policy suggestions to improve economic performance.

Not all theories of the economy's functioning have such implications. The stance of cycle theorists is that the course of the economy is determined by factors that are beyond manipulation; so policy of any sort, even the undoing of current policy, is unable to affect the economy's performance. Marxists, the subject of the next chapter, hold that steps could be taken to deal with the economy's ills, but only radical steps which would require a fundamental change in the system. Any such change could not be implemented as part of a conscious economic policy, but would be the result of political struggle.

We feel that there are pragmatic policy alternatives for the U.S. economy, and later chapters will detail them. Nonetheless, completeness and the possibility that the cycle theorists or the Marxists correctly understand the nature of the economy necessitate their inclusion.

THE CYCLE OF CYCLE THEORIES

Although the origins of cycle theories can be found in the Greek or Roman traditions or those of other cultures, the starting point for theories of *economic* cycles is the work of the Russian author, Kondratieff, whose major work was published in English in 1935.[1] He theorized that the economy's performance was dominated by "long waves" in economic activity, cycles of some fifty years in length. The appearance of long-wave theory and its popularity during the Depression are hardly accidental; and interest in long-wave theory has mirrored the performance of the economy ever since. It was dismissed by Russian encyclopedists as "wrong and reactionary"[2] and by English philosophers as "blasphemy."[3] Finally it was ignored by American economists for decades after Garvey's "definitive" review article found its statistical basis defective. Improved economic performance pushed it further into the shadows. A turning point in the life-cycle of this idea was apparently reached several years ago when the U.S. business cycle reappeared and interest in the long waves was on the upswing; however, the long recovery since 1982 has dampened the enthusiasm. Prior to that, economists of widely different political persuasions looked again at Kondratieff's views in hopes of finding some clues to the origins and probable outcome of the economic difficulties. Geoffrey Barraclough used Kondratieff quite effectively to organize the views presented in nine books on economics in the middle 1970s.[4] And that was just a small part of the cycle-theory work that was underway. We can be sure that the next downturn, just over the horizon, will rekindle the interest in cycle theories.

Many analysts beside Kondratieff have used cycle theories to explain economic phenomena. Schumpeter and Kuznets were early writers in this genre; Rostow and Mandel are more recent examples. Their common claim is that there are long waves in economic life, and that simple policy prescriptions cannot counteract them. Theorists' suggestions of the cause of the cycle differ substantially, and no single explanation is very satisfactory. Another shortcoming is that none provide clear guideposts of the exact position of today's U.S. economy in the long cycle. So they could suggest to their readers an extreme optimism for the future—or extreme pessimism.

The many limitations of specific cycle theories, and their periodic popularity, indicate that their value may be as metaphors for how the economy functions at times when it seems clearly to escape any conscious control. So an overview of cycle theories and theorists will be useful.

ANALYTICS OF CYCLES

The interest and excitement which Kondratieff's long-wave theory engendered came from its apparent explanation of economic cycles. It is important, therefore, to understand the meaning of economic cycles.

The Concept of the Cycle

The definition adopted by the National Bureau of Economic Research is a good starting point:

> ... a cycle consists of expansions occurring at about the same time in many economic activities followed by similarly general recessions, contractions, and revivals, which merge into the expansion phase of the next cycle; this sequence of changes is recurrent but not periodic. ... [5]

The connections in the sequence are important. The values of the economic indicators cannot simply be random fluctuations about the mean of that indicator. There must be a rhythm, a systematic variation in the level of economic activity, even if it is not a precise regularity.

One way of expressing this idea is that the cause of the depression phase of a cycle is the prosperity. As Oskar Lange put it: "to prove this theory [i.e., of long-range cycles] it would be necessary to show that there exists a causal relation between two consecutive phases of the cycle. ..."[6] This implies that the different phases of the cycle are self-reinforcing: once a downswing begins, it feeds on itself, creating further movement in the same direction; once an upswing has begun, it too is cumulative.

Lee expressed very well the root attraction of the idea of cycles:

> [the cycle idea] implies a regular succession of *similar* fluctuations, constituting some sort of *recurrence,* so that, as in the case of the phases of the moon, the tides of the sea, wave motion, or pendulum swing, we can forecast the future on the basis of a pattern worked

out from past experience, and which we have reason to think will be copied in the future.[7]

So a cycle is different from a trend, because the values of economic variables tend to recur; it is different from random fluctuations because there is a systematic variation in the values of these variables over time. And a cycle is different from economic fluctuations because cycles are internally caused and tend to be cumulative.

Detailed study of cycles has been based upon a historical review of economic data which suggest a number of cycle varieties, distinguished primarily by their length.[8]

Types of Cycles

According to the National Bureau of Economic Research business cycles may last from more than one year to ten or twelve years; and the Kondratieff cycle is considerably longer. Among the shorter business cycles is the "Juglar Cycle," with a period of nine to ten years, discovered by Juglar in the 1860s.

Juglar cycles have typically been associated with different rates of investment. In one view, the investment cycle corresponds to the life-cycle of major product and equipment innovations. In order to embody a new technical innovation in process or product, substantial new investment is needed. When the new capital equipment is constructed, or the new product fully marketed, investment subsides, and the economy sinks back into a trough.

The "Kitchin" cycle lasts from two to four years, although Joseph Kitchin (1923) put the figure at forty months. These shorter cycles are associated with short-term adjustments and are sometimes labeled "inventory" cycles, since they could result from minor over-accumulation of inventories leading to a slowdown in production to draw the inventories down. This pattern of marginal increases and decreases in the quantity of output gives the shorter cycles their rhythm. The inventory control aggressively used by modern firms casts some doubt on such an explanation, though inventories were certainly a factor in the 1975 recession.

Cycles of intermediate length have been called "Kuznets" cycles. These are growth rate changes in a wide variety of variables:

output, population and size of the labor force, supply of money, or stock of capital. They are of intermediate length, varying from fifteen to twenty years in duration, and are often associated with cycles in construction. Building cycles originate when a strong "outside" stimulus, such as a wave of immigration, sets up a strong demand for housing. The financial institutions in the building industry facilitate speculation and uncontrolled construction after this increase in demand. The boom lasts until an oversupply of houses has built up, and the construction binge halts. Since houses are relatively durable, it is a long time before enough houses deteriorate to allow a new upswing.

LONG-SWING THEORIES

Economic policy does seem to have been effective in dampening these shorter cycles, and so most interest has focused on the long waves which are of considerably greater duration. The period of long cycles varies from forty to sixty years and they have been noted in the behavior both of prices and of production. There are four main theorists of long cycles.

Kondratieff

In "The Long Waves in Economic Life" (1935), Kondratieff admitted the existence of the Juglar and Kitchin cycles, but was most interested in demonstrating the existence of fifty-year cycles. He examined various indices of economic activity, concentrating on two: prices and production. He found that the wholesale price index for the United States, England, and France exhibited no long-term trend, but did exhibit long wavelike movements about an average level. Data were available only from the close of the eighteenth century on. However, his examination of these data prompted him to set up the following chart of the long waves:

First Long Wave:	Upswing	End of 1780s until 1810–17
	Downswing	1810–17 until 1844–51
Second Long Wave:	Upswing	1844–51 until 1870–75
	Downswing	1870–75 until 1890–96
Third Long Wave:	Upswing	1890–96 until 1914–20[9]

Measured from trough to trough, Kondratieff's price waves lasted sixty years and forty-seven years respectively. There were similar long waves in the rate of interest, in wages, and in foreign trade, which were obviously price-related movements. In addition Kondratieff tried to demonstrate the existence of physical cycles by examining the growth rates of production and consumption of coal and pig iron, and of the production of lead, an effort which generated considerable criticism and skepticism about long-wave cycles in production. Garvey argued persuasively that the choice of periods in estimating the trend line was arbitrary, as was the choice of dates for turning points. With different choices, the Kondratieff waves in production vanished. He concluded that only the price waves were successfully established by Kondratieff.[10]

Nevertheless Kondratieff thought he had established parallel movements in a large number of economic indicators and thus had made a persuasive case for long waves. He had allowed a five- to seven-year range in the dating of the turning point. Several other characteristics of Kondratieff's long waves are important as well. First, the cycles were international in scope, for data from all major capitalist countries exhibited cyclical behavior. Second, the shorter business cycles were affected by the long waves. A long upswing did not preclude a short slump period, though it did make slumps less severe both in amplitude and duration. Similarly, on the downswing, years of depression dominate, even though there are some years of prosperity.

Granting Kondratieff's claims, what caused the long waves? Theoretical controversies abound in this area. Leon Trotsky argued that the strong trends which Kondratieff had discovered were exogenously determined.

> Their character and duration is determined not by the internal interplay of capitalist forces but by those external conditions through whose channel capitalist development flows. The acquisition by capitalism of new countries and continents, the discovery of new natural resources, and, in the wake of these, such major facts of a 'superstructural' order as wars and revolutions, determine the character and the replacement of ascending, stagnating or declining epochs of capitalist development.[11]

In short, these long-term movements were simply not cycles. They were determined not by internal forces—the prosperity did not cause the depression—but by accidental combinations of unique historical forces. They were a mere succession of trends, each more or less independent of those that precede and follow.

Kondratieff replied by insisting that the long waves were as regular as the shorter business cycle. First, the long waves recurred at more or less regular intervals. While the length of the business cycle varies between seven and eleven years, i.e., 57 percent, "the length of the long cycles fluctuates between 48 and 60 years, i.e., 25 percent only."[12]

Second, Kondratieff argued that the so-called external causes of the long waves were not really external at all. He listed four such causes: (1) changes in technique; (2) wars and revolutions; (3) the assimilation of new countries into the world economy; and (4) fluctuations in gold production. Changes in technique, for instance, are not independent of economic conditions. The impression that they are stems from the confusion of the process of discovery, which is indeed a creative act not determined by economic conditions, with the use of these discoveries. Once the new technical knowledge is available it is still necessary for the economic conditions to be ready for its use. In particular, the relative prices of labor and the new technology must make it more profitable to invest in the new technology than to use more labor. Even where the new technology is capital saving, it must be more profitable to introduce the new technology than to continue the old. And this criterion of profitability in turn relates to availability of loanable capital and to its rate of interest. Hence, it is correct to suggest that changes in technique are not entirely exogenous factors.

Kondratieff is less convincing in the other cases. He argues that most wars have an economic basis, though he presents no compelling argument that religion or race are inadequate explanations for some wars. He also maintains that opening a new country to the world market is economically determined. The discovery of the new country may not be so determined, he says, but its entanglement in the world economy is. Again he does not present a clear mechanism which would explain this economic determinism.

Finally, he makes the point that gold production is very much like the introduction of a new technique: the discovery of gold may be accidental and creative but its production is based upon how profitable it is to dig it out of the earth. Hence, it is more likely that gold production will increase when gold has its highest purchasing power, i.e., when prices are low. So, gold production is not independent of economic forces.

Kondratieff's major point was that all these factors could be explained internally (endogenously) to the economic system; and so even if they caused the long waves, the conclusion that long waves were the product of external, accidental forces was not warranted.

Kondratieff's third point was that his critics "see an accident where we have really to deal with a law governing the events."[13] The claim that the long waves were governed by laws implies that theoretically explaining them was possible. Unfortunately, Kondratieff did not proceed very far in developing "an appropriate theory of long waves." His point was that the long waves exhibited the characteristics of lawlike phenomena: they were recurrent, more or less regular, sequences of changes in economic life. Chance or accident would not explain the recurrence or the regularity. So, Kondratieff could claim that the phenomena of long waves were lawfully governed, despite the absence of a fully developed theory which formulated laws governing the waves.

Kondratieff actually did develop a theoretical model to explain the long waves, a model which was never presented in English. By building upon the idea that the shorter business cycles were produced by periodic reinvestment of fixed capital with an average life expectancy of ten years, Kondratieff suggested that the long waves were simply the economic reflection of the life cycle of "basic capital goods." To this category of "basic capital goods" belong big plants, railroads, canals, large land improvements, and the training of skilled labor. Investment in basic capital goods proceeded in spurts rather than continuously, and so the basic capital goods produced by one spurt of investment were allowed to deteriorate until the next round of investment. The upswing of the cycle corresponded to the initial investment, while the tapering off of investment in basic capital goods corresponded to the downswing of the long waves.

To explain why the investment process was discontinuous, Kondratieff argued that investments in basic capital goods required large amounts of loanable capital, and that these amounts were available only under certain conditions: (1) high propensity to save; (2) large supply of loan capital at low rates; (3) funds placed at the disposal of powerful entrepreneurial groups; (4) a low price level. These conditions implied that large amounts of loanable capital were available only at the bottom of a downswing. Once the upswing started, Kondratieff explained, it would come to a halt because interest rates would rise and a shortage of loanable capital would develop. However, nothing in the theory explained why an upswing must start. Kondratieff's conditions were only conditions for the possibility of an upswing. Although no precise mechanism was offered, Kondratieff asserted its existence and that the long waves were a lawlike process in which each phase created the conditions which produced the next phase.

Kondratieff provides the general outline of long-swing approaches. There are precious few policy implications in the analysis. The best a policymaker can do is to watch the economy and hope that the upswing will appear to save the day.

Joseph Schumpeter developed a more elaborate attempt to explain the long waves, though he again gave little policy guidance.

Schumpeter

Joseph Schumpeter was one of the preeminent economists of the twentieth century and wrote widely on a variety of economic questions. Perhaps the best indicator of his contribution is that whenever there are changes in the economy or doubts about its functioning, other economists are able to find important and helpful insights in Schumpeter's writings—though they may have appeared over forty years ago!

Schumpeter wrote about economic cycles because he thought they were important to the functioning of the capitalist economy.[14] His analysis had three central components: first, a historical reconstruction of cycles in the capitalist countries; second, an analytical model of the course of a typical cycle; and third, his notion of leading sectors as explanatory factors in cycles.

Schumpeter reviewed the historical data and resolved the course of development in capitalist countries into the interplay of three types of cycles: the long-wave Kondratieffs, the middle-range Juglars, and the short-term Kitchins. His first Kondratieff ran from 1787 to 1842, and contained several Juglars; the second from 1843 to 1897, also with several smaller Juglars; and the third Kondratieff upswing ended with World War I, and contained one complete Juglar. In general, Schumpeter saw Kondratieffs as composed of six smaller Juglars, in turn broken down into three Kitchin cycles. This did not follow from any imposed theory, but simply emerged from the data available to him.

Schumpeter's analytical model contained two steps. In step one, he imagined the entire economy in a state of equilibrium, where firms set prices equal to average costs, profits are zero, and there is no involuntary unemployment. Into this situation comes an innovation and an enterprising person or firm decides to develop it. A loan from a bank is required which bids up the interest rate, and the enterprising firm bids scarce resources away from other firms, causing a price increase. The new innovation is a success, imitators follow, and soon a boom is underway. At some point, the innovation plays itself out: new investment declines, loans are paid back, prices decline, and a recession eventually returns the economy to equilibrium. So step one is a two-phase model of boom and recession.

The next step adds two more phases. The recession, in step two, forces the economy down past the equilibrium point into a depression. At some point this depression gives way to a revival which brings the economy back up to equilibrium. Schumpeter provided no novel ideas on how the economy pulls itself out of the depression trough. He mentioned the need to let prices sink until investment became profitable again and the need to pay off debts before embarking upon a new round of investment. He also emphasized the psychological expectations of businessmen. His novel idea was that the whole process began and ended from equilibrium, and was guided by the innovation process.

For all three types of cycles, Schumpeter proposed the same mechanism. The only difference lay in the scale of the new invention: innovations requiring little investment generated the smaller cycles; huge innovations resulted in the long cycles. Schumpeter distinguished three different sectors within which innovation took place and whose life-cycle paralleled the long cycles. First, there was a revolution in cotton textiles and iron which set off the first Kondratieff wave. Schumpeter called this the Industrial Revolution. Next was the revolution in the construction of railroads and in the use of steam and steel which set off the second Kondratieff. Finally, developments in electricity, industrial chemistry, and the internal combustion engine set off the third Kondratieff upswing.

Several criticisms of Schumpeter's views have been made. First, he associated the beginning of an upswing with the start of an innovation process. But the innovation process usually produces a decrease in prices in the innovating industry. It is hard to reconcile this with the fact that prices tend to rise during the upswing of a long cycle.

Second, although Schumpeter maintained that cycles were an inherent part of the economic process and not determined by outside physical or institutional forces, his idea of the great innovator seemed to be just such an outside force.

Third, and related to this last point, one of the defining characteristics of cycles is their continuity, that the prosperity breeds the depression. Schumpeter's view allowed that sort of continuity, but also implied that the entire economy could perch at an equilibrium point indefinitely until the innovation process started again. The continuity between the revival period which dragged the economy out of the depression phase and the prosperity period was broken, and nothing about the revival forces would ensure that prosperity would follow. The continuity of the cycles was made to rest on the historical accident that someone developed enough nerve to initiate the innovation process.

So Schumpeter provides a much richer treatment of cycles and it corresponds well with performance in the pre–World War I period. There have been more recent efforts to find long swings in economic performance, and to them we now turn with Simon Kuznets's and Walt Rostow's analyses.

Kuznets and Rostow

In addition to updating the work on long cycles, Kuznets and Rostow did not try to explain the long-wave phenomena via a unitary theory; instead, a number of forces were isolated, and their historical interplay examined. Their approach was also less mechanistic and more historical, though again they provided no policy guidance.[15]

Kuznets examined trends in production, and discovered evidence that swings in the production of certain sectors correspond to the life-cycle of certain innovations. However, in contrast to Schumpeter he found that the initial stages of the introduction of an innovation were periods of price reduction, and not price increase.

In his later work, Kuznets found that long trends in various economic variables were linked to population growth. Housing construction and building of the railroads, for example, were found to be population sensitive, particularly to waves of immigration.

But these trends in the growth rate of various economic quantities were of shorter duration than the observed long waves and so Kuznets could not use them as an explanation of long waves.

Rostow built upon the work of Kuznets and his followers by using several of the forces they had found significant. The first was the rise of a new leading sector in production. For example, Rostow maintained that around 1900 the growth of the old leading sector composed of the railroad and steel complex was decelerating, while the new leading sector of the automobile, electricity, and chemicals complex was only beginning to emerge. Hence, the period of 1900–1914 was one of decelerating output per capita.

The second force was the movement in trade and capital in response to shortages of raw materials and foodstuffs. For example, in 1896 there was a worldwide shortage of wheat, causing a price explosion. This immediately triggered an adjustment mechanism when production of wheat in Australia, Canada, Argentina, and Russia increased. The increase in production was facilitated by large imports of capital into these countries, which was used to build up the infrastructure, especially the railroads.

Into this interplay of forces Rostow introduced the third force—the large movements of population highlighted by Kuznets. The key factor which produced the large flows of immigration was the growth of the new countries' agricultural and construction activity. Another result of the migration was that the large numbers of people produced increased demand for still further housing and infrastructural development.

In this way, Rostow tried to reconcile the different accounts of trends in all the economic indicators. He also tried to apply his historical results to the situation of the 1970s by suggesting that the high prices of raw materials and foodstuffs indicated an upswing of a new Kondratieff wave, and that the development of new countries associated with these upswing periods should be expected.

With Rostow, the idea that there should be a necessary connection between different trends was lost. The basic change from an old leading sector to a new leading sector which he presented as part of the deceleration of output from 1900 to 1914 was not analyzed. He offered no explanation of why this change took place. Similarly, the shortage of wheat which produced the price explosion in 1896 was not analyzed. Again why did this shortage take place then? The net result of these unanswered questions is the feeling that the whole process was rather accidental, and could just as easily have gone the other way. It would have the same implication for our current situation; and again the policymaker would have simply to observe with little ability to affect the economy's direction. So Rostow implied that long waves have no inner necessity at all. This conclusion differed from Mandel's in his attempt to revive Kondratieff. Since Mandel is a Marxist, his framework will also provide a good transition into the Marxist analysis of the next chapter.

Mandel

Mandel's *Late Capitalism* contributed to the analysis of long waves by presenting in summary form new statistical evidence suggesting that there are indeed long waves in the economic life of capitalist countries.[16] He used the data to claim that the economic crisis of the 1970s was likely to get worse, for we were in the downswing of a Kondratieff cycle.

The statistical information he provided was all in terms of physical output, and thus supplemented the price series generally accepted as showing long-wave behavior. Using data from the United States, Great Britain, and Germany, he found fluctuations

in industrial output which matched the price fluctuations Kondratieff had found. Most interesting was his projection into the future: since 1967, he said, we have changed from a long wave of
expansion to a long wave of contraction, seen most clearly in a
remarkable reduction in the percentage growth of industrial product. This implies that capitalism is entering a crisis, a theme that
will be dealt with at much greater length in the next chapter.

Mandel, in explaining the long swing, did not simply credit
the development of these waves to outside forces acting directly
on the rate of profit. Instead, he proposed a version of Schumpeter's theory of innovations. Each of the long cycles was characterized by the spread of a different kind of innovation in the technology of productive motive machines. The first cycle lasted from the
end of the eighteenth century until 1847 and produced the spread
of the steam engine, made by a manufacturing process. The second long wave began in 1847, ended in the 1890s, and was characterized by the use of the machine-made steam engine. The period
lasting from the 1890s to the Second World War produced the
widespread use of electric and internal combustion engines. Finally, during and after World War II the generalized control of
machines by electronics was introduced, as was the beginnings of
the use of nuclear energy. The peak of this period was reached in
1967, when we entered the downswing.

The mechanisms Mandel cited are the usual ones: as the new
technology becomes more widespread, there is less and less of a
need to invest huge sums; all the basic investments have been
made. The force that gave the upswing its power is gone. There
are, so to speak, no more fields to conquer. So, the boom turns
into a period of decline.

A theory which relies upon large-scale innovations in motive
machinery is an attempt to give a genuine explanation of the cycles. But it is incomplete, and insofar as it must rely upon external
unique forces it is no longer an explanation of a cycle.

One attempt to amend Mandel's view was briefly sketched
by David Gordon. According to his view, large-scale investment
could not take place after the initial phase of building up the new
technology because "so much had already been set in concrete and
billed for future repayment."[17] These investments in motive machinery and, he adds, in infrastructure, thereby locked us into a

pattern which could not be broken. The boom had to be followed by a period of recession until the old technology and infrastructure simply wore out.

Gordon added at one point that this process was not simply a matter of physical decay. The class struggle must enter in as well. Only when the class struggle becomes intense, and labor puts a profit squeeze on capital will it become profitable once again to embark on a huge investment scheme in some new form of technology, or some new type of infrastructural development.

With Mandel and Gordon we begin to get to theories which see cycles as inherent in capitalism and which look to Marxism for the explanatory theory. Indeed much of the current work on cycles in capitalism is from the Soviet Union and Eastern Europe.[18] It generally operates out of the Schumpeterian tradition of waves generated by clusters of innovations. We will deal much more with the Marxist tradition of analysis in the next chapter.

The interest in cycle theories in the Eastern bloc and the difficulty in developing a convincing theoretical and empirical basis for them should emphasize that in one way they are simply metaphors for understanding the working of the capitalist system. They suggest a system which is not stable and which cannot finally be controlled by conscious effort, by economic policy. Completeness suggests that we should mention a new metaphor which has been applied to many systems, mainly physical but also biological, and which may also correspond with the behavior of the economic system. This is the theory of "chaos."

CHAOS THEORY

Implicit in much of our thinking about economics is that relations between economic variables are basically linear. We draw linear supply and demand schedules and our production functions are usually linear, or easily transformed into linear relations. Such simplifications may not distort reality too greatly and may allow approaches to problems which are quite powerful, such as linear programming which can solve some complex optimizing problems, or input-output analysis which allows detailed insight into many of the production relations of the economy. Their clearest value, however, is their simplification of the mathematics of modeling which becomes quite complex when non-linear relations enter.

Of course cycles are of their very nature non-linear. Think of the simplest regular wave motion, the "sine-wave," whose regular and rounded peaks and troughs are anything but linear. One of the earliest mathematical models of cycles was developed by Paul Samuelson.[19] He started with two economic constructs. The first was the Keynesian multiplier, that the effect of a ten-dollar increase in government expenditures will have a multiplied effect on income. The second was the accelerator, that if this period's investment depends on last period's saving, as saving starts to increase there will be rapidly increasing or accelerating investment. By putting the two together into a model, he was able to show that under certain circumstances, the economic variables would exhibit cyclical behavior. The "certain circumstances" were a set of mathematical values or parameters in the underlying economic relations. If these circumstances were not met, if the values were different, the system would become unstable and might literally do anything.

Samuelson had developed a simple non-linear description of the economy. Similar descriptions had been developed in many other areas: populations or epidemics in biology, simple weather systems, pendulums, or cooling processes in hot liquid.[20] These were non-linear systems and had traditionally been solved by finding the "certain circumstances" that gave a neat result, perhaps a cycle, perhaps a dampening of the cycle to a stable point. But what happens if those certain circumstances are not met, a very likely event? It turns out that "chaos" often results in such systems, but a very different chaos from the random disorder we usually associate with the term. In general a chaotic system has some very important properties:

1. It is very sensitive to initial conditions, so a slightly different saving rate would give a radically different pattern to how the economy evolves.

2. It is locally very unstable. If the economy once moves to position "b" from position "a," the next time it arrives at position "a" there is no reason it will move to position "b." In the extreme we can say that the pattern *never* repeats itself. This is a very different view from the recurrence assumed in cycle theories.

3. However, it is globally stable, for there are bounds to the patterns of the economy. For example, during the Depression the economy did finally stabilize; there was a floor to its fall. Perhaps the experience of the 1970s shows there are bounds to growth rates as well.

One of the earliest applications of chaos theory to economics, to the behavior of cotton prices, illustrates these elements. Each particular cotton price change was random and unpredictable, so there was local instability. But the sequence of changes was independent of the time scale; curves of daily price changes and of monthly price changes matched perfectly.[21] So there was a global stability to the process.

Gleick sums up the worldview of the chaos theorists as follows: "Simple systems give rise to complex behavior. Complex systems give rise to simple behavior. And most importantly, the laws of complexity hold universally, caring not at all for the system's constitutent atoms.... For [chaos theorists] chaos was the end of the reductionist program in science."[22]

The next time the economy escapes our control it might be better to think in terms of chaos rather than in terms of cycles, which ultimately are mechanistic and deterministic. The complexity of human beings and the social systems they create would seem to be reflected in the idea of chaos much more successfully than in the usual cycles.

SUMMARY

A theory of cycles has three tasks according to Mass.[23] First, it must explain why the cycle gets started, and once started in a particular direction, why it continues to develop in that direction. Second, it must have an explanation of why this cumulative movement in one direction comes to a halt. And finally the theory must explain why there is movement back in the opposite direction.

One extreme views each and every cycle as explainable by one and only one type of cause, e.g., innovations. At the other extreme, only a narrative of the exact historical events can explain each separate cycle. The correct view is probably in the middle:

each cycle is a unique historical event, but it must share certain causal features with other cycles. Otherwise, there would be no cycles, only a succession of trends moving in opposite directions. So, a theory of cycles must allow for enough generality to expose the common elements in each cycle without mechanically imposing upon each cycle a pattern which does not fit.

The Kondratieff theory is stimulating and obviously has important implications at certain times. But it finally is of little help to policymakers or to us. For it has no suggestions for steps to be taken to deal with the cycle, nor does it have a theoretical base that could tell us where we are in a cycle until it is long past! Though it is an intellectually appealing approach to understanding past fluctuations in economic activity—and those that certainly will take place in the future—it is far less well-developed than the Marxist theories of the next chapter.

In some sense all of these theories are metaphors for understanding our economy and its instabilities. In a very real sense the idea of chaos may finally be the most appealing of these metaphors and may finally lead us to the richness of understanding that human society requires.

7. Marxism: Inherent Cycles and Inevitable Crises

One body of economic theory is unlikely to play a central role in the policy debate of the United States: Marxism. As part of the Western political struggle against the Soviet Bloc countries, Americans slowly, but inexorably, have learned to treat evil as synonymous with communism. Ronald Reagan's characterization of the Soviet Union as the "evil empire" spoke to the contemporary American psyche much more strongly than his later efforts to work toward mutually beneficial agreements on arms control and in Southern Africa.

Sadly, but understandably, Karl Marx himself is often portrayed as a perverted, evil, and maladjusted man, since he is easily associated with the terrorism and revolution that rings the globe today. However, there is a vast gulf between Libyan revolutionary advocacy and the economic thought that originated in Karl Marx's innovative theories of the market (Marxists prefer to call it "capitalist") economy.

The current problems of socialist countries are taken by many as a refutation of Marx's theory of capitalism. This is a complete misunderstanding. Marx attempted to construct a theory of how *capitalism* works. It is not a theory of how to manage a *socialist* economy. An open-minded approach would show that Marxist interpretations and explanations of our current economic and social dilemma have a surprising degree of coherence and relevance.

Over the years more and more well-known (and often conservative) economists have begun to lend a sympathetic ear to some of Marx's work on the economics of capitalism.[1] Part of this interest stems from the well-developed economic theories with which Marxists claim to understand the dynamics behind intermittent capitalist crises. It is in this spirit that we move forward into Marxist theories of the crises and social malaise of the seventies and eighties, for any complete understanding of the U.S. economy must take these Marxist insights into account.

MARXIST POINTS OF DEPARTURE

Much of Marx's thought on capitalist economies centered on a dual tendency thought to be inherent to the structure of the capitalist system. The first tendency is toward fluctuations from short booms to temporary recessions, the cycles of the last chapter. These short cycles are an inevitable aspect of capitalist growth. Because of their transitory nature they are not that disruptive and there is, therefore, no compelling reason to consider them as unnatural and cataclysmic.

The second tendency, though, is substantially more serious; for a series of these short cycles could, over the long run, develop into an economic stagnation of critical proportions. In Marxist terms this is "the tendency toward crisis." Crises such as these will not cure themselves, as will the shorter periodic fluctuations. In contrast with our earlier long-swing theorists, there is no tendency to recovery and upswing. Instead, only major shifts in structural and social relations will relieve a crisis and allow the system to resume its normal, if somewhat altered, mode of cyclical expansion.

Most economists of Marxist persuasion claim that the U.S. is currently in one of the long-run crises which beset the economy every fifty years or so. A serious crisis threatened the nation shortly after the Civil War, lasting from 1870 until about 1890. The next severe crisis began with the stock market crash in October of 1929. And now, beginning somewhere in the 1970s, we have entered a third major economic crisis, perhaps the worst of all in terms of long-run events.

In the first two cases capitalism was saved, but not without major institutional and behavioral revisions. The system was saved from complete collapse at the end of the nineteenth century by a proliferation of new monopolies that did away with the ravages of uncontrolled competition, by a surge in global expansion that reduced the costs of raw materials, by new technical innovations, e.g., the entirely new industry created by electric power, and by relatively progressive labor policies undertaken "voluntarily" by the newly created large firms.

When capitalism floundered again in the 1930s, government took on the role of stabilizer under the guidance of the New Deal–Keynesian consensus; and the government's role grew along with the economy. Finally, Marxists argue, before we emerge from the crisis of the seventies and eighties the economy will undergo another major shift. Some predict that shift will be toward increased economic planning. Others expect more substantial structural reform. They all agree that whatever direction the economy actually moves, there must be a dramatic change in the economic and social system before it can begin a stage of renewed vitality.

What clearly distinguishes Marxist economics from that of the traditional economics quoted in the newspapers, heard on radio and television, and used for advising in Washington is its rejection of traditional economics, as embodied in either CEI or Keynesian garb, and the claims that the economy can be kept on a stable growth path. CEIs believe it will grow of its own accord, and Keynesians believe it needs management; but neither anticipates major crises to crop up periodically. Marxists, on the other hand, fully expect that any capitalist country, by its very nature, must not only go through cyclical fluctuations, but must also struggle through rarer, though inevitable, crises of monumental proportions. It is this sort of crisis that we find ourselves in right now.

In this chapter, therefore, we will look at the Marxists' critique of capitalism, see why they confidently foretell capitalist crises, assess whether their explanation has any validity, and finally confront the Marxist call to change. Our procedure is initially to discuss some of the core elements of Marxist theory in order to lay open its vision of the world. We will draw heavily on quotes from Marxist writers to ensure a proper presentation of their views. Second, the theory will be applied to events of the 1960s–1980s to explain in Marxist terms why and how we have arrived at the current problems. Third, we will take a brief look at the Marxist solutions.

ELEMENTS OF MARXIST THEORY

Although economics forms a large part of his general system, Marx is much more than an economist. Economics, sociology, political theory, history, and philosophy are all mixed into his sweeping analysis. In this section we cover only those portions of Marx's thought relevant to crisis theory.

Historical Materialism

His general framework analysis is the materialist interpretation of history. Marx rejects philosophies of history based on metaphysics or psychological laws of human nature. He denounces metaphysical explanations as meaningless mysticism. Psychological explanations are dismissed with the remark that "it is not the consciousness of men that determines their existence, but, on the contrary, their social existence determines their consciousness."[2]

Marx views the general shape of any given historical epoch as determined by the prevailing mode of production. By "mode of production" he refers not simply to technique (included among what he terms the "forces of production") but also to the "relations of production"—the relations with one another which people enter by reason of the various positions they occupy in the productive process. The mode of production and the relations of production breed a superstructure of ideas and institutions. As Marx put it, "The sum total of these relations of production constitutes the economic structure of society, the real foundation, on which rises a legal and political superstructure and to which correspond definite forms of social consciousness. The mode of production of material life conditions the social, political, and intellectual life process in general."[3] However, Marx does not insist that all ideas and institutions represent passive adaptations to the mode of production; some cultural expressions might rise quite independently. He contends, nevertheless, that such autonomous noneconomic forces exert only secondary influence on long-run historical development.

For Marx, social reality is more than a specified set of relations; it is the process of change inherent in such a set of relations. In other words, social reality is the historical process. The process of social change is not purely mechanical; it is the product of human action, but action which is definitely limited by the kind of society in which it has its roots. "Men make their own history," Marx wrote, "but they do not make it just as they please; they do not make it under circumstances chosen by themselves, but under circumstances directly found, given and transmitted from the past."[4] Society is both changing and, within limits, can be changed.

Evolution in society occurs because the elements that make up the mode of production change. Different forms of society may accelerate or retard the development of these economic factors, but some change in the productive forces takes place under all economic conditions. In the early stages of a particular social system, the material forces of production are compatible with the relations of production and the superstructure of ideas and institutions. In this period the existing relations of production are "forms of development of the forces of production." Changes in the relations of production and the cultural superstructure lag behind the development of the material forces of production. And then, "at a certain stage of their development, the material productive forces of society come in conflict with the existing relations of production, or—what is but a legal expression for the same thing—with the property relations within which they have been at work hitherto." The existing property relations now "turn into fetters" on the forces of production. When this occurs there "begins an epoch of social revolution. With the change of the economic foundation the entire immense superstructure is more or less rapidly transformed."[5]

The class struggle is the vehicle of social change. Or as Marx expressed it, "The history of all hitherto existing society is the history of class struggles. Freeman and slave, patrician and plebian, lord and serf, guild-master and journeyman, in a word, oppressor and oppressed, stood in constant opposition to one another, carried on an uninterrupted, now hidden, now open fight, a fight that each time ended, either in a revolutionary reconstitution of society at large, or in the common ruin of the contending classes."[6] In medieval society the dominant relationship had been between feudal lords and serfs. In the classical world it had been between master and slave, the relationship of servitude between them depending on the fact that the master-class possessed not only the instruments of production and the product of labor, but also the very producer as a personal chattel. In capitalist society the legal bonds which tied the producer to a lord or master no longer existed. The laborer had been emancipated and was a free agent before the law, entering into a contractual relationship with an employer which was in form akin to any other market contract. In other words, labor for a master was no longer obligatory. Employment occurred by an act of sale of labor power in the free market. This marked the essential difference between the social relationships typical of capitalist society and those characterizing earlier forms of class society. With the market it appeared that free and equal contractual relationships had been substituted for a relationship of exploitation; that freedom and equality had been realized; and that there was now no resemblance to the older class societies. But Marx said, "The modern bourgeois society that has sprouted from the ruins of the feudal society, has not done away with class antagonisms. It has but established new classes, new conditions of oppression, new forms of struggle in place of the old ones." Or again, in place of "exploitation veiled by religious and political illusions, it [the bourgeoisie] has substituted naked, shameless, direct, brutal exploitation."[7]

As the relations of production mature and harden in any social system, while the forces of production continue to develop, the lines between the ruling and oppressed classes sharpen. The oppressed class, which stands to gain by a modification of the existing property relations, asserts itself and attempts to secure political control. Since this class is aligned with the all-powerful productive forces, its eventual success is guaranteed. A new set of property relations develops which is appropriate for the expansion of the new productive forces. With the change in property relations, the entire superstructure of ideas and institutions is modified and changed. All history, according to Marx, follows the cycle of revolution, progressive evolution, the rise of and need for resistance to institutional change as a part of further progress, degeneration, and again revolution. What Marx says about capitalism applies to all previous social systems as well: "not only has the bourgeoisie forged the weapons (the forces of production) that bring death to itself; it has also called into existence the men who

are to wield those weapons—the modern working class—the pro-
letarians." And again, "The development of modern industry . . .
cuts from under its feet the very foundation on which the bourgeoisie produces and appropriates products. What the bourgeoisie
therefore produces, above all, are its own grave-diggers. Its fall
and the victory of the proletariat are equally inevitable."[8] Marx
contends that after capitalism has been replaced by socialism, and
socialism by communism, the evolution of social systems will come
to an end, because class conflict will then have been eliminated.

> In broad outlines Asiatic, ancient, feudal, and modern bourgeois
> modes of production can be designated as progressive epochs in the
> economic forms of society. The bourgeois relations of production
> are the last antagonistic form of the social process of production—
> antagonistic, not in the sense of individual antagonism, but of one
> arising from the social conditions of life of the individuals; at the
> same time the productive forces developing in the womb of bour-
> geois society create the material conditions for the solution of that
> antagonism. The social formation brings, therefore, the prehistory
> of human society to a close.[9]

This, then, is Marx's conception of the historical process:
economic factors play the decisive role in shaping the evolution
of society, because the relations of production determine the ideological, political, legal, and institutional structure of the community. Since the forces of production are continually changing, the
form society takes is also subject to constant change, not in a simple
mechanistic fashion, but inexorably nonetheless. Indeed, four different historical stages can be identified—primitive communism,
the ancient slave state, feudalism, and capitalism—each of which
arose out of the previous stage as a result of the conflict between
the forces of production and the relations of production. In each
case the internal contradictions generated by this incompatibility
led to the breakdown of the older system and to the emergence
of a new one. In each instance, the agents of change were the
social classes that were created by the particular mode of production that was used; the method of change was a struggle between
classes arising from the internal contradictions of the system. Nor
is the capitalist mode of production exempt. It, too, has created its

internal stresses and strains. Like the previous stages, therefore, it will eventually be swept away, according to Marx, in favor of other forms—socialism at first, and then communism.

The Capitalist Mode of Production

Marx set out to probe the secret of capitalism as a mode of production and he attempted to reveal the specific character of the conflicts within this mode of production which would determine its place in history, its growth and movement, and the future society that was destined to supplant it.

Marx's theory of surplus value provides the framework on which he bases his analysis of capitalism. The essence of capitalism, in his view, is the division of the population into two classes. "The epoch of the bourgeoisie possesses ... this distinctive feature: It has simplified the class antagonisms. Society as a whole is more and more splitting up into two great hostile camps, into two great classes directly facing each other—bourgeoisie and proletariat."[10] One class, the capitalists, owns all the means of production; the other class, the workers, have only their own labor power to sell. The available supply of labor and the existing means of production can produce a greater flow of commodities than that needed to maintain intact the labor supply and the means of production. The economy, in other words, is able to produce a surplus over and above the value of subsistence needs of the workers and the value of the raw materials and equipment used up in production. Marx calls this "surplus value." The surplus is expropriated by the capitalist class in the form of net profits, interest, and rent.

How does surplus value arise and why are the capitalists able to expropriate it? According to Marx, labor power, which the capitalists purchase in the market and consume in the productive process, possesses the unique characteristic of yielding more than its own value as it is used. The excess value created by labor power is the surplus value that capitalists expropriate. Since labor power is a commodity its value "is determined, as in the case of every other commodity, by the labour-time necessary for the production, and consequently also the reproduction, of this special article ... in other words, the value of labour-power is the value of the means of subsistence necessary for the maintenance of the labourer."[11]

The capitalist buys labor power at its value and since he "acquired the right to use or make that labouring power work during the whole day or week,"[12] he is able to force workers to work longer than is necessary to produce a value equivalent to their labor power. In other words "the value of the labouring power is determined by the quantity of labour necessary to maintain or reproduce it, but the use of that labouring power is only limited by the active energies and physical strength of the labourer."[13] The surplus value which is generated goes to the capitalist because "wherever a part of society possesses the monopoly of the means of production, the labourer, free or not free, must add to the working-time in order to produce the means of subsistence for the owners of the means of production."[14] But why can't wages rise above the subsistence level, above the value of labor power, so that the workers could obtain part of the surplus value? Marx's answer draws on his famous concept of the "reserve army of labor." The reserve army of labor consists of unemployed workers who, through their active competition on the labor market, exercise a continuous downward pressure on the wage level.

> The industrial reserve army, during periods of stagnation and average prosperity, weighs down the active labour-army; during the periods of overproduction and paroxysm, it holds its pretensions in check. Relative surplus-population is therefore the pivot upon which the law of demand and supply of labour works. It confines the field of action of this law within the limits absolutely convenient to the activity of exploitation and to the domination of capital.[15]

Marx maintains that only labor can create surplus value, but could it not originate from the raw materials and capital equipment utilized in production? Since the value of all commodities is determined by the amount of "socially necessary labor time" they incorporate, raw materials and capital equipment can only transfer this value in the production process. They have no value in and of themselves separate from the labor embodied in them. The capitalists who sell the raw materials and capital equipment obtain the surplus value when they sell them to other capitalists for use in production. The capitalists who purchase them get back merely the value they paid for them. Although Marx admits that better machinery increases surplus value, he holds that it is the embodied "socially necessary labor time" that is responsible, not the machinery.

The value of the total product produced in the economy during any period is the sum of three components. The first part, which merely represents the value of the raw materials and capital equipment used up, "does not, in the process of production, undergo any quantitative alteration of value,"[16] and is therefore called constant capital (c). The second part, that which replaces the value of labor power, does in a sense undergo an alteration of value in that "it both reproduces the equivalent of its own value, and also produces an excess, a surplus-value, which may itself vary, may be more or less according to circumstances."[17] It is therefore called variable capital (v). The third part is surplus value (s) itself. Therefore total value (V) can be shown as $V = c + v + s$. Marx uses three ratios of these components of total value. The ratio s/v is the rate of surplus value or the rate of exploitation. He expresses this as a division of the working time into the period that labor works for itself and into the time that it works for the capitalists. If s/v is 50 percent, this means that it only takes labor two-thirds of the work day to produce its means of subsistence, and the other one-third of the workday is spent producing surplus value which the capitalists expropriate. The ratio s/c + v is the "rate of profit" on the total capital invested. Finally, the relation between constant and variable capital c/v is what Marx terms the "organic composition of capital."

The goal of the capitalist is to increase the mass of surplus value received. It is not the production of goods for consumption or even for a particular profit. As Marx says:

> . . . it is only in so far as the appropriation of ever more and more wealth in the abstract becomes the sole motive of his operations, that he functions as a capitalist, that is, as capital personified and endowed with consciousness and a will. Use-values must therefore never be looked upon as the real aim of the capitalist; neither must the profit on any single transaction. The restless never-ending process of profit-making alone is what he aims at.[18]

With a given employed labor force the capitalist can increase the mass of surplus value by raising the rate of exploitation. There are three ways of doing this. First, the length of the working day can be extended, and if the value of the means of subsistence remain unchanged, the surplus labor time and hence surplus value is increased. Second, real wages can be reduced; but since real wages are normally at the subsistence level, this can only be temporary if the labor supply is to be maintained. Third, the productiveness of labor can be increased through a change in the state of technology. The improved technique increases the total output produced by a given labor force, and thus increases the difference between total output and subsistence output.

In Marx's model technological improvements are endogenous and occur at a rapid rate. By the very nature of the capitalist process technological change must occur. The capitalist is constantly seeking ways to increase the mass of surplus value. Since the methods of lengthening the working day and reducing wages have physical limits, to increase surplus value the capitalists must rely primarily upon increasing the productivity of labor via technological improvement. Each capitalist firm discovers that it can temporarily gain on its competitors by introducing more productive instruments. By doing this, it immediately lowers the cost of production, while the price of the product falls only gradually as other capitalists follow. Those who are among the first to introduce a new technique, therefore, gain extra profits. Thus each capitalist firm tries to get the jump on its competitors or, failing this, introduces new machinery merely to hold its relative position in the industry.

Marx believes that there is a strong tendency for technological progress to increase the quantity of machinery and equipment per worker. Thus, to take advantage of new techniques capitalists require a larger stock of capital. Another way an individual firm can increase its total profits or surplus value is to expand its output under existing methods of production. This requires an increase in the outlay on labor, raw materials, and capital equipment. Thus, whether the capitalist firm increases its total surplus value via technological change or simply an expansion of output, it finds that it must accumulate more and more capital. This, then, becomes the goal of capitalist activity. As Marx says, "Accumulate, accumulate! That is Moses and the prophets! . . . reconvert the greatest possible

portion of surplus value ... into capital! Accumulation for accumulation's sake, production for production's sake ... this [is] ...
the historical mission of the bourgeoisie...."[19]

Marx viewed capitalism as a powerful engine of economic
growth. The capitalist is driven by the system to accumulate more
and more capital. But, capitalism uses harsh and inhuman methods to accumulate this capital. In one of his more emotional pas-
sages Marx says, "If money ... comes into the world with a con-
genital bloodstain on one cheek, capital comes dripping from head
to foot, from every pore, with blood and dirt."[20] In spite of the
role it plays in generating wealth, capitalism—by its very nature—
is not able to maintain sustained economic growth. It is plagued
with both cyclical fluctuations and periodic crises. And, in spite of
the great increase in wealth, the great mass of people benefit little.
Economic development continues, accumulation and more accumulation, but with the capitalists reaping most of the benefits and
workers remaining near a susbistence level of existence. Life-sustenance is not delivered to all. Esteem and freedom are reserved
to the elite that controls society. Where does it all end? What is the
path which lies before capitalism? Marx says:

> As soon as this process of transformation has sufficiently decom-
> posed the old society from top to bottom, as soon as the labourers
> are turned into proletarians, their means of labour into capital, as
> soon as the capitalist mode of production stands on its own feet,
> then the further socialisation of labour and further transformation
> of the land and other means of production, as well as the further
> expropriation of private proprietors, takes a new form. That which
> is now to be expropriated is no longer the labourer working for
> himself, but the capitalist exploiting many labourers. This expro-
> priation is accomplished by the action of the immanent laws of
> capitalistic production itself, by the centralization of capital. One
> capitalist always kills many. Hand in hand with this centralisation,
> or this expropriation of many capitalists by few, develop, on an
> ever-extending scale, the co-operative form of the labour-process,
> the conscious technical application of science, the methodical culti-
> vation of the soil, the transformation of the instruments of labour
> into instruments of labour only usable in common, the economising
> of all means of production of combined, socialised labour, the en-

tanglement of all peoples in the net of the world market, and with this, the international character of the capitalistic regime. Along with the constantly diminishing number of the magnates of capital, who usurp and monopolise all advantages of this process of transformation, grows the mass of misery, oppression, slavery, degradation, exploitation; but with this too grows the revolt of the working-class, a class always increasing in numbers, and disciplined, united, organised by the very mechanism of the process of capitalistic production itself. The monopoly of capital becomes a fetter upon the mode of production, which has sprung up and flourished along with, and under it. Centralisation of the means of production and socialisation of labour at last reach a point where they become incompatible with their capitalist integument. This integument is burst asunder. The knell of capitalist private property sounds. The expropriators are expropriated.[21]

Countervailing Tendencies

Marx undoubtedly hoped that his version of capitalism's demise would come true. His life was spent trying to promote this end. It would seem, though, that the "expropriation of the expropriators" is not so much a prediction that must follow from his model as it is a vivid description of a tendency. For, in volume three, while speaking of the centralization of capital into a few hands, he says, "This process would soon bring about the collapse of capitalist production if it were not for counteracting tendencies, which have a continuous decentralizing effect alongside the centripetal one."[22] A present-day Marxist deals with this question in the following terms: "In a real sense it can be said that Marx's entire theoretical system constitutes a denial of the possibility of indefinite capitalist expansion and an affirmation of the inevitability of the socialist revolution. But nowhere in his work is there to be found a doctrine of the specifically economic breakdown of capitalist production."[23]

Most American Marxist economists no longer believe that capitalism will destroy itself any time soon. Rather they focus on the nature of the crises that periodically disrupt capitalist development and on the ways that it resolves those crises.

Regardless of the final outcome the two classes are always

posed in a fundamentally irresolvable conflict, neither side fully content, and both sides always scheming about how to improve their own position at the expense of the other.

The capitalists, however, always enjoy an advantage; for when workers begin to gain, capitalists have numerous means to keep labor in its place. One result of this continual class conflict is economic cycles as treated below. However, one element which Marx did not foresee, and which is crucial in the historical evolution of the capitalist system, is intervention of the state in the economic system on behalf of groups other than capitalists. It is possible that this historical fact may have so changed the nature of capitalism that Marx's analysis must be severely amended. Therefore, modern Marxists have been forced to analyze New Deal–Keynesian government intervention by developing a "theory of the state," which can take into account the state's willingness and ability to counter the tendencies to crisis which Marx found inherent in capitalism.

Without too much simplification, Marxist theories of the state can be reduced to a sort of grand conspiracy theory of how to keep laborers in their place by keeping them from being discontented or at least by convincing them that nothing better is possible. In his book, *Fiscal Crisis of the State,* James O'Connor illustrates one such interpretation.[24] O'Connor maintains there are two primary economic roles for the state: accumulation and legitimization. Government expenditures in the area of social capital correspond to the accumulation function, while expenditures for social objectives correspond to the legitimization function. Social capital refers to government investment in physical capital like highways and utilities and to investments aimed either at improving labor skills or at improving techniques via research and development. The best case of social investment designed to improve labor skills is the massive amount of money that goes into public education.[25]

Aside from these expenditures which go directly to increase the potential accumulation of capitalists are the explicit social expenditures. These include social security, unemployment benefits, welfare, and medicare. Such programs are responses to expressed needs of the working class; and through these programs the government, which is an agent of the ruling class, in effect buys off the workers. Any incentives to rebel against the system are effectively squelched as the government moves an inch to satisfy the demands of the working class. But this is just a sop, for workers still do not get what they deserve. In reality this type of government expenditure merely legitimizes the continuation of a system which caters to the needs of the capitalist. If a majority of the workers became rebellious, business would stand the chance of losing everything. So they allow the government to involve itself in such social affairs. The end result is that the tendencies to capitalist crisis have been offset, and the demise of capitalism which appeared imminent to Marx has yet to occur. Nonetheless there are limits to the success of these policies, and their greatest challenge comes from the inherent cyclical tendencies of the capitalist economy.

MARXIST THEORIES OF THE BUSINESS CYCLE

From the Marxist viewpoint the cyclical nature of the capitalist economy can only be understood historically. Furthermore, and of more importance, societies undergo their major upheavals during periods of crisis. Thus, Marxists see underway a fundamental restructuring of the social institutional framework that orders all social and economic activity, termed the "social structure of accumulation." The starting point for understanding their view is the specific Marxist models of the business cycle, which then suggest how these cycles turn into crises.

Marxists propose three principal sources of inherent capitalist instability. The first focuses on the tendency for the organic composition of capital to rise over time. The second examines the inevitability of an aggregate underconsumption of goods. And the third analyzes the effects of the exhaustion of the reserve army of labor. All have one thing in common: each centers its attention on capitalist profits as the motor force of the economy. Because profits fluctuate between high and low rates, the level of investment activity and economic growth fluctuate as well. The ensuing business cycles may not be greatly disruptive at first; however, they compound over time, with each downturn becoming more serious than the previous one. Finally the steady progression of cycles builds to a crisis, a situation where fundamental change must occur in order for profits to rise again and for growth to proceed.

The Organic-Composition-of-Capital Thesis

The problem engendered by the rising organic composition of capital can be seen in a review of Marx's explanation of the source of profits: they are the direct result of exploitation of labor. A worker is paid, say, ten dollars per hour, but may create value at the rate of twelve dollars per hour. The two dollars per hour difference is the surplus value, and it is the owner's profit. To get total profits one multiplies the number of workers by the surplus value produced by each, and it is impossible to make profits except by employing labor. Machines, for example, produce no extra value. If a machine costs $50,000, then that machine will, on the average, work to create $50,000 worth of output over its life, and not a dollar more.

Now, because firms are motivated to increase their profits, they wish to increase the productivity of their workers. With wages unchanged, they must increase the rate at which workers are exploited. If a worker were creating a value of twelve dollars per hour, and if labor productivity could be increased to, say, fifteen dollars per hour, then profits per worker would increase as long as wages remained below thirteen dollars per hour. Increasing productivity is essential to the competitive capitalist firm, which cannot allow its competition to get the advantage. At first glance the drive to enhance productivity appears to be a lucrative venture, but it has a serious drawback. A firm engaging in a productivity drive usually opts to purchase more machines, allowing each worker to produce more output. As the capital in use rises, so does the organic composition of capital; that is, the value of capital in use rises faster than the value of labor employed. This process is accelerated if some workers are laid off with the introduction of labor saving technology. So even though productivity of each employed worker increases, the number of workers employed often falls, and the ratio of workers to total capital outlay always falls. Hence the base upon which profits are realized shrinks.

This can be seen by further examination of the above example. If productivity increases to fifteen dollars per hour, then the same level of production can be maintained with fewer workers. If wages rise to around thirteen dollars per hour, profits per worker would remain about the same; but profits on total outlays would decline since there are now fewer workers per machine. Even if demand for the product increased, it is very possible that higher sales would not adequately compensate for the proportionate loss of the profit base.

Why, then, one asks, would firms introduce labor saving technology? For anyone not well versed in Marxian thought and theory the firm behavior seems silly. Everyone knows that new machines are introduced in order to increase profits, not lose them. Robert Heilbroner offers an explanation. He notes that the capitalist firm is obligated to mechanize in order to stay competitive. Says Heilbroner:

> He is only obeying his impulse to accumulate and trying to stay abreast of his competitors. As his wages rise, he must introduce labor saving machinery to cut his costs and rescue his profits—if he does not, his neighbor will. But since he must substitute machinery for labor, he must also narrow the base out of which he gleans his profits. It is kind of a Greek drama where men go willy-nilly to their fate, and in which they all unwittingly cooperate to bring about their own destruction.[26]

A second reason for substituting machinery for labor is the need for more control over the work force, a need which could push firms to overinvest in machines regardless of the lower profit rate.

Nonetheless, the effect of capital accumulation on the rate of profit clearly places limits on that process. Once a firm reaches the limit of capital accumulation, the only mode of further expansion beyond forcing the labor force to work harder is through an improvement in technology which can increase the output per worker without reducing the number of workers. However, dependency on technology is an obstacle to expansion because technological innovation occurs slowly and gradually. Furthermore, many firms do not have the money to invest in technology.

As capital accumulation proceeds, the profit rate will eventually fall so low that there is no longer sufficient incentive to invest. A recession begins, wages drop, and the weaker firms, whose profit rates have become negative, go bankrupt. When upward wage pressures end, and when the stronger firms buy up the bankrupt ones at prices below their real value, profit rates can rise again and another expansionary period can begin.

This is the earliest Marxist theory of the business cycle; it is also the weakest. For example firms and industries with a high organic composition of capital do not necessarily have lower profit rates. The oil companies are a good example.*

The Underconsumption Thesis

A second Marxist theory of capitalist instability, known as the theory of underconsumption, relies on an analysis of the dynamics of consumer demand. Again firms are driven by the desire to increase profits. This time, though, they try to stretch profit margins by raising their prices. Once more they eventually do themselves in, because the general rise in prices has the effect of reducing the purchasing power, or the real wages, of their workers. As the real income of the laboring class declines, so too does their ability to purchase all the goods that are produced in the capitalist enterprises. In other words, aggregate demand shrinks, and when demand shrinks so does economic activity in general.

Two modern Marxists, Baran and Sweezy, refer to the problem of underconsumption as the inability of firms to realize full profits on total output.[27] As the real income of workers declines they are unable to purchase the output of firms operating at capacity. There will be a surplus of production, and firms must choose among several options. They may be able to take the surplus and find new markets in which to sell. This tendency, say many Marxists, is the source of much of the overseas development of multinational corporations. If this is not feasible, or if they

---

*Technically the organic composition of capital argument can be represented as $p' = s/v(1-c/v)$. If the rate of surplus value (s/v) is taken as constant, then a rising organic composition of capital (c/v) will result in a falling rate of profit. However, capitalists use new capital to raise s/v. And while it is true that in the nineteenth century capital accumulation resulted in a rising c/v, in the twentieth century new capital has been both labor saving and capital saving.

cannot get rid of the entire surplus, they will have to cut back on production, reduce prices, or do some of both. Workers thus lose their jobs, real income falls because of unemployment, and a recession is at hand. Eventually prices may fall far enough so that real income levels are restored and underconsumption no longer bedevils the system. And as the potential of profits once again becomes a reality the same process will begin again.

Once again one wonders how firms could be so stupid. From a long-run perspective, any self-respecting business firm ought to recognize that it has little to gain from its attempts to increase short-run profits. But since each business firm operates individually in competition with its fellow firms, it is blinded to the larger picture. As a consequence, actions taken by single firms to enhance their own relative positions are compounded by similar decisions by competing firms to the detriment of all.

Did Marx think it was possible to maintain a permanent and steady growth in the capitalist economy? This would only be possible if everything went perfectly. For example, Marxist theory claims that capitalist firms are able to control both supply and demand. Supply is controlled via simple output decisions, and demand is controlled by business expenditures on investment goods, a category in the Marxist schema which includes wages. Marx formalizes the problem as a process which takes place over several time periods. Production occurs in period one, but this production is purchased with the wages and capital expenditures of period two. So there is always a one period lag in the consumption of goods. Now, suppose that productivity increases 10 percent in period two. The firm plans to give workers just enough wages to buy up all that was produced in period one. This means that the firm will have 10 percent profit in period two and will be able to invest that profit to increase productivity again in period three. The capitalist pays the worker 10 percent less than what was produced, which enables last period's market to clear. The system could thus enjoy uninterrupted expansion.

But this could only occur once in a million times, for such a delightful scenario would require perfect planning. And the capitalist system operates entirely too anarchically. Each individual firm operates autonomously. If one firm's planning is off, or if several firms just blunder, then the drop in demand could reverberate through the whole system and the permanent expansion would come to an end.

Thus the system will be subject to cycles of recession and expansion. As profits expand in the up cycle, investment will increase and the output capacity of the firm will rise. Eventually the firms realize that demand is not strong enough to purchase all their produced goods. They must cut back and a downward trend takes shape.

Empirically underconsumption would show up as too little consumption demand and thus too much savings for the available investment demand. So far in U.S. history this has not been a major problem with the possible exception of the late 1920s when lagging real wages contributed to the onset of the Great Depression.

The Reserve Army of Labor Thesis

The third theory of the business cycle is more convincing and realistic than the preceding two when considered in light of the U.S. economy today. It concentrates on the labor market and uses the concept of the reserve army of labor. Whereas underconsumption theory centers on the effects of consumer demand for goods, the reserve army theory stresses the changes in the demand and supply for labor during the process of capital accumulation. During an expansion capital accumulates and the demand for labor increases. As demand increases, wage rates also begin to rise since labor becomes relatively scarce. Furthermore, as labor becomes scarce, those working become relatively more powerful in their bargaining position and are able to demand not only higher wages, but better working conditions as well. Workers, of course, are always struggling to gain better wages and working conditions; since labor is now scarce, they start winning the struggle. If capitalists wish to continue production, they either give in to their workers, lose them to other firms, or face strikes, slowdowns, or other industrial action. As labor makes real gains, unit costs spurt upward and profit margins are squeezed to where the capitalist firm cuts back on production, an action that creates unemployment. The solidarity of workers is thus splintered through fear of job loss, and each individual now concentrates more on finding or keeping a job than on winning more job benefits. Accordingly, as worker power jockeys back and forth, a cycle of recessions and expansions becomes the rule. Marx thought that in the long run the solidarity of workers would grow so strong that short-run unemployment would no longer destroy labor's unity. When this happened, capitalism would end, for workers would stay united to overthrow the system collectively.

One aspect of the reserve army theory deserves special mention. The decline in the rate of profit is not traced back to basic instability in the process of capital accumulation. Rather, the profit squeeze results from workers' response to the process. In this scenario the source of instability is class conflict between labor and capital, and thus it is class relations which become the ultimate barrier to the progressive accumulation of capital.

When these three theories of capitalist instability were conceived, the final outcome was presumed to be the demise of the capitalist order, brought about by the overwhelming solidarity and singularity of purpose of the mass of exploited workers. Cycles were considered to be characteristic, with each becoming more disruptive than the previous one, until finally the whole system would collapse in utter chaos. As we all know, capitalism has not disappeared, and there is no compelling reason to believe it will topple and crash in the near future. Instead capitalism has adjusted to the pressures, meeting some difficulties with government regulations on business, and confronting others with some controlled income redistribution to the poorest members of society.

The theories just discussed deal primarily with the reasons for the existence of the business cycle in capitalist economies. Behind all of these theories, however, is the implicit notion that one day the cycles will build into an economic crisis and threaten the demise of capitalism.

For contemporary Marxists a cyclical downturn is no longer an indicator of imminent capitalist collapse. Instead, periodic cycles build up the inherent contradictions of capitalism over time and eventually resolve into economic crises, crises which presage major change, not necessarily total collapse. Many Marxists claim that the U.S. economy is in the midst of just such a crisis. In the next section we will look at the nature of these crises and see how Marxists apply the concept to the present day.

CRISES IN THE SOCIAL STRUCTURES OF ACCUMULATION

There are several competing Marxist theories which explain the nature of crises in a capitalist economy, though they have more similarities than differences.[28] We will focus on the "social structures of accumulation" theory.[29]

This theory builds on Marx's insight that capitalism is a historical product that evolves through stages. The capitalist accumulation process destroys earlier economic systems such as feudalism and slavery, transforms the class structure of society, generates massive social change, and, most importantly, creates changes in the institutional setting within which accumulation takes place.

The stages through which capitalism evolves are defined by different social structures of accumulation—"the set of laws, institutions, and social customs that provides the institutional environment for accumulation. Accumulation—the making and reinvesting of profits by individual capitalists or firms—occurs within this 'social structure' or institutional setting and is shaped by it."[30]

Each stage or social structure of accumulation is long-lived, typically lasting for several decades. It is long-lived because it is embedded in highly durable social relationships:

> sets of laws, institutions, class relationships, organization of political parties, and customary ways of producing and consuming. Each of these arrangements, once established, works to the advantage of particular groups in the society, who become this accumulation structure's natural defender. Unless these groups are weak or divided, the social structure of accumulation thus typically takes a long time to change.[31]

Each stage is itself marked by phases. If the social structure of accumulation results in high profit rates and capitalists have good profit expectations for the future, capital accumulation will be rapid and all will appear well with the economy. This phase is labeled the "period of consolidation." This is followed by a phase called the "period of decay," during which the social structure of accumulation becomes ever less favorable to capitalist enterprise, profit expectations decline, and the rate of capital accumulation slows. This results in long swings in the performance of the economy. Consolidation generates lengthy periods of economic boom and decay results in lengthy periods of economic hard times. Applying this to the U.S. economy, it is argued that the 1890s were hard times, 1899–1929 were boom times, 1929–1941 were hard times again, 1941–1973 saw the return of good times; and now, since 1973, we are in hard times again.

What makes a social structure of accumulation evolve from the phase of consolidation into the phase of decay cannot be answered in general since it is a historical process that differs in each case. However, there are some general points that can be made.

Each social structure of accumulation is characterized by several important relationships—among capitalists, between capitalists and workers, among workers, and between government and the economy. The institutional structure gives a particular form to these relationships and it tends to change slowly while the accumulation process that is embedded within it develops very rapidly. The result is that the old institutional structures become less supportive of the accumulation process. The period of decay may create a crisis, during which many people become disaffected and the various relationships noted above become marked by social conflict.

A typical response would be for capitalists to speed up their efforts at technological and organizational innovation, for workers to seek new ways to get a better deal through government or their own organizations, and for those groups losing their favored positions to propose new ways of organizing the economy.

As a result, the old alignments may change, and new electoral coalitions emerge, sometimes reforming the dominant political party from within, sometimes establishing a new dominant party. Electoral realignments took place at the height of the last two crisis periods, around what political scientists call the critical election years, 1896 and 1934–36.

Out of this period of crisis, decay, conflict, and change may come the construction of a new set of social relationships—a new social structure of accumulation. Such reconstruction is by no means inevitable, since it depends on the outcome of many specific conflicts and deals.

Nonetheless, the crisis creates a situation in which the inadequacies of the old social structure of accumulation become visible, the problems more pressing, and the demand for action urgent. Thus the conditions have been laid for overcoming the inertia of the old institutions and implementing a new set of relationships.[32]

The Stages of American Capitalism

Marxists argue that the U.S. economy has evolved through three social structures of accumulation during the past 150 years. The first was competitive capitalism (1840–1890); the second, monopolistically competitive capitalism (1890–1940); and the third, contemporary capitalism (1940-present). Contemporary capitalism is in crisis with the 1980s and the 1990s the period during which a new social structure of accumulation is being created. The chart[33] below illustrates these stages and the key social structure relationships—relations among capitalists, between capitalists and workers, among workers, and between government and the economy.

The growth of large national corporations led to crisis in the social structure of accumulation of competitive capitalism and to the rise of monopolistically competitive capitalism. Contemporary capitalism was inaugurated by the spread of monopolistic competition on a world scale.

Contemporary Capitalism in Crisis

After World War II, U.S. corporations dominated the world economy, since most industrial countries were still recovering from the war. By the mid-1950s, however, they increasingly had to compete with large firms from western Europe and Japan. By the 1970s firms from the Newly Industrializing Countries (NICs) provided additional competitive challenges.

Until the 1980s, the organized section of U.S. workers were powerful enough to bargain with large firms over sharing productivity gains, producing an arrangement called a labor accord or social contract. This led to segmented labor markets where workers employed by large firms received high wages and benefits along with job protection, while workers in the more competitive sectors had to accept lower wages, few benefits, and unstable employment.

Stages of American Capitalism

Key relations in the social structure of accumulation	Social structure of accumulation I: Competitive capitalism (1840–1890)	Social structure of accumulation II: Monopolistically competitive capitalism (1890–1940)	Social structure of accumulation III: Contemporary capitalism (1940–present)
Capital-capital relations	Small business, local, competitive capitalism	National monopolistic competition, large corporations (trusts)	Monopolistic competition on a world scale, U.S. corporations dominant
Capital-labor relations	Strong craft-based unions in some industries, extensive workplace control exercised by skilled workers	Capitalists are dominant, unions weak, not recognized	Labor accord, unions recognized with legal rights
Labor-labor relations	Craft-based distinctions between skilled and unskilled workers	Homogenized labor semiskilled factory, operatives become important	Segmented labor markets, unions among mass production workers
Government-economy relations	Limited government	Limited government (some regulation, e.g., Federal Reserve)	Keynesian regulation of macroeconomy, United States as world policeman for capitalism

Government played a major and expanding role in the economy. It engaged in macroeconomic policy to regulate the overall level of economic activity, used taxes and welfare policies to redistribute income and to build a safety net under the poor, used regulations to intervene in the economy to change market outcomes, and absorbed a significant share of GNP to maintain a large military force, extended over much of the world.

The postwar boom generated by the new social structure of accumulation came to an end in the early 1970s. It ended because the changing nature of production and distribution (Marx's forces of production) resulted in the social structure of accumulation (Marx's relations of production) becoming a fetter upon further development. The result was a long-term decline in the profit rate with a consequent lower rate of investment and slower economic growth.

The decay of the social structure of accumulation was a product of its very success which generated social movements, conflict, and the rise of new economic conditions—new worldwide competitors, new technologies, and new organizational forms.

More specifically, because of its geographic advantage and increased industrial might, the U.S. emerged from World War II as the leading economic power. In 1944 at the Bretton Woods conference, the U.S. solidified its position as the provider of economic order among capitalist trading nations. New York replaced London as the financial center of the world, and the U.S. dollar was to serve as both international money and a reserve currency.[34]

This new position in the international economy made foreign markets more accessible to U.S. business concerns. European countries needed to build up reserves of U.S. dollars since the dollar had become the standard currency for most of international trade. Thus, they welcomed expansion by U.S. corporations as a source for building up their reserve currency. Both foreign countries and the U.S. benefitted from this expansion; the U.S. found other markets to consume its excess supply and foreign countries built up their reserves with the influx of U.S. dollars from capitalist expansion. Given this scenario of mutual advantage, the U.S. accelerated its penetration of the old European and Japanese empires. It built up a system of military bases around the world which Marxists claim was designed to maintain access to cheap raw materials and provide military security to the multinational corporations. Those countries which complied with U.S. imperialism received military assistance. Governments which opposed U.S. penetration were overthrown. Examples are Iran and Guatemala. In this regard U.S. support of Britain in the Falklands/Malvinas war with Argentina was a foregone conclusion.

Between the end of World War II and 1980 the foreign direct investments of U.S. corporations grew from $10 billion to $213 billion. Domestic opposition to imperialism was deflected through the accusation of communism, and those who disagreed with foreign policy were blacklisted and humiliated. Marxists see the collaboration between the government and business during this period of imperialistic expansion as evidence that the state serves the interests of the capitalist class. U.S. hegemony worked to protect business firms from the effects of low demand, using a combination of political and economic power.

However, the very nature of this expansion portended a long-run breakdown of power. The more investments were made in foreign countries, the greater became these countries' competitive stance among trading nations. Eventually Western Europe and Japan became capitalist rivals with the U.S., and the mutual advantage of imperialistic expansion collapsed.

In addition to the increasingly more powerful bargaining position of Europe and Japan, Third World revolutionary forces were becoming more difficult and more expensive to contain. Perhaps the ultimate threat to continued U.S. hegemony manifested itself in the U.S. failure to maintain power in Vietnam. This defeat highlighted the U.S. inability to organize and control the competitive order of the world capitalist system.

The various forces threatening U.S. hegemony culminated in the breakdown of the Bretton Woods Agreement. Fixed exchange rates were replaced by a system of floating exchange rates. Floating rates can be very unstable because of the increased currency speculation and because capitalist countries may try to manipulate the exchange rates through banking practices and currency controls. Such instability has a profound effect on the quantity of foreign investment. In times of political and economic instability, such as those engendered by the move to floating exchange rates, financial assets are favored over capital accumulation. That is, corporations will delay their capital investments and await the reestablishment of international stability.

Such corporate behavior can easily be analyzed in the Marxist terms of underconsumption. During an expansion corporations find themselves producing a surplus. Hence, they look for other markets to absorb this surplus. If these other markets are not stable and profitable, corporations will naturally choose to defer investment until stability and profitability return. In the meantime they will attempt to build up their financial assets while waiting for stable market conditions to evolve. One repercussion of this drop in investment is an increase in the balance of trade deficit; for as corporations cut back foreign investments, exports also will decline. Hence, the stability of the international economy has serious implications for the capitalist system.

Accompanying the decline in U.S. hegemony was the end of easy access to the raw materials of Third World countries. Third World nationalism and mutual cooperation combined with Soviet support to those opposing the U.S. to restrict U.S. influence on international markets. Of most importance, the U.S. could no longer buy unlimited amounts of raw materials at inexpensive rates. The price of oil, for example, rose more than tenfold in the years since 1973.

The importance of access to raw materials can best be understood through an analysis of its effect on profit rates. Before the decline in U.S. hegemony, the price of raw materials would not increase during an expansion because the U.S. had control over unlimited supplies. That is, increases in demand for raw materials could easily be met without price increases. However, with the decline of U.S. ability to control the world economy, the supply of raw materials became more inelastic. Now, when demand for raw materials goes up, the prices rise, for Third World countries have gained more control over their resource deposits.

Marxists claim that imperialism and U.S. hegemony clearly enabled corporations to avoid the inherent capitalist problems of aggregate demand.

Another way of controlling consumer demand is to use Keynesian demand management in the domestic economy. Throughout the 1960s the government adopted a policy of expansion through spending. However, as the expansion continued for a number of years, corporate profits were squeezed. In this case much of the squeeze on profits was brought about by the exhaustion of the reserve army of labor, for the unemployment level fell below 4 percent.

But if the government serves the capitalist class, why did it continue a policy of expansion in these circumstances? The answer to this question centers on the Vietnam War. From the Marxist viewpoint, the state was aiding the owners of production by fighting in Indochina, for they were attempting to protect and provide for imperialistic expansion. However, in doing this, the state simultaneously overstimulated the economy at home because increasing taxes to pay for such an unpopular war was politically unfeasible. The failure to allow a recession to discipline workers led not only to declining profit rates for corporations, but ignited the fires of inflation.

What was the corporations' response to the continued decline in profits? In order to meet the increased demand, capitalists needed to expand their capacity to produce. But profits generate the money needed to expand capacity output, and profits were declining. Thus, in order to meet the demand of consumers, corporations were driven to dramatically greater borrowing for investment.

The effects of borrowing to maintain corporate investments were not seen until the economy was allowed to go into recession and then begin another period of expansion. According to Boddy and Crotty,[35] in the first half of expansion corporate profits increase and investment also increases as corporations expand their output capacity. However, when the expansion began, after the light recession of 1973, corporations were unable to put their increased profits into investment; rather, they had to pay off the debts and the interest on those debts. Capital expenditures did not increase, preventing the growth in production and employment necessary for the recovery. This same explanation can be applied to the 1980s which has witnessed extremely lethargic investment performance. Keynesian demand management policies no longer worked.

In addition, Marxists suggest that after World War II the U.S. was able to sustain lower unemployment rates than in the prewar period mainly due to a social contract negotiated between organized labor and the largest corporate employers. But this social contract broke down in the crisis of the 1970s. After the purging of left-wing elements in the late 1940s, organized labor agreed to maintain labor discipline and refrain from actions which would threaten profitability, management prerogatives, or political stability. The largest corporations agreed to maintain economic growth and low unemployment rates in the organized sectors. Increased unemployment rates during the 1970s reflected the breakdown of this social contract. Organized labor was unable to

172 Beyond Reaganomics

fulfill its part of the contract due to its declining influence among
workers. Corporations were unable to fulfill their part of the contract due to the intensification of foreign competition and the
other aspects of the 1970s' crisis which forced a slowdown in the
growth rate of real wages.

The rising influence of unorganized groups of workers and
sun belt capitalists also hastened the breakdown of the social contract. Since the 1960s, women, black, and Hispanic workers have
demanded a greater share of the national income, while medium-
sized and newer large firms operating out of the sun belt have
begun to compete for a greater share of economic and political
power. Therefore, even if organized labor and the largest corporations had agreed to maintain the social contract, unorganized
workers and sun belt corporations would have hindered its implementation.

The breakdown in U.S. hegemony, the ineffectiveness of demand management, and the breakup of the social contract meant
that the social structure of contemporary capitalism was no longer
viable and entering a stage of decay.

Marxists see the Reagan administration's economic policies
as an attempt to restore profitability by creating a new social structure of accumulation similar to that of monopolistically competitive capitalism. Needless to say they do not believe that it will be
successful because the forces of production have changed radically
since 1890–1940. Rather they see the Reagan era as an interlude
before the next stage which probably will see an even more state-
directed capitalism.

THE MARXIST ANSWER: A REDISTRIBUTION OF
ECONOMIC POWER

Based on the above analysis, Marxists traditionally have proposed one policy: "Workers of all countries, unite!" Marx himself
envisioned the capitalist system ending in a revolution of the proletariat. However, present-day Marxists do not predict that the
system will crumble in glorious revolution; they believe that workers, through the organization of trade unions, can increase their
power in the production process and eventually take control.

In effect, then, Marxists offer no stabilization policy prescriptions that government can be requested to implement, for they have no confidence in the present form of government. Instead of prescribing policy, they present a critique of the entire capitalist system, showing why capitalist economies are subject to recurrent business cycles and intermittent major crises. Roger Alcaly sums up the problem of capitalist instability: "In the most basic sense, crises can be said to dominate the dynamics of capitalist development because capitalism is a system of production for profit rather than production for use."[36] When profits are not high, investors hold back, causing recession. When profits are high, they invest and an exaggerated boom ensues. In this way instability is unavoidable in a capitalist environment.

According to Marxists this problem can only be resolved through fundamental social change. The pattern of ownership, the distribution and control of profits, and the locus of production decisions must all be taken out of the hands of the few. Marxists argue that capitalists will never take the initiative to carry this out on their own. Nor can government be expected to sponsor such radical changes. Therefore, Marxists rely on the working class to unify and work forcefully through the creation of large and powerful labor unions. Labor must use its collective influence and power to demand participation in the decisions that are normally reserved for the capitalist.

The conclusion of an article by David Gordon on the need for restructuring the economy gives a flavor of this position:

> . . . we face a critical choice: Will internal corporate systems of control become even more centralized? Or shall we finally begin to move toward more participatory and democratic systems of worker coordination and self-management![37]

The immediate response to any demand for labor participation in management, particularly investment decisions, is to write it off as ideological and impractical. However, if the labor movement in the U.S. is to regain its bargaining position in the struggle with large conglomerates, it will have to expand and reorganize. Perhaps the key to success in establishing a position in corporate investment decisions is political influence. Working collectively through unions, labor must break away from its traditional tie with the Democratic party and help form a new political party. In this way the working class will assure itself of representation in the legislation of public policy. What labor needs now is education; workers must understand the structure of the market and its intrinsic instability in order for them to oppose that structure for their own good and for the good of the country.

CONCLUSION

Marxists are the only group of economic theorists who have a fully developed theory that explains business fluctuations and recurrent economic and social crises. Right now, they say, we are suffering through one of the times of crisis. But these could be avoided, they tell us, if major changes in the social, economic, and political structure took place. First, productive resources must be owned by a much wider range of people, and labor must participate in the decisions of how to distribute profits. Second, stability in the world economy needs to be restored via international cooperation rather than competition and antagonism. And third, labor unions must be allowed and encouraged to evolve into partners in production.

Few people, however, are willing to lend a very sympathetic ear; for although Marxists provide a coherent critique of the present crisis, their proposals are vague and sound like slogans. Moreover, the Russian, Chinese, and Polish claims to having built socialism in accordance with Marxist theory is a terrible albatross for American Marxists.

Capitalism has seen the U.S. through a great number of prosperous years. True, admit the Marxists, but the curtain is falling fast on the era of contemporary capitalism. If prosperity is to continue, and if progress is again to prevail, then an unbending allegiance to the free market system must fall by the way. Marxists warn that one day they will be vindicated and proven right. We shall see.

But whatever our views on the validity of Marxist analysis, let us appreciate it for the insights it provides as the only coherent theoretical structure which does not treat recurrent cycles and depression-like conditions as an accident. In its framework, they are predictable.

Let us turn now from these theoretical frameworks which have dominated economists' thinking on the modern macro-economy and its problems. We will start with our own theoretical stance, then look more closely at our contemporary economy, and finally in the last chapter offer our own menu of policies for dealing with the current problems.

PART THREE

The Alternative:
Post-Keynesian Institutionalism

8. Toward a New Political Economy: Methodological and Historical Considerations

The previous chapters have shown that the methodology, the theoretical bases, and the historical experience with the competing approaches leads to one conclusion: all are inadequate in dealing with the current situation of the U.S. economy. Thus they should be used cautiously while searching for an alternative. Long-swing theories provide no policy guidelines nor even a clear picture of where we are in the cycle. Marxian analysis has useful insights into our current economic difficulties; however, Marxism as an ideology is so uncongenial to the American temper that there is little possibility it could ever become the core of a new political economy.

In addition, both Conservative Economic Individualism and mainstream U.S. Keynesianism appear incapable of coping with the myriad problems confronting our economy and our society; problems rooted in the creative-destructive nature of capitalism. CEI and traditional Keynesian theories are limited because they adhere to a narrow economic approach that focuses on the problems of scarcity and choice. Concentration on the logic of individual choice misses the reality that choices are conditioned by historically specific institutional structures, power relations, and belief systems.

The economy is more complex than the simple theory of choice can handle. Business firms are more than mere profit maximizers. Workers choose jobs for other reasons than relative wages and the opportunity for leisure. Job satisfaction, personal fulfillment, location preference, screening devices by employers all play a part in allocating labor in the economy. The U.S. industrial economy is not exclusively competitive in nature. Monopoly practices, implicit contracts with suppliers, and imperfect information limit competitive forces. Workers' earnings are not simply a reflection of what they contribute to production: sexual and racial discrimination are realities.

Does it matter that the real world differs from the ideal one of CEIs and Keynesians? They respond that they do not claim their models can simply replicate the economy, that since their conception of human behavior captures the essence of motivation in the economic world, their theories perform adequately in terms of economic understanding and of prediction. So their conclusion is "No, differences between the real economy and our theory do not invalidate the theory." Milton Friedman has constantly reiterated their methodological stance that the reality of the theory's assumptions is unimportant; the important issue is the ability to predict correctly.

The first step in developing an alternative understanding of our economy is to reexamine this methodology.

FORMAL THEORY, PREDICTION AND STANDARD ECONOMICS

Both traditional theories claim to be scientific, "positive economics." Positive economics, with its logical positivist model of explanation, has found wide acceptance among economists since the publication in the 1950s of I. M. D. Little's *Critique of Welfare Economics* and Milton Friedman's *Essays in Positive Economics*.[1] Predictability is the crucial element in positive economics. Economic science is advanced by logically deducing hypotheses from a general theory which then act as predictions of correlational relationships in the real world. That is, the "positive science investigator" tries to test the degree of correspondence between his or her predictions and the empirical evidence provided by the real world. A high degree of correspondence or a "good fit" supports the theory (or at least keeps the hypothesis among the not-yet-falsified); a low level or lack of correspondence indicates a flaw. Disputes are resolved by testing, and if the predictions derived from one model prove "better" than those from another, the former is tentatively selected as preferable. In every case, the theory which best explains the observable phenomena of the economic world is preferred. Thus, empirical testing is the key to theory selection in economics.

Since the validity of a model is to be judged by its predictive ability, the realism of its assumptions or the static nature of its structure become irrelevant issues. In a formal model, all assumptions are more or less abstract and unrealistic because a model, by definition, cannot capture or reproduce the whole of reality. Consequently, assumptions facilitate abstraction, which enables the economist to explain the underlying order.

Since standard economists place so much weight on the ability to predict as the means of theory selection, what has been the success of this endeavor in economics? In a word, successful prediction of economic phemonena has been notably absent over past years. This failure is mirrored in the models' inability to deal with the nation's recent experience with unemployment, inflation, and the energy crisis. Insofar as positive economic theories are to be "judged solely by [their] predictive ability," why is it that, in practice, when economists' theories fail to fit the facts, they are not rejected?[2]

An example can illuminate the issue. The controversy over the central issue of the causes of changes in output and the price level can illustrate that differences between Keynesians and the "monetarist" wing of the CEIs cannot be resolved on the basis of empirical results. We will find that since prediction is not sufficient, the reality of the theory's basic assumptions and propositions becomes important. In addition, the example will show that underlying economic philosophies provide better guidance to understanding the differences between the two groups.

In a study for the Commission on Money and Credit,[3] Milton Friedman and David Meiselman set out to test empirically the predictive power of monetarist versus Keynesian theories of business fluctuations. They predicted consumption expenditures for each year between 1897 and 1958 using two different equations. They divided nominal income Y into autonomous expenditure A and induced expenditure B. The "Keynesian" equation used autonomous expenditure A as the independent variable and induced expenditure B as the dependent variable or the variable to be explained. The "monetarist" equation used the quantity of money M as the independent variable and induced expenditure B as the dependent variable. Autonomous expenditure A was defined as the sum of net private investment plus government deficit on income and product account plus net foreign balance. Quantity of money M was defined as currency plus demand deposits adjusted, plus time deposits at all commercial banks.

Friedman and Meiselman claimed that their tests over the entire period 1897–1958 indicated that the quantity of money M was a better predictor of induced expenditure B than autonomous expenditure A. Tests of various sub-periods confirmed these results. They also claimed that the change in nominal M was a better predictor of the change in nominal B than the change in nominal A. Finally, any correlation between autonomous expenditure A and induced expenditure B was claimed to reflect the effect of the quantity of money, M, on A and B simultaneously. Thus Friedman and Meiselman concluded that the CEI monetarist interpretation of business fluctuations was more accurate than Keynesian theory.

Keynesian rebuttals were quickly forthcoming. *The American Economic Review* printed two articles attacking the Friedman and Meiselman work, one by Albert Ando and Franco Modigliani and the other by Michael De Prano and Thomas Mayer.[4] Friedman and Meiselman wrote a reply in the same issue defending their procedures and results.[5] The following paragraphs briefly summarize the criticisms.[6]

One line of attack was to argue that the equations used in the test were so simplified that the results were relevant only to the abstract world represented by the models. Friedman and Meiselman gave no reasons the results should be relevant to the actual economy. In addition, the two theories should be represented in equations that have been simplified to the same degree. However, Friedman and Meiselman presented no objective way of determining relative simplicity for two different models or equations.

The critics argued, further, that the test results need not hold for different, and particularly for more complex, specifications of the two theories; that is, the results were not statistically robust. Different definitions of the A and M variables could make the

Keynesian autonomous expenditure A outperform the CEI monetarist quantity of money M.

Ando and Modigliani argued that Friedman and Meiselman's
specification of autonomous expenditure A and, therefore, of induced expenditure B were incorrect in Keynesian terms. Friedman and Meiselman's simplification of Keynesian theory specified
all investment, government spending, taxes, and imports as exogenously determined. At the same time, they assumed that all
consumption was endogenously determined and that the bal-
anced-budget multiplier was zero. Ando and Modigliani used a
different specification of the Keynesian model and claimed that
the Freidman-Meiselman definition was selected to maximize support for the CEI monetarist position. Friedman and Meiselman
retorted that their definition was not incorrect, merely selective.
De Prano and Mayer offered twenty different reasonable definitions of autonomous expenditure A and cast further doubt on the
Freidman-Meiselman results, since the conclusions were sensitive
to different definitions.

One implication of the above controversy is that the results
of testing competing theories are dependent on the statistical testing procedures. Because there is no way to determine objectively
the relative degree of simplicity or the proper definitions of the
variables, it becomes impossible to settle disputes between rival
theories by appeal to empirical testing. In fact, empirical testing
has been unable to determine whether the predominant causation
is the Keynesian A to Y to M, or the CEI monetarist M to Y to B.
Consequently, there is no basis for deciding between the theories.

William Poole and Elinda Kornblith replicated the tests of all
the previous contestants and, in addition, extended the tests to
cover the 1959–1970 period.[7] Their conclusions are worth quot-
ing:

> Our findings emphasize the futility of the R^2 [a measure of statisti-
> cal correlation] game. The F-M critics all came up with definitions
> of autonomous expenditures that produced regression R^2s rivaling
> or exceeding the R^2 for M_2. But beyond the period of estimation
> many of these relationships fall apart. Whatever one's biases in
> terms of the Keynesian and quantity theory approaches, these find-
> ings indicate that none of the single equation models predict the

future very well. . . . In terms of verified empirical knowledge,
economists have good reason to be modest.

The first implication of the Keynesian-CEI monetarist debate
is that, contrary to the logical positivist position of standard economics, empirical tests seldom resolve theoretical disputes. This is
true because there are insurmountable testing problems.

The testing process in economics is flawed in several serious
ways. First, there are substantial problems in specifying the key
variables. For example, what is the proper empirical definition of
the theoretical concept "M," the quantity of money? Should it be
M_1 (currency plus demand deposits), M_2, M_3, or some other definition? Should large certificates of deposit be included and then
excluded as their importance changes over time? Should it be the
size of M or its rate of change that is used? Monetarists cannot
agree even among themselves. The same problems plague the
empirical specification of the Keynesian theoretical concept of
autonomous expenditure A. There is no objective way to decide
these questions. Friedman has, of course, argued that the defini-
tional issues can be settled empirically—use the definition that
works. But this ultimately fails because different empirical approaches give different empirical results when applied to different
time periods.

A second problem that plagues econometric testing is the
selection of leads and lags. What is the proper time lag structure
for testing the impact of M on Y? Problems of lag specification (we
simply do not know what they are) make estimating the true lag
structure next to impossible. The temptation is to select the structure that maximizes the R^2 between M and Y or A and B, as the
case may be.

A third difficulty is distinguishing cause from effect in the
test. For example, as mentioned earlier, does causation run M to
Y to B as the CEI monetarists say, or A to Y to M as the Keynesians
maintain? In other words, is M exogenously determined (by the
Federal Reserve) or endogenously determined by other variables
within the system, or are both views partially correct? While causal-
ity tests do exist and are used with increasing frequency, they are
not powerful enough to enable us to resolve the issue.

Finally, both the data collection methods and the procedures for calculating economic variables are open to judgment, and such judgment can affect the final results.

These econometric difficulties imply that the choice among alternative theories cannot be made solely on empirical grounds. In addition, the desirable qualities of a logical model—simplicity, generality, specificity, and aesthetics—must be taken into account, and their relative evaluation is largely determined by one's own vision of the economic process and attendant policy implications.

A second implication of the debate is that empirical verification does not provide an adequate basis for theory selection. Our review of the theories and of the methodological issues convinces us that the empirical controversy has always been secondary. The underlying issue is the difference in policy orientation, and theories are chosen because they yield policy implications compatible with one's vision of the economic process.

And at a fundamental level CEIs and Keynesians share a common worldview: the economy can best be understood as a simple summing-up of all of its atomistic individuals, with the market the optimal mechanism for their coordination. Their main difference, which is not broached in the debates, is the degree of stability of a market economy.[8] Monetarist CEIs believe that the economy is basically stable and that an activist policy will destabilize it. The Keynesians, also firm believers in the efficacy of the market system, believe that the economy has fundamental instabilities that require active intervention by government. No amount of empirical testing can settle this difference. In any case it is probably less important than their common support of the market view of the economy.

The result is that economic policy proposals are guided by a free market worldview, whether CEI or Keynesian, whose "scientific" (in the sense of empirical proof) basis is questionable, at best. Since theoretical controversies cannot be resolved by appeal to statistical testing and since adverse results always can be explained away, economists are left only with their worldview as support. Examples of the persistence of theoretical claims in the face of contrary evidence abound. For example, in 1984 Milton Friedman predicted that because of earlier discretionary policy (a rapid rise in the money supply), "we shall be fortunate indeed if prices are not rising in . . . double digits by 1985." Despite actual inflation of

3.6 percent that year, Friedman did not hesitate recently to claim that 1989's increase in inflation was just "a delayed reaction to the very high rates of [money supply] growth in 1985 and 1986."[9] So the worldview of a stable market economy disrupted by misguided stabilization policy persists even when prediction fails.

There is a growing realization of these problems in mainstream economics. For example, Donald McCloskey suggests that acceptance of a theory is based more upon the general "persuasiveness" of its argument to a peer group than to its ability to survive empirical tests. Thus, agreement among the leading economists is what counts in the final analysis.[10] Clearly, therefore, the worldview of those economists is important.

Economists would do well to drop these "scientific" pretensions and accept that they are "storytellers."[11] Then, statistical testing would become merely one more piece of evidence contributing to the realism and coherence of the "story." At the minimum, this methodological approach would generate caution and humility. It might also direct economists' attention to questions of institutional structure, relations of power, and systems of belief that have been neglected by economists because they cannot be investigated econometrically.

TOWARD A NEW POLITICAL ECONOMY: POST-KEYNESIAN INSTITUTIONALISM

An increasing number of economists, including ourselves, believe that the essential characteristics of the economic world are not incorporated into either CEI or Keynesian theory. Consequently neither approach adequately explains economic activity, predicts economic results accurately, or proposes appropriate public policies. The seventies gave ample evidence against the Keynesians and the 1980s have provided the same sort of evidence against the CEIs.

In the remainder of the book we synthesize our work and that of like-minded economists into a "story" of the way the economy operates, why it is malfunctioning, and what can be done to make it perform better. This synthesis we call Post-Keynesian Institutionalism (PKI) to give it a label comparable to Keynesianism,

Conservative Economic Individualism, and Marxism. The label has its roots in Keynes and in the American Institutionalists.[12]

The remainder of this chapter presents the contrasting worldview from which PKIs operate. Succeeding chapters deal with the central features of PKI theory and the derived policy recommendations.

Methodology of Post-Keynesian Institutionalism:
Look at the World, then Theorize

In general the PKI starts with a given situation and seeks to explain the dynamics of existing structures and institutions. What moves the economy? What makes it work? What kind of values does it support and instill? What motivates individuals to do anything? What is the nature of conflict and who has the power to get what they want and to influence structures and other people? By asking such questions, the PKI economist hopes to come to an understanding of the way the economy actually functions.

PKIs believe that no two societies are alike. Each is the unique product of a set of historical events and the society's response to those events. Societies may be similar, but none are exactly the same. Nor are the people the same. Each social system is thus its own unique evolutionary system, one that changes over time in response to varying historical conditions.

Traditional economics, both CEI and Keynesianism, believes in the possibility of universal laws which transcend historical, cultural, and institutional differences between societies. Thus a market is a market is a market. Marxism similarly holds that there are economic laws, though they are historically specific to a particular social system. Thus capitalism is capitalism is capitalism, no matter the country or the time it operates.

On the other hand, Post-Keynesian Institutionalists believe that so-called economic "laws" are nothing more than empirical generalizations that are historically specific and must be revised as culture and institutions change. Any evidence about actual behavior is accepted as a piece of information that must be fitted into the whole picture of the society.

Does all this have anything to do with the problems now faced by the U.S. economy? Certainly; it implies that to understand the nature of the current problems, we must focus on the current economic structure and not on the U.S. economic structure of the nineteenth century or on some theoretical ideal of perfect competition. And not surprisingly PKIs find that the root source of many of the ills facing the U.S. economy resides in the evolutionary developments of the structures or institutions that make up society—markets, corporations, labor-management relations, government.

The PKI approach to economic understanding, however, does have at least one serious drawback. Different economists may develop different explanations of the core motivating factors in society. This cannot be avoided. The CEI and Keynesian schools have developed a very formal, logically consistent and sophisticated (however unrealistic) body of theory from which most knowledgeable economists will derive the same results. No such corpus of theory exists among PKIs. As a result, different PKI economists highlight different economic factors as crucial; and different PKI economists offer different solutions to economic problems.*

In spite of their differences PKIs still have much in common. At the methodological level, PKI economics can be characterized as holistic, systemic, and evolutionary. Social reality is seen as more than a specified set of relations; it is the process of change inherent in a set of social institutions which we call an economic system. The process of social change is not purely mechanical; it is the product of human action, which is shaped and limited by the society in which it has its roots. Thus PKI is holistic because it focuses on the pattern of relations among parts and the whole. It is systemic because it believes that those parts make up a coherent whole and can be understood only in terms of the whole. It is evolutionary because changes in the pattern of relations are the very essence of social reality. PKIs focus on capitalism as an evolving socio-economic system that requires continuing changes in

---

*In fact, some of the economists we would place in this category would be uncomfortable being classed in the same school of thought with some of the others.

policies if its creative-destructive and uneven development tendencies are to be controlled.

At a more concrete level, PKI economics has an appreciation for the centrality of power and conflict in the economic process.

> The preoccupation with the role of conflict, power and coercion is an intellectual heritage which ... early American institutionalists like Veblen and Commons have reformulated and integrated ... into their analysis of "vested interests," absentee ownership, the economic role of the state, the legal foundations of capitalism, the importance of collective and political bargaining, public utility regulations and the analysis of collusion between financial, industrial and political power.[13]

This heritage is carried on today by John Kenneth Galbraith's work on the "planning system,"[14] Warren Samuels on law and economics,[15] Willard Mueller on antitrust,[16] Charles Craypo on the impact of conglomerate mergers on collective bargaining,[17] Michael Piore on dual labor markets,[18] and a host of scholars[19]— Alfred Eichner, John Cornwall, J. A. Kregel—on macrodynamics; Charles Sable and Michael Piore on technical change; Bennett Harrison and Barry Bluestone on the labor market; Hyman Minsky on the financial system; Ajit Singh on the world economy; and the list could go on and on. They concentrate on the effect of changes in technology, social institutions, and distribution of power, treating them as an inherent part of the economic process.

PKIs emphasize the predominant role of technology in defining various power groups. Present technological levels that require mass production pit worker against management. Since technological developments have led to the growth of huge corporate enterprises, consumers are often pitted against producers, government bureaucrats square off against corporate planners, and so on. While given technologies do not in themselves absolutely determine the shape of society, changing technology leads to conflict between different groups, realigns power, and initiates grand systemic change.

At the motivational level, PKI economics always has recognized the importance of "nonrational" human behavior in economic decision making.[20] A thirst for power and adventure, a sense of independence, altruism, idle curiosity, custom, and habit may all be powerful motivations of economic behavior. Thus, PKIs have been particularly critical of the rational economic actor assumption: the CEI or Keynesian rational, calculating individual, harnessed to utility and profit maximization.[21]

These characteristics of PKI—holistic, systemic, evolutionary—combined with the appreciation for the centrality of power and conflict, and the recognition of the importance of nonrational human behavior, differentiate PKI from standard economics. CEI and Keynesian formal models simply cannot handle the range of variables, the specificity of institutions, and the variety of behavior that are a part of PKI theory.

Beyond these characteristics of PKI thought, the central feature which links PKIs is their methodological predisposition, or simply put, the way they go about their work.[22] This link is found in the PKI propensity to explain their knowledge by "telling stories."[23] In other words, PKIs explain an economic or social system by means of a pattern model, a model which incorporates all relevant features of social action, gives them meaning, and orders them into a coherent whole. The whole system is thus understood by linking these various parts (or subsystems) into a pattern of interaction which characterizes the essential nature of the larger system.

For the PKI, then, explanation of reality cannot come through the application of universal laws, with successful predictions the only form of verification. Rather, an event or action is explained by identifying its place in a pattern that characterizes the ongoing processes of change in the whole system.

Thorstein Veblen, the recognized founder of the American Institutionalist tradition, brought this holist methodological orientation to the study of the U.S. economy. Veblen conceived of the economic order as an evolving scheme or a cultural process. His construction of a "systems economics" was to remain the point of reference from which later PKIs would criticize the narrow "market economics of choice" of standard economics. As Samuels remarks: "The institutionalist paradigm focuses upon ... an holistic and evolutionary view of the structure-behavior-performance of the economy ... in a system of general interdependence or cumulative causation."[24] This could also serve as a summary of PKIs' methodology.

With such a starting point, that everything is affected by everything else, the PKI must develop a means to study given problems in the whole social system; otherwise it would be a hopelessly gigantic task. Obviously, though, if it is economic phenomena that are of most interest, the PKI will begin looking at the particular structures, or subsystems, that seem to have the most pronounced impact on economic performance.

Alfred Eichner, a pioneering PKI, describes what a new political economy must do in a typical, Western developed society:

> Under the systems approach, economics is no longer the study of how scarce resources are allocated. It is instead the study of how an economic system—defined as the set of social institutions responsible for meeting the material needs of society's members—is able to expand its output over time by producing and distributing a social surplus. [25]

So the job of the economist is to study the system and all its different elements to understand how it can best function to create and maintain a growing level of output. Eichner goes on to argue that the acid test for the validity of an economic theory in the systems framework is whether or not certain actions (or policies) produce predicted results. If they do not, the system has not been properly understood.[26] Whether PKIs will be any more successful in testing their theory in this way is a question only time will answer.

One of the important implications of the systems approach and of the assumption that social systems are evolutionary is a different characterization of the economic process. PKIs see uneven development and creative-destructive processes in our modern economy and their terminology includes historical time, dynamic behavior, and continuous change.

The concept of historical time was developed to counter the orthodox tendency to construct and refer to equilibrium models which require the use of what is known as logical time. Logical time takes no account of history and assumes that any point in the past can be reached again in the future; and past and future are terms not frequently used. The essence of the PKI claim is that individuals and society are travelling through time and can never return to previous states. When viewed in this way the concept of equilibrium rings resoundingly hollow, for who will know at what time, or in what situation, an equilibrium will be reached? The past is over and known with certainty, but the future is unknown and the road society travels is of uncertain destination.

The importance of the point is illustrated by a few relevant examples from the recent past. Who, for example, would have predicted the formation and success of OPEC during the 1970s? Certainly not orthodox economists whose knowledge tells them that it is impossible for OPEC to exist. Milton Friedman predicted OPEC would survive less than six months. Few business analysts were able to foresee its advent either. Similarly, there seems to be no appropriate way of logically and rationally predicting what, where, and in what way corporate managers will choose to invest. Even the CEIs and Keynesians, who have developed wonderfully "precise" models, have a dismal record of predicting economic circumstances of the future over even relatively short time periods.

Consequent to an emphasis on historical time is the conception that the economy is in a continuous evolutionary pattern, characterized by creative-destructive processes and uneven development. Dynamic behavior is thus central to PKI theories. In orthodox theories the central analytical construct has traditionally been static equilibrium, ignoring the reality that institutions and circumstances change (sometimes dramatically) over time.

This is one area where PKIs part company with their cousins, the Keynesians. While the mainstream U.S. Keynesians invest their efforts in understanding the dynamics of change from one equilibrium position to another, PKIs argue that it is much better to forget about equilibrium altogether and think instead in terms of continuous transition, or constant disequilibrium. PKIs are thus led to explain circumstances in one period of time by analyzing the causes in the previous time period(s). Such an approach, focusing on the historical time-sequential links, leads into the PKI analysis of the historical determinants (or causes) of the price level, investment, and income distribution.

Eichner sums up the benefits:

> the advantage which it offers social scientists is that it can incorporate within its analytical structure (a) purposeful activity, (b) cumulative processes, and (c) the interaction of subsystems, both as part

of a larger systems dynamic and in response to feedback from the environment.[27]

Once again, this approach is attractive because it allows the analyst to examine the actual nature of an economic system without sifting everything through the framework of traditional economic theory. It discourages trying to fit everything into a preconceived framework which assumes the basic nature of the system's activity is known already.

The Evolution of the Self-Regulating Market System: The PKI View

The PKI stance that economic analysis should be structured as holistic, systemic, and evolutionary, with an appreciation for the centrality of power and conflict, requires a historical view of the market economy. For the market is the key construct in all the theories. Whereas CEI and Keynesian analyses take it as a datum, for PKIs the market is an institution in constant evolution. The capitalist economy is an evolving system of self-regulating markets that had a beginning in historical time and has been in the process of transformation ever since. Let us develop this argument in some detail, building on the original work of Karl Polanyi.[28]

Most historians, whether their orientation is political, cultural, or economic, clearly recognize that the eighteenth century was a turning point in the nature of the Western world which saw momentous movements and events—intellectual, political, military, social, cultural and economic. The Enlightenment, with its emphasis on reason, natural law and progress, and its avant-garde—the philosophes and physiocrats—opened new vistas, although most of the population of Europe and the remainder of the world scarcely glimpsed those vistas. The writings of the philosophes, Rousseau, Montesquieu and Voltaire in particular, infected the rising bourgeoisie of France and, together with the maladministrations of Louis XV and XVI, brought on the French Revolution, the second momentous event of the eighteenth century. The twilight of the divine right monarchies had arrived on the Continent and would move to its inevitable end, despite the best efforts of the more enlightened despots.

In economic affairs, the eighteenth century began with Francois Quesnay's campaign against mercantilism and ended with the completion of the campaign by Adam Smith. In the process, the classical school of economics, a new social science, came into being. Finally, in the course of the century, the agricultural and commercial revolutions of the previous two centuries initiated the Industrial Revolution in England in four key industries: mining, metallurgy, munitions, and textiles.

Polanyi pinpointed the emergence of the self-regulating market in this historical context; and it was truly one of the momentous changes of the eighteenth century. He observed:

> Since the middle of the eighteenth century national markets had been developing; the price of grain was no longer local, but regional; this presupposed the almost general use of money and a wide marketability of goods. Market prices and incomes, including rents and wages, showed considerable stability. The Physiocrats were the first to note these regularities, which they could not even theoretically fit into a whole as feudal incomes were still prevalent in France, and labor was often semiservile, so that neither rents nor wages were, as a rule, determined in the market. But the English countryside in Adam Smith's time had become part and parcel of a commercial society; the rent due to the landlord as well as the wages of the agricultural laborer showed a marked dependence on prices. Only exceptionally were wages or prices fixed by authorities. Malthus' population law and the law of diminishing returns as handled by Ricardo made the fertility of man and soil constitutive elements of the new realm the existence of which had been uncovered. Economic society had emerged as distinct from the political state.
>
> The circumstances under which the existence of this human aggregate—a complex society—became apparent were of the utmost importance for the history of nineteenth century thought. Since the emerging society was no other than the market system, human society was now in danger of being shifted to foundations utterly foreign to the moral world of which the body politic hitherto had formed part.[29]

Significantly, however, it was England of the later eighteenth century which provided the fertile ground in which the self-regulating market could and initially did take root and mature. Not only had the Industrial Revolution begun in the four industries cited above; of equal or greater importance, the Industrial Revolution began in a period in English history when poverty and its tragic result, pauperism, showed an alarming increase. Even more to the point the poor laws were modified to throw a great mass of English paupers upon the mercy of market wage levels.

Now that the self-regulated market had arrived, what were its characteristics? A capitalist market economy is controlled, regulated, and directed by markets alone. Order in the production and distribution of goods is entrusted to this self-regulating mechanism, based on the expectation that human beings behave so as to achieve money gains. It assumes markets in which the supply of goods, including services available at a definite price, will equal the demand at that price. A market economy assumes the presence of money, which functions as purchasing power in the hands of its owners. Production will then be controlled by prices, for the profits of those who direct production will depend upon them; the distribution of the goods also will depend upon prices, since prices form incomes and it is with the help of these incomes that the produced goods are distributed among the members of society. Thus, order in the production and distribution of goods is ensured by prices alone.

In contrast, during preceding historical periods, markets were never more than accessories of economic life. Generally, the economic system was embedded in the social system. In Babylonia and even Greece the local markets (trading centers) were compatible with the established social way of life; markets did not expand at the expense of the society. Even under the mercantile system of the previous two centuries, where markets had expanded to involve a large part of the nation, they were not free markets as described above but were subjected to centralized administration. In Karl Mannheim's words, the market was transformed from a regulatory mechanism utilized by society into the very organizing principle of society itself.[30]*

------

*China's and Russia's current policies which are encouraging more market activity are attempts to use the advantages of the market as a regulatory mechanism while keeping socialism as the organizing principle of their societies.

On the eve of the Industrial Revolution, the English economy could be characterized as follows: (1) although the new national markets were in some degree competitive, the overriding feature of these markets was regulation; (2) the self-sufficing household of the peasant remained the basis of the economic system and was being integrated into large national units through the formation of an internal market; and (3) agriculture was supplemented by internal commerce, although at the beginning of the eighteenth century the system of internal commerce was one of relatively isolated markets.

This new phenomenon, the self-regulating market, would include some additional ingredients: (1) self-regulation implied that all production was for sale on the market and that all incomes derived from such sales; (2) there were markets for all elements of industry including goods, labor, land, and money, whose prices were respectively commodity prices, wages, rent, and interest; (3) the state would do nothing to inhibit the formation of markets and incomes would be formed only through sales; and (4) there would be no interference in adjustment of prices to changed market conditions.

The self-regulating market, which came into existence during the latter part of the eighteenth century and became fully operative with the creation of a true labor market in 1834, and the repeal of the Speenhamland system,* was an economic utopia along the lines envisaged by Adam Smith. The transition from regulated to self-regulating markets represented a complete transformation in the structure of society. A self-regulating market demanded nothing less than the institutional separation of society into an economic and a political sphere, a singular departure from previous societies whose economies were embedded in the social system and "economic" decision making was determined by larger needs and values.

Moreover, such an institutional pattern could not function

---

*During the most active period of the Industrial Revolution, that is, between 1795 and 1834, a true labor market did not come into being due to extensive poor relief, specifically the Speenhamland system which was not finally eliminated until 1834. Thus, in England, both land and money were mobilized through markets before labor.

unless society was subordinated to its requirements. A market economy could only exist in a market society, as the following examination of the institutional nature of a market economy will serve to illustrate.

Labor, land, and money, as well as commodities, form a vital part of the economic system. They are, in fact, just like commodities, to be bought and sold on the market. However, labor, land, and money are obviously not commodities since they are not "produced" primarily for sale. Labor is only another name for a human activity which is part of life itself, and which is not "produced" for sale but occurs for entirely different reasons. In addition, that human activity cannot be separated from the rest of life. Land is only another name for nature, which is not produced either. Actual money is merely a token of purchasing power that is not produced but comes into existence through the mechanism of banking or state finance. None of the three is produced for sale, so the commodity description of labor, land, and money is purely fictitious. Never before in history had there been true self-regulating markets in labor, land, and money. As Polanyi notes however:

> ... it is with the help of this fiction that the actual markets for labor, land, and money are organized; they are being actually bought and sold on the market; their demand and supply are real magnitudes; and any measures or policies that would inhibit the formation of such markets would ipso facto endanger the self-regulation of the system. The commodity fiction, therefore, supplies a vital organizing principle in regard to the whole of society affecting almost all its institutions in the most varied way, namely, the principle according to which no arrangement or behavior should be allowed to exist that might prevent the actual functioning of the market mechanism on the lines of the commodity fiction.[31]

This meant that the self-regulating market mechanism became, in fact, the sole director of the fate of human beings and of their natural environment. Polanyi observed that:

> ... in regard to labor, land, and money such a postulate cannot be upheld. To allow the market mechanism to be sole director of the fate of human beings and their natural environment, indeed, even of the amount and use of purchasing power, would result in the

demolition of society. For the alleged commodity "labor power" cannot be shoved about, used indiscriminately, or even unused, without affecting also the human individual who happens to be the bearer of this peculiar commodity. In disposing of a man's labor power the system would, incidentally, dispose of the physical, psychological, and moral entity "man" attached to that tag. Robbed of the protective covering of cultural institutions, human beings would perish from the effects of social exposure; they would die as the victims of acute social dislocation through vice, perversion, crime, and starvation. Nature would be reduced to its elements, neighborhoods and landscapes defiled, rivers polluted, military safety jeopardized, the power to produce food and raw materials destroyed. Finally, the market administration of purchasing power would periodically liquidate business enterprise, for shortages and surfeits of money would prove as disastrous to business as floods and droughts in primitive society. Undoubtedly, labor, land, and money markets are essential to a market economy. But no society could stand the effects of such a system of crude fictions even for the shortest stretch of time unless its human and natural substance as well as its business organization was protected against the ravages of this satanic mill.[32]

This was, indeed, a creative-destructive process which would have annihilated society but for protective countermoves. Accordingly, no sooner had the utopia of the self-regulating market been established than it was challenged in order that society itself might survive. Polanyi observed:

> Social history in the nineteenth century was thus the result of a double movement: the extension of the market organization in respect to genuine commodities was accompanied by its restriction in respect to fictitious ones. While on the one hand markets spread all over the face of the globe and the amount of goods involved grew to unbelievable proportions, on the other hand a network of measures and policies was integrated into powerful institutions designed to check the action of the market relative to labor, land and money. While the organization of world commodity markets, world capital markets and world currency markets under the aegis of the gold standard gave an unparalleled momentum to the mechanism of markets, a deep-seated movement sprang into being to resist the

pernicious effects of a market-controlled economy. Society protected itself against the perils inherent in a self-regulating market
system—this was the one comprehensive feature in the history of
the age.[33]

It is appropriate to review, however briefly, the course of this
market system both in its national and international context.
Polanyi's basic premise regarding the market and society is worth
repeating:

> Production is interaction of man and nature; if this process is to be
> organized through a self-regulating mechanism of barter and ex-
> change, then man and nature must be brought into its orbit; they
> must be subject to supply and demand, that is, be dealt with as
> commodities, as goods for sale.... But, while production could
> theoretically be organized in this way, the commodity fiction disre-
> garded the fact that leaving the fate of soil and people to the market
> would be tantamount to annihilating them. Accordingly, the coun-
> termove consisted in checking the action of the market in respect
> to the factors of production, labor and land. This was the main
> function of interventionism.[34]

Interventionism, of course, did not occur simultaneously
both on the national scene and in international affairs. On the
national scene it did not become a potent force until after mid-
century while the international market system was not placed in
jeopardy until the last quarter of the nineteenth century. The
forces of intervention gathered only slowly; as they accelerated, all
was swept before them.

By 1820, in England at least, three tenets of classical laissez-
faire economics had been clearly identified: that commodities (including labor) find their price on the market; that the creation of
money should be subject to an automatic mechanism; that goods
should be free to flow from country to country without hindrance
or preference. Policy called for a free labor market, the gold standard, and free international trade. Between 1820 and 1850 economic laissez faire was fully implemented in England, France, and
the Low Countries.

In England, the Poor Law Amendment Bill terminating the
Speenhamland system became effective in 1834, thereby ending

the system of poor relief and creating a free labor market. By 1825, despite inflation and a business slump following the Napoleonic Wars, it was clear that Parliament intended to adhere to the classical principle of a sound currency; its method was to support and defend the gold standard. However, the gold standard implied deflation and monetary stringency in the face of depression. The chief supporter of laissez faire and the self-regulated market, the manufacturer, had therefore to be protected. Wages had to fall at least in proportion to the general fall in prices so as to allow the exploitation of an ever-expanding market. Thus, the repeal of the Corn Laws in 1846, a corollary of Peel's Bank Act of 1844, was undertaken to bring laissez faire to world trade, to allow the free flow of grain into Britain, and to insure that wages and prices would tend to a free market equilibrium. By 1850 in England, therefore, it appeared that the self-regulating market was triumphant as these three elements, a true labor market, the gold standard, and free trade now formed a coherent whole. It might also be added that in France, Louis Philippe saw to it that the expectations of the rising middle classes were fulfilled.

The utilitarians, including Bentham, however, had long since reflected on the shortcomings and contradictions inherent in this classical utopia and were more than mildly distressed at the sacrifices such a system exacted from the people. The utilitarian critiques and the excesses of the market system in general sparked a revolt among not only the working class but more significantly among the rising middle class. Polanyi termed this revolt the collectivist movement. In England, the collectivists, led by the utilitarians, looked to the government for redress. On the Continent, after the unifications of Germany and Italy and the creation of the Third Republic in France, the governments of these countries followed the utilitarian lead. Scarcely more than a decade after the self-regulating market appeared to be triumphant, it was already in retreat, however grudgingly.

Then on the Continent and in England, particularly after the English Parliamentary Reform Act of 1867 which gave the working class the right to vote, a series of "protectionist" legislation was enacted. Factory laws, social insurance, municipal trading, health service, and public utility laws were passed in close succession. New tariffs, embargoes on immigration, national subsidies, formation of cartels and trusts, and curtailment of capital movements were also enacted, all of which inhibited the self-regulating mechanism of the market. German, Japanese, and American growth in the late nineteenth and early twentieth centuries took place behind high tariff walls; and in the first two countries, government intervention was pervasive.

The countermove against economic liberalism and laissez faire possessed all the unmistakable characteristics of a spontaneous action. At innumerable disconnected points it set in without any traceable links between the interests directly affected or any ideological conformity between them. Even in the settlement of one and the same problem, as in the case of workmen's compensation, solutions switched from individualist to collectivist merely as a result of the increasing realization of the nature of the problem in question. The change, interestingly enough, took place in several countries at a similar stage in their industrial development. Finally, even free-market liberals were forced to support government intervention to prevent monopoly and so secure the preconditions of the self-regulating market. Indeed, such a market, in all of its manifestations, threatened society—which undertook measures to protect itself.

Despite ample evidence that the self-regulating market, and with it nineteenth-century market society, had broken down, efforts were made during the post–World War I years to rehabilitate both. The chief instigators of this effort, of course, were the laissez-faire economists. Polanyi observed:

> Economic liberalism made a supreme bid to restore the self-regulation of the system by eliminating all interventionist policies which interfered with the freedom of markets for land, labor and money. It undertook no less than to solve, in an emergency, the secular problem involved in the three fundamental principles of free trade, a free labor market, and a freely functioning gold standard. It became, in effect, the spearhead of a heroic attempt to restore world trade, remove all avoidable hindrances to the mobility of labor, and reconstruct stable exchanges. This last aim had precedence over the rest. For unless confidence in the currencies was restored, the mechanism of the market could not function.[35]

The root problems of market society, interventionism and currency, reappeared after Versailles and these issues became the center of politics in the twenties. A singular effort was made in Geneva during the twenties, particularly by Britain, France, and the United States, to reestablish stable exchanges through a return to gold. Increasingly the responsibility for carrying this burden fell on the United States; and when the Depression struck in 1929, the effort dissolved with the stock market. The effort, however noble, to recreate free trade, a free labor market, and a freely functioning gold standard went the way of the inflated stock. The self-regulating market had succumbed to its own nemeses.

The response to this collapse was Fascism in some countries and the expansion of the welfare state in others. The conclusion we draw is that the free market economy, in the sense of a self-regulating system, is an utopian vision in the minds of economists and was at best a temporary aberration in the history of humankind. Individual markets may have always existed (at least for commodities), but an economy run by free markets was anything but natural and required specific actions of government to come into existence. The mercantilist controls over the economy that laissez-faire economics fought against were merely that era's way of embedding the economy into the social system. The attempt to "free" markets (particularly for the fictitious commodities of labor, land, and money) from societal control was a failure. Society was not willing to live with the creative-destructive process and the uneven development results of a pure market system. In practice, few would accept the notion that everything and everyone's worth was measured by a market determined price. Workers formed trade unions to eliminate competition in the labor market, business firms merged or sought government regulation to eliminate competition. Farmers sought government price supports. And consumers sought government protection from the free market in the form of pure food and drug acts. Professionals convinced government that the public welfare demanded the licensing of lawyers and physicians.

CONCLUSION

If anything is "natural," it is social control of the economy as a way of embedding it in the total social system; and, if anything is "unnatural," it is a laissez-faire system of self-regulating markets. Government may interfere with our private lives; an unregulated market system with its creative-destructive processes and uneven development has an even greater negative effect in most lives. Therefore, we and most PKIs argue that the burden of proof should lie with the free market devotees. History and common sense make the real issue, "what type of policies will harness the creative side of the capitalist market economy to achieve our economic goals without allowing the destructive side to override our social and political values and needs."

This historical analysis casts serious doubt on the long-term success of CEI policies in the United States and Great Britain. The attempts to dismantle the protective devices created by previous generations are fraught with danger. "Freeing-up" labor markets and creating an enterprise culture will release the destructive forces of the market system upon individual lives and society itself. "Freeing-up" land use and an emphasis on unfettered economic growth threaten the environmental system within which we all must live.

In brief, it is incorrect to assume with the CEIs that the problem is too much government intervention. The Polanyian position suggests that the problem is the specific structure of government intervention. This implies that more, and different, government intervention might be necessary to overcome our current economic problems. The Polanyian view implies that government interventions are constitutive of a market economy—without them capitalist society could not exist. Thus it does not make sense to speak of a contradiction between government intervention and the internal logic of a market economy. Some economic policies are more effective than others and an explanation for the difference will be found at a more concrete level of analysis than the general incompatibility theses propounded by both Marxists and CEIs.

Of course government cannot have an unlimited range of action either. The problems of the communist economies and their move to greater use of markets attest to this. It must be limited to actions that clearly enhance the three goals of the economy. And there must be a balance of government and the market, a mixed economy which must be guided to serve human needs of life-sustenance, fellowship, and freedom.

In the remaining two chapters we will focus on PKI theory and on policy to control the capitalist market economy, to enhance the benefits from its creative side while limiting suffering from its destructive side. The old Keynesian way no longer works. Nor does the CEI approach which exacerbates the tendency toward uneven development because of its refusal to control the destructive side.

9. Structure and Operation of the U.S. Economy: The PKI View

The PKI's recognition that a pure free market economy was an historical aberration and that today's economy is the outcome of both private and public attempts to re-embed the economy into the social system provides a useful starting point for viewing its actual functioning. The PKI view also leads to a close examination of contemporary institutions which provide both explanations and solutions for contemporary economic problems. The origins of this institutional structure were traced out earlier.

The New Deal–Keynesian economic consensus that emerged in the 1930s provided a theory and program to save the market economy by utilizing government intervention to correct the major destructive aspect of capitalist development—unemployment. New Deal politics and Keynesian economics rescued capitalism by providing a new mainstream consensus. The "golden age" of the New Deal–Keynesian consensus was 1960–1973. Per capita income and consumption expanded dramatically, and Keynesian economics seemed to meet its test, for full employment and stable prices were achieved. But trouble began in 1968–69, with inflation becoming serious. In 1973–75 came the longest and deepest recession since the 1930s, followed by seemingly endless stagflation.

The rapid inflation set off a struggle over income shares among income classes and between workers and employers. Increased international competition made business resist wage increases, exacerbating the struggle and further breaking down the social consensus. The faltering economy led to calls for deregulation and reductions in social welfare expenditures. By the end of the 1970s the New Deal–Keynesian consensus was in disarray.

As a result the American electorate once again embraced unfettered free enterprise under the guise of supply-side economics. This was in preference to Carter's enfeebled version of the New Deal–Keynesian consensus. Under the Reagan administration the efficiency and optimal welfare concepts of free market economic theory were translated into growth of GNP, which became the key to solving all economic problems.

Government programs established under the New Deal–Keynesian consensus came under attack for reducing incentives and thus productivity. Unfortunately, the economy's performance has not matched the claims of the CEIs, and in the process we have allowed it to become our master instead of using it as our servant. We close industrial plants, create unemployment, devastate whole communities, and call it an efficient reallocation of resources. We who are prospering from CEI policies caution that nothing can be done because natural economic forces are at work. It is the poor, the unemployed, the underemployed, and the homeless who bear the burden of this free market myopia.

The task of reversing this situation and making the economy our servant in the effort to attain our three goals must begin by attempting to understand the political-economic structure of the U.S. economy. The following step is to devise new policies which can help shape a future consensus. In this chapter we analyze the political-economic structure inherited from the New Deal–Keynesian era as modified by the Reagan revolution.* We attempt to show why this amalgam is no longer able to control capitalism's uneven development. In the final chapter we present a set of policy guidelines with which to build a new political-economic structure and a new social consensus to control capitalism's destructiveness while benefiting from its creativity.

U.S. economists distinguish between the private economy and the public economy. In actual practice, the division is anything

---

*The economic policies of the 1980s must be taken into account. For while the Reagan administration was unable to fulfill its 1980 promises, it certainly succeeded in changing the nature of the debate and in altering, often quite profoundly, the institutional structure of the U.S. economy. It also incubated an additional set of problems that will face economic policy in future years.

but neat; and many other economies do not even attempt to make such distinctions.[1] The effort to escape the destructive side of the market has resulted in some institutions in the private economy that can insulate themselves from the discipline of the market, and most that cannot. Thus, the private economy can be classified into two sectors. In the first, economic power prevails; this is the oligopolistic, core, planning or fix-price sector of the large corporation. The second, the market sector, is made up of small competitive firms which are disciplined by the market; it is termed variously the competitive, periphery, market or flex-price sector. A new extension of the market sector, the underground or informal sector, seems to be growing in importance in recent years.

In the public economy, government operations at federal, state, and local levels now absorb about one-third of the national income. Government functions as an actor in the economy and does so with significant independence and substantial impact.

THE PRIVATE ECONOMY

The planning and the market sectors are composed of qualitatively different types of firms which operate in substantially different economic environments. Each of these sectors may affect the other, but in large measure they act and respond to different sets of conditions.

The planning sector is composed of about 800 of the largest corporations in the U.S. which had 1984 sales greater than $500 million and generated nearly 75 percent of total output.[2] They are typically highly capital-intensive in their production methods so they provide jobs to less than 25 percent of the entire labor force. Their workers' generally have had, until recently, strong unions and have been well-paid. Because these firms are large and oligopolistic, because it is very difficult for newcomers to enter the market, and because each producer substantially differentiates its product lines from those of others, corporations in the planning sector have traditionally been able to obtain considerable control over the supply of particular goods and to influence market price. In addition, they have substantial influence on the determination of government policy.

The late 1970s and 1980s have seen a qualitative change. It is still next to impossible for new domestic firms to enter the industries of the planning sectors; however, foreign firms, often aided by their governments' policies, have done so with dramatic effect on the internal structure of the sector and on worker-employer relations. Aided by an overvalued dollar and the ease of entry into the U.S., Japanese, South Korean, and European firms have become players in many oligopolistic markets. This has undermined the power of unions which has allowed firms to adjust by forcing wages lower. In addition, leveraged buyouts using "creative" financing have forced even large firms such as RJR Nabisco, which was purchased for $25 billion, to concentrate heavily on their financial structure and performance.

The market sector is composed of the remaining 15 million firms: corporations, partnerships, and proprietorships. They are primarily engaged in the provision of services, wholesale and retail trade, or in construction. Production in the market sector is typically labor intensive (especially and naturally in services) and over two-thirds of the private formal sector labor force works in this sector. Virtually all of the new jobs created in the 1970s and 1980s originated in the market sector (or in the public economy). Services accounted for almost 9 million of the 20 million new jobs between 1975 and 1985. Even so, less than half of the national product originates in the market sector which is characteristically competitive: it is easy for newcomers to set up a business, and firms are small and produce only a small fraction of the total output of that particular good. As a result, no single firm has enough power to affect either total supply or the price of the good. Nor does a firm have more than marginal political impact.

The result is not idyllic. There is substantial inefficiency as many new firms go bankrupt within five years of birth. In recent years the failure rate has risen, from 43 per 10,000 in 1975 to 120 in 1986. Wage levels and security are far lower than in the planning sector, and many firms remain in business only because the owners "exploit" themselves with long hours and low profits.

The planning sector is very different. The economic environment is consciously manipulated by the large corporations. Thanks to their almost bottomless pit of resources they advertise widely, they spend great sums on research and product innovation, and ordinarily they "create" the demand they need to sell their products and make a profit. Together with their control over supply, under normal conditions planning sector corporations are able to plan, control, and protect their prices, profit margins, and other elements of their business environment.

Planning sector firms traditionally have not taken prices as a given. The top 800 firms have traditionally been "price-makers," and not "price-takers." The increased activity of foreign firms in the U.S. has put limits on this ability. In response, planning sector firms have pushed the burden of adjustment onto their workers by lowering wages, having massive layoffs, changing work-rules. Even during 1981–83 when business bankruptcies reached their post-depression highs,* few of the 800 were so threatened. The Braniffs were the exception rather than the rule. Even with the depressed auto production, the Big Three were able to adjust so as to have very profitable quarters. Despite growing Japanese imports, and with the help of "voluntary" quotas, U.S. auto firms' profits have remained high, between 1983 and 1987 averaging $6.4 billion per year.

One rapidly developing part of the market sector has a variety of names—the irregular economy, the underground economy, the informal sector. In many ways it carries to an extreme the idea of the competitive firm: small, often only one person, and easy entry; all one needs is a street-corner to sell some goods on. This sector includes those economic activities which go unreported in our present system of economic and tax measures—the exchange of services by craftsmen, illegal transactions, small unincorporated operations such as street vendors.[3]

The underground economy seems to be growing as a component of total economic activity. Of course estimates are difficult to make with any precision; there is evidence that substantial growth has occurred and total activity might sum to one-third of the officially reported output. In addition, there is evidence that the sector plays the role of a shock absorber to disruptions in the labor

---

*The fragility of the Reagan recovery is evidenced by even greater numbers of business failures in 1986 than had occurred during the earlier recession.

market and increases in unemployment rates. It provides a means of support for those who cannot obtain formal sector jobs, thus, leading to an underestimate of unemployment.

We turn now to an analysis of how the private economy operates, placing primary emphasis on the planning sector, because it has been and still is the dominating force in the present-day economy. Within the planning sector the firm is the major actor and its relationship with organized labor was the main private sector pillar of the New Deal–Keynesian consensus and structure.

The Oligopolistic Firm

The central institution in the American economy is the firm, which in the present day is the modern corporation. Historical changes in the corporation, often in response to economic policy, are at the root of the economic problems we experience today. Through mergers, outright purchases of competitors or of firms in entirely different lines of business, expansion drives which push smaller firms out of the industry, or international expansion, planning sector firms in the U.S. have become continually larger since the first days of the country's industrialization in the mid-1800s. Traditional economic theory—whether CEI or Keynesian—views the firm as a smallish entity whose product is dictated by the consumer and whose method of production is dictated by competition. The reality of the typical firm in the planning sector is light years away.

Periodic government efforts at antitrust have been ineffectual, and the Reagan administration abandoned the effort with the result that nothing has stood in the way of the drive to grow ever bigger. The problem this entails was highlighted in John Blair's study of certain critical industries (e.g., steel, oil, autos, drugs, rubber, chemicals) which found conclusive evidence that a larger firm is more likely to engage in pricing activities which are non-competitive in nature.[4] The prices set by large firms differ from those expected under the competitive circumstances assumed by Keynesians and CEIs. He suggested that prices are set on the basis of target return pricing (a practice which seeks a certain level of profits no matter the quantity of goods sold), mark-up pricing (a system of pricing which automatically sets the price at, say, 40 percent over the cost of production), or perhaps price following (setting prices according to what the dominant firm in the industry decides).

This view of the nature of price determination and of the behavioral goals of the large planning sector corporations leads to a reconsideration of the microeconomic core of theory which underlies standard macroeconomic policy proposals. Contrary to the orthodox economist's profit maximization rule, i.e., set output and price at levels which equate marginal revenue to marginal costs, corporate managers set prices and output at levels which achieve a target level of profits. Therefore the strategic variable is the price markup over direct costs.

In a mark-up pricing system direct costs are calculated, profit requirements are added on, and investment plans are thrown in on top of that. Thus there are now three components of price: (1) direct costs (labor, materials, rent, etc.), (2) a target level of profits to satisfy shareholders, and (3) funds to reinvest for further growth. This third component ensures an optimum growth of sales revenue and reflects that large oligopolistic firms in the U.S. rely primarily on internal sources of funds (i.e., retained earnings) to finance their fixed capital expenditures. Firms estimate the growth in demand for their product and then compare that with their existing capacity to determine their investment needs. Once future investment plans are determined, the target level of profits necessary to finance the investment is fixed. Corporations then set prices at the level necessary to generate that target level of profits.

The central implication of this pricing behavior is that actual market prices do not simply reflect the current state of demand but also include planned investment which reflects expected future demand. Thus, prices cannot be viewed simply as short-run market clearing devices since, in addition, they signal shifts in the allocation of resources over time. The end result is that prices set by the large corporations in the planning sector reflect investment needs more than current market demand.

Several aspects of recent economic performance become less puzzling when this pricing framework is utilized. For example, prices were quite stable after the 1982 recession, and investment was quite lethargic despite wide-ranging incentives provided in Reagan administration policies. This model of the planning sector firm could explain both as reactions to the deep recession and its effect on investment plans of firms. Until recovery from the recession was far along, firms had no need of added investment in capacity. Thus this element in their pricing decision held prices down. Now as pressure on capacity has grown, investment will increase as will the prices firms charge in order to generate the needed investment funds.

Blair argued that the effects of the pricing behavior of these highly concentrated firms is seen in three areas. First, there is an income effect, i.e., such practices redistribute income from truly competitive firms in the market sector to those in the planning sector large enough not to be immediately threatened by lower prices of a competitor. Second, there is a potentially adverse effect on production because the firms will adjust the quantity of their output rather than their price. And third the policy effect is that macroeconomic policies based on a freely competitive model may be ineffective or erroneous because the firms are not subject to competitive pressures. A classic example is the automobile companies who raised prices on 1976 models in the face of the steepest decline in demand experienced to that date.

Many characteristics of planning sector firms allow them to ignore market discipline. The absence of competitors, the ability to collude with the few that do exist, or a differentiated product all facilitate this. In our modern mixed economy another facilitating factor is the power to lobby politically for laws and resolutions favorable to their business. The whole defense industry is little affected by price competition, as has become painfully apparent in the breakneck effort to throw money at defense since 1981. And the auto companies, whose competitive position should have been aided by the falling dollar from 1985–1988 apparently raised their prices to keep pace with the increase in the price of imported autos, rather than competing on the basis of price.

This pricing behavior occurs even in supposedly more competitive international markets. In the face of a 89 percent rise in the value of the yen compared to the dollar between 1985 and 1987 most American corporations did not take the opportunity to cut prices on the goods they exported to Japan. In fact many actually increased prices. The Japanese Ministry of International Trade and Industry has compiled figures that show that American microchip manufacturers, which complain that the Japanese will not let them into the market, increased their average price of digital integrated circuits 66 percent between August 1986 and May 1987.[5] Managers of U.S. firms reply that cutting prices does not increase demand in Japan. Rather the opportunity for increased profits allows the companies to improve their images by constructing fancy office buildings, increasing advertising, and other ways of becoming part of Japan's planning sector. Jerald Blumberg, president of Du Pont's Japanese unit, says: "Unless you have the presence you will not be part of the network."[6]

While the planning sector continues to dominate the economy and price setting, a qualitative change did occur under the Reagan administration. The continuation, for the most part, of a free trade policy opened ever greater areas of the economy to international competition, though it was usually from planning sector firms of other nations who were unlikely to compete on price. The continued deregulation of industries such as the airlines did open them to competitive activity. Apathy in the antitrust area made takeovers and buyouts a threat to inefficient firms.

The results will be felt for many years, and a complete assessment is difficult to make. The clearest result is the shift in wealth to the financial wizards involved in the hostile takeovers, leveraged buyouts, and junk bond purchases, and the major revaluing of admittedly undervalued assets seen most clearly in the increase in share values of the stock market. It has also fundamentally changed the balance sheet of the corporate sectors with debt rising an estimated $840 billion in five years while equity was falling $300 billion.[7] The end result may well have been to weaken firms' ability to withstand increases in interest rates or declines in production. A worst-case scenario would be a replay of the Savings and Loan bailout where federal funds were required to bailout or stabilize important segments of our domestic corporate sector.

In any case, in the real economy of goods and services, the benefits of Reagan policies are hard to find. Free trade has decimated certain of our industries, often because prices were held artificially low by foreign firms in order to gain entry to the U.S. market. The process has resulted in the massive trade deficits which we now face.

Deregulation of the airlines lowered barriers to entry and

permitted an increase in the number of firms, a change in the organization of the service, such as hubs, an increase in passenger miles, and apparently lower prices on certain kinds of tickets. It also resulted in poorer service for many small cities and for the many customers whose bags were lost or who had long delays on runways or on arrivals, and it raised real questions about safety. Only the threat or reality of government action led firms to respond. And there is every expectation among airline analysts that the final configuration of the industry, after deregulation and all of its changes, will be one of equal or greater concentration than before. This is already true for particular airports such as Minneapolis or St. Louis where over 90 percent of the flights belong to one airline. Prices have risen in those markets as competition decreased, and in the last two years there has been a general increase in prices throughout the industry for the same reason. Analysts predict that there will finally be six major airline companies in the industry, an ideal setting for planning sector behavior. So much for the competitive benefits of deregulation! Competition destroys itself.

Similarly the benefits of the takeover binge are hard to find. Has U.S. productivity increased dramatically? Not at all. Is there clear evidence that the reorganized firms operate more efficiently? No, and subsequent reorganizations and economic difficulties of many of the firms seem to point in the opposite direction. What seems to have occurred is a major financial game where the winners are the financiers.

Underlying all of these changes in competition during the Reagan administration is one significant change in the behavior of planning sector firms. Previously their major form of control was through prices. Under Reagan administration policies their margin of control has been wages, and these firms have used every tactic possible to maintain their profits by forcing their wage bill lower. Givebacks, two-tiered wage systems, layoffs, decertifications, and in the extreme case, bankruptcy to avoid pension costs have all been tactics used by planning sector firms. Much of the "competition" in the airline industry depended on which company could operate with lowest wages.

So the planning sector continues to dominate the economy despite all of the changes of recent years. And those changes have failed to provide the promised increases in real efficiency. Thus the underlying assumption of Keynesian and CEI analysis is unrealistic. Any policy framework which ignores planning sector behavior will be inadequate to meet the challenges of the 1990s.

The Labor Market and the Organized Worker

Analysis of the labor market indicates more fully how the behavior of workers, particularly organized workers, helped result in the breakdown of the New Deal–Keynesian consensus. A structural analysis of the labor market reveals little relation to the orthodox labor theory of how wages and hours worked are determined. Keynes himself was one of the first to notice that the demand for labor in dominant sectors of the economy is not greatly affected by changes in the real wage level. Wage decreases do not elicit large increases in employment since a business's desire to hire labor is not particularly responsive to wage rates. Neither is the supply of labor determined exclusively, or even primarily, by levels of the real wage.[8]

The structure of the labor market parallels that of American industry. Just as there is a dual industrial structure, so too is there a dual, or segmented, labor market. The primary market for labor is linked to the oligopolistic, or planning, sector of the economy. Workers in this sector have typically received high wages, been highly educated and/or skilled, enjoyed substantial job security and opportunities for advancement: the benefits garnered by their membership in a relatively strong union. The other sector of labor which corresponds to the market and the irregular sector is termed the "secondary market for labor." Here the job characteristics are exactly the reverse of those in the primary sector: low wages, low levels of education and/or skill, little job security or opportunity for advancement, and typically an absence of union activity. In general, the workers from the one sector have not openly competed for jobs with the workers employed in the other sector. And the irregular or informal sector absorbs workers who cannot or will not work in the market sector.

The demand for labor, the supply of labor, the level of real wages, and the employment level are all determined by distinctly different processes.

In the world of big business the demand for labor is the direct result of the decision on how much to produce and not a result of the going wage rate. In much of the oligopolistic core the degree of automation is extremely high, so the cost considerations of hiring or laying off workers are swamped by the need to make the best use of the extremely expensive capital stock. In addition strategic considerations of oligopolistic competition can play an important role. So in this sector wages have only a subsidiary influence on hiring practices.

If the basic demand for labor is not determined by the real wage, market forces might still affect the supply of labor. Do people decide where to work and their occupation according to different wage offers, or are there other considerations? Keynes observed in the twenties and thirties that the supply of labor is affected little by wage changes, for households are such that one member generally has to work a full-time job, and often another member of the family does too. The same is certainly true today, and the increase in labor force participation rates is at least partially a response to this necessity. Changes in real wages generally affect consumption patterns more than hours worked. Also there have been many recent periods when wide variations in desired employment levels have occurred even when the real wage was not changing at all. There is some evidence that declining real wage rates since 1967 have increased the labor force participation rates of women and teenagers. In this case the effect is the opposite of the model's prediction: decreases in real wages increase the household supply of labor, in an attempt to maintain the old (1967) level of consumption.

The central issue in understanding the labor market in the past was the process by which some workers supplied labor to the planning sector which provides job security, higher wages, and better working conditions, and other workers supplied their labor to the market and informal sectors where turnover is high, wages are low, and working conditions are poor. Continued profitability in the planning sector required uninterrupted production, so personnel managers in this sector required a relatively stable work force. Moreover, the greater technological sophistication of production meant the work force must receive on-the-job training if productivity was to be maximized. Because of the imperative of

uninterrupted production and the high costs of on-the-job training, these personnel managers sought inexpensive screening devices to predetermine the potential job stability of prospective employees. The menu of screening devices typically included: dis-
criminating against such groups as blacks, women, and teenagers,
who historically have had unstable work patterns; drawing on the
firm's internal pool of labor to fill job slots through promotion up
(or down) the firm's internal career ladders; or requiring educational credentialism which in effect certified the trainability and
internalized self-discipline of the worker. Thus, workers were segmented primarily by differences in sex, ethnicity, class background, and through unequal access to educational institutions,
and the supply of labor to the planning sector was determined
largely by the demographic and sociocultural characteristics of the
worker. This effectively limited equality of job opportunity and
job mobility. Therefore, the supply of labor had little if anything
to do with the real wage or the leisure-income choice of the individual worker.

As a result money wages are not determined by labor's supply
and demand on the market; money wages are usually arrived at
through a process of collective bargaining. So it is improbable that
a reduction in primary sector wage rates will lead to a drop in
unemployment. The automatic and stable adjustment to full
(natural) employment assumed by the CEIs is not likely in our
oligopolistic economy. And in the secondary labor market there is
not much possibility of the wage rate being lowered to reduce
unemployment because as Eileen Appelbaum says: "Unemployment is concentrated among secondary workers and is related to
the characteristics of their jobs rather than to wage rates. [And
therefore] no further reduction in wage rates is likely to reduce
unemployment rates for workers in the secondary sector."[9] So at
the base of the problem are structural questions. Market adjustment or simple government fine-tuning will not solve the problem
of unemployment. Structural problems demand structural solutions.

The adjustment in the planning sector in response to Reagan
administration policies has made this even more true. The distinction between the primary and secondary sectors has become
blurred. The implicit job guarantee of the skilled worker no lon-

ger exists, as many auto workers discovered, and the wholesale attack on labor was designed to lower the wage differential between the two sectors. It has become common for large firms to contract out work to small firms and to hire significant numbers of part-time workers at low wages, no benefits and no security. The sum of changes in the Reagan years was to destroy the implicit agreement between big business and its unionized employees and to increase the number of workers in the secondary sector. Union membership fell rapidly, from 20.1 percent of workers in 1983 to 17.5 percent in 1986. The goal again was to raise the profitability of planning sector firms in situations in which they could not raise their prices, particularly in industries faced with competition from imports and deregulation. The employment decisions now became subsidiary to the strategic choices of the planning sector firms which might lead them to close down entire plants, move production to other areas or countries, or "outsource" production of major components of their products. Wage rates were subsidiary concerns to these strategic issues.

Though average real weekly earnings fell from 1975 on, the sluggishness of the unemployment rate showed that this lowering of wages would not bring the desired decline in unemployment, for wage setting in planning firms still dominated the wage structure. Unemployment only began to fall significantly when exports began to increase, supporting the demand stimulus that government deficits had provided to that point. Also much of the decline in unemployment was the result of being forced to accept part-time employment or low-pay work with subcontractors.

So once again in their assumptions about the operation of the labor market, Keynesian and CEI approaches do not capture the planning sector's behavior.

THE PUBLIC ECONOMY

The New Deal–Keynesian consensus was built on the cooperation of big business, big labor, and big government. Thus we need to look at the role of the public economy and its relation to the other two economic actors. The government sector, as measured by taxes at all levels as a percentage of gross national product (GNP), accounts for about one-third of the total economy.

The not-for-profit sector can be classified as part of the public economy because of the similarity of goals and motivations. Unfortunately we do not collect statistics separately for the not-for-profit sector. An estimate for 1973, made by Burton Weisbrod from a survey of 432 organizations, indicates that the total revenue for the not-for-profit sector was $530.9 billion.[10] Were this figure directly comparable to GNP, the not-for-profit sector would have accounted for 41 percent of GNP in 1973. Unfortunately, it is not comparable since these figures contain an unknown amount of double counting. For example, the premium paid to Blue Cross/Blue Shield by the individual and the subsequent payment to the physician are both counted in Weisbrod's revenue estimate. However, it is clear that the not-for-profit sector is large, and it is growing. Its role in any future consensus will be vital.

Let us focus on the role of the government sector, or to use the more common term—the state—in a capitalist market economy. This involves the double problem of what *is* the role of the state and what *should be* the role of the state. The positions of the Conservative Economic Individualists and the Keynesians differ in their view of the role of the state depending upon their evaluations of the market economy—whether they believe it capable of meeting peoples' basic material needs; whether they believe it inherently equitable and fair, thus, encouraging self-esteem; and whether they believe that it promotes human freedom.

The CEI and Keynesian Views

For the CEIs, government is the most likely nexus for power concentration and so its size and role must be strictly limited. In the CEI program there are some important roles for the government which the market cannot perform. The protection of property rights is the key to successful operation of the free market system; otherwise, contracts, copyrights, patents, and the like, would carry little meaning. There are the obvious governmental functions which few, except perhaps anarchists, would argue with: maintaining law and order, providing for national and civil defense, constructing public works that the private sector is unable to, and providing a stable monetary framework.

The scope and spectrum for state activity varies widely from the most conservative CEIs to the most liberal Keynesians. Liberal Keynesians, like Paul Samuelson, see more pervasive market failure, ranging over a wide spectrum and including extensive imperfections in the market mechanism. The central task of our affluent capitalism, by liberal standards, is to strike an appropriate balance between the market and the polity, taking account of the strengths and weaknesses of both.

For the Keynesian, the government in our democracy is an authentic reflection of the interplay of pluralistic interests of the modern, complex society. It must be relied upon to balance competing interests since market imperfections have led to concentrated economic power; reliance on market forces would simply allow the economically powerful to rule the society. In Keynesian eyes, one very important part the government plays is its effect on the goal of equity, thus far ignored in our discussion. A perfectly functioning competitive market would guarantee an efficient allocation of resources, but it in no way would assure society of an acceptable distribution of those goods and services. Such a belief leads many liberal Keynesian economists to claim that government must address the question of redistribution of income.

CEIs and Keynesians see the government sector as exogenous to the economic system, as determined by the political process independently of economic factors. In the CEI view the state enforces the rules of the game or it intervenes to the detriment of all. In the Keynesian view the state intervenes when the rules of the game yield widely unacceptable results and it represents society in stabilizing the economy. In either case the real action is in the private market economy. As a result both CEI and Keynesian theory have had difficulty in incorporating the government sector in their models.

Their best attempt has been a CEI use of competitive equilibrium theory to explain behavior in the public economy as an instance of "public choice" akin to consumer choice. Their argument has two parts. First, they deny that market failures are extensive. Furthermore they claim that most externalities will be "internalized" by private agreements among the affected parties. For example, parties that suffer from the water pollution of a factory can band together and seek remedy through legal means.

Second, they claim that "government failure" is far more pervasive than market failure. By this they mean that both elected officials and government bureaucrats are motivated by self-interest, not by the public interest. Elected officials will maximize their chances of reelection and thus cater to the demands of organized special interest groups regardless of merit. The result will be excessive spending and regulations to win the support of all types of special interest groups—environmentalists, minority groups, industries such as ship building, and on and on. Likewise government bureaus have an interest in seeing their programs expand, not contract. Thus they propound ever new regulations as a justification for more staff. Again the result is excessive spending and regulations.

Despite a certain appeal of the theoretical argument there is little empirical evidence to support it. It does give reason to be cautious in the development of new government programs and in the continuation of old ones. And one of the legacies of the Reagan years was a reexamination of existing government programs. Senator Proxmire never failed in his search for "Golden Fleece" candidates in government programs. However, the most egregious examples of the meat cleaver approach, e.g., declaring catsup a vegetable in the school lunch program or removing government control on offshore oil exploration, were rejected in the wider interest of society.

The PKI View

Several areas of contention exist between CEIs and Keynesians on the one side and PKIs on the other which will serve to highlight the different roles of the state each favors. Traditional economists maintain that society is simply a collection of individuals, while PKIs see society as an organic whole greater than the sum of its individual parts. In addition, their views vary greatly on the nature of human behavior. Whereas traditional economists believe human behavior is fundamentally rationalistic, atomistic, and hedonistic, PKIs conceive of a broader human nature, including habit, custom, sense of adventure, even perversity, in addition to acquisitiveness.[11] PKIs also utilize a broader conception of the economic system. Whereas traditional economists downplay the existence or importance of power in the hands of any individual economic agent, PKIs place at the center of their analysis an explicit consideration of certain powerful institutions: large corporations, unions, the state. Much of the story of the Reagan years is of a joint effort on the part of major corporations and the administration to limit societal constraints on corporations and to check and reverse the power of unions.

Finally, while PKIs value freedom no less than CEIs, they contend that the market system restricts rather than promotes freedom for some. Basic freedom requires adequate food, shelter, health care, and education which, PKIs assert, is necessary for the exercise of freedom and which the private market system seldom provides for all. Thus, intervention by the state, by taxing some (thus limiting their freedom) and transferring it to others, is frequently necessary to make freedom real for the poor:

> The issue is one of whose freedom rather than freedom in the abstract. The great moral choice in any society is whose freedom counts when interests conflict in the face of scarcity. Where people conflict, global freedom is without meaning and can only obfuscate the real conflict and the ethical question.[12]

The free market response is to argue that the *status quo* distribution of property and income has priority because it in fact exists. The PKI rebuttal is that this *status quo* distribution is actually the result of past public decisions over the distribution of property rights and thus the ethical question of *whose rights shall count* remains to be answered. Clearly PKIs believe that the small loss of freedom due to taxation of the wealthier is more than compensated by the gain in freedom to the less advantaged which results from transfers that provide for basic needs.

CEIs see the growth of the government sector as an aberration caused by misguided political philosophy. Keynesians see the growth as a response to the need to provide macro-stabilization, correct market failures, and care for the losers in the economic game. They admit that the growth of government has gotten out of hand and public policies should be redesigned to use rather than override the market.

PKIs see the growth of government as a natural phenomenon required to re-embed the economy into the social system and
thus control the destructiveness of capitalism's uneven development. As various groups in the economy have sought to control
the workings of the free market system they have called on government for help: pure food and drug legislation for consumers,
price supports for farmers, minimum wage and maximum hour
laws for workers, licensing for attorneys and physicians, tariffs for
business, and on and on. In addition, government was needed to
facilitate private arrangements to circumvent the market: endors-
ing collective bargaining as a national policy, allowing the elimination of competition through corporate mergers, and allowing professional organizations to set standards for their members.

In fact, no one (except CEIs) wants the free market system
to be the organizing principle of society itself. At most, it should
be the primary (but not sole) regulatory mechanism utilized by
society to achieve its goals.

As a result of the need to oversee this re-embedding process,
government has become a primary economic agent along with
business firms and labor unions. Government, as the key actor in
the public economy, operates with a degree of independence un-
thinkable to the Marxist, but bounded by constraints ignored by
CEIs and Keynesians. The historical evidence is overwhelming
that government is not merely the servant of the capitalist class.
On the other hand, it is clear that government is an integral part
of the political-economic system.

Any relevant economic theory must provide a central role for
government as an actor not just a referee or umpire. PKI theory
attempts to do this by focusing on the distribution of power as the
key to understanding the economy.

THE SOCIAL CONSENSUS AND ITS DEMISE

The glue that had held this political-economic structure together was the social consensus on the roles of government, business, and organized labor which it embodied.

Large corporations would be tolerated as long as their monopolistic power was not abused. They in turn would tolerate in-

dependent labor unions as legitimate representatives of their workers. The struggle over income shares would be institutionalized through the mechanisms of collective bargaining focused on sharing of productivity increases. Expanding aggregate demand muted that struggle by making it easy for firms to absorb wage increases through productivity gains and to pass on wage increases above productivity in the form of price increases.

Government policies would provide minimum economic security through old age benefits, unemployment insurance, minimum wage laws, and guarantees of the right of workers to organize unions to bargain with firms. In addition, government would cushion the operation of the secondary labor market by providing welfare benefits, minimal education, and strong enforcement of property rights. It also had the responsibility to use macro-stabilization policies to maintain full employment with stable prices. Finally, government was expected to establish a general environment that would encourage long-run economic growth. A variety of policies might be used for this purpose: support of higher education, tax incentives for investment, subsidies for scientific research.

The resulting structure of big government, big business, and big labor was expected to tame the destructive side of capitalism while aiding its creative side. This it did quite successfully in the post–World War II, post-depression period. By the late 1970s its success declined dramatically, and the Reagan administration represented an attempt, albeit unsuccessful, to destroy that consensus and establish a new mode of organizing the economy. Three factors resulted in the demise of the consensus: changes in the structure of the economy; limits on the growth possibilities in the economy; and loss of U.S. international hegemony. They will be examined below. The PKI program which will be suggested in the next chapter is another alternative which deals with the problems in a very different manner from that of the Reagan administration.

THE STRUCTURAL ROOTS OF THE PROBLEMS

The dynamics of our explanation of the inability to overcome the unacceptable mix of unemployment, inflation, unstable growth, and increasing poverty are found in the nature of the planning sector and in its interaction with the market sector and the public sector.

The starting point is that the operation of the planning sector in recent years contributed to inflation, unemployment, and instability. Since planning sector firms have been generally protected from the discipline of the market, their price-setting behavior has had an inflationary bias. Despite the long-running debate in economics whether inflation is "demand-pull" or "cost-push," it is actually a result of the social conflict over who will receive what share of the national income. In the planning sector, this is a battle between owners and workers over who will receive the income from production, based upon some concept of a fair distribution of income.

Since planning sector firms generally set the price of their product using mark-up pricing, their incentive for hard bargaining on labor contracts or supplier contracts was not strong. Thus there was a tendency for costs to rise and as a result for prices of products to be higher as well, especially in the planning sector.

What made this inflationary pressure acute in the late 1970s and led to the current problems was a decline in the performance of the planning sector firms, the "falling productivity of American industry." If firms had become more efficient and gotten more output from their operations, higher input costs would not have resulted in actual price increases. Such increases in efficiency were not forthcoming during the 1970s (or the 1980s) for a series of complex reasons. Workers were most often blamed, with little justification, or government was another favorite culprit. One contributing factor was the effect of technology: the dearth of new productivity-increasing technology and the exhaustion of benefits from large-scale production. Another factor was the change in the mix of the economy from industrial products open to productivity increases to service industry products. Another important factor was the U.S. corporation itself and the type of manager that reached its upper echelons.[13]

To summarize an extensive debate, in U.S. firms the financial analyst seeking short-run goals rather than the production specialist concentrating on long-run growth tended to reach the top; and this led to an inability to compete in production with the Germans,

Japanese, and others. Technology is where the dynamism of our economy is generated. R&D expenditures fell over the previous twenty years as managers improved this year's—and even this quarter's—"bottom line" through mergers, short-run product re-design, and other cosmetic changes.[14] The large corporation was becoming ever more bureaucratized, resulting in greater ineffi-ciency and lowered productivity. Lester Thurow said, "American government may be bureaucratic and inefficient, but American industry is just as bureaucratic and inefficient."[15]

By the early 1980s there was some awareness of this problem. For example, General Electric's president, John Welch, radically altered management practices:

> Mr. Welch blames the foreign threat to GE and other American companies on many of the management principles that GE itself helped shape in the 1960s and 1970s—a time, he says, when compa-nies were "managed, not led." He fears that managing assets as if they were investment portfolios, seeking short-term profits at the sacrifice of long-term gains, and stressing conservatism over inno-vation may have permanently crippled many of America's major industries.[16]

It was significant that Welch was a chemical engineer who started in production at GE in 1960. Ross Perot, the founder of Electronic Data Systems, sounded a similar theme in talking with the Associ-ated Press in 1988, saying that business leaders and not politicians are to blame for the decline in U.S. leadership in world affairs: "We've become a people who want to feel good now, at any cost, and let tomorrow take care of itself. We and not the elected offi-cials are the dwarfs and the wimps."[17]

The leveraged buyout craze of the mid-1980s could only in-crease this concentration on financial issues and short-run goals.[18]

Lower productivity growth slowed the growth of aggregate supply and contributed to stagflation. The government validated this wage-price structure when the Federal Reserve allowed the supply of money to grow in accordance with the new demand for money. This masked the owner-worker struggle for greater shares of the national output. If the increased money supply were not forthcoming to validate increased money wages, the struggle over income shares would become clearer and thus more dangerous.

In addition the functioning of the planning sector would be severely disrupted.

Keynesian fiscal and monetary policy seemed effective as long as inflation was not a problem, as long as productivity increases in the planning sector were able to offset the higher input costs. Once this was no longer the case and inflation had become a serious problem, Keynesian prescriptions became unacceptable. Government efforts to offset reductions in aggregate demand due to declines in investment merely exacerbated inflation. And to stop inflation, a major decrease in aggregate demand and employment was necessary. Thus the advent of inflation was really the demise of the New Deal–Keynesian consensus.

The CEI policies which were implemented under the Reagan administration destroyed the remnants of the New Deal–Keynesian consensus without solving the fundamental problem of the creative-destructive nature of capitalism. The consensus on social welfare and government regulation was ended with the move to deregulation and cutbacks in social welfare programs. The Reagan administration's breaking of PATCO through the firing of the striking air traffic controllers led to the wholesale repudiation by business of its implicit contract with organized labor with the result of wage rollbacks, plant relocations, massive layoffs, and substitution of non-union for union labor. Also the prolonged recession of 1981–83, combined with the offensive against unions, shifted the balance-of-power into the hands of business, effectively ending the struggle over income shares in favor of business. This enabled the Reagan administration to reduce inflation but at the cost of high unemployment, increased poverty, and massive trade and budget deficits. As the economy moves back toward lower unemployment rates, we can expect inflation to increase, and the only CEI response will be another recession. All the while those left out, those who haunt the prosperity, grow in numbers and any recovery benefits ever smaller protions of the population.

EMPHASIS ON ECONOMIC GROWTH

The key to much of the past success of the U.S. economic system has been economic growth. As a consequence, the New

Deal–Keynesian economic structure, particularly the planning sector and its financial component, operated on the premise of continuous economic growth. But for reasons of physical and social limits and increasing loss of U.S. international hegemony, that premise became ever more untenable and indeed dangerous. The interruption in the 1970s of the pattern of continual growth contributed to stagflation and the downfall of the New Deal–Keynesian consensus. The continued sluggishness of economic growth under the CEI-led Reagan administration had its effect cushioned by the exceptionally high trade and budget deficits, though it resulted in increased poverty.

Present and future prospects do not warrant much optimism on the renewal of historic growth rates. This does not mean an era of zero growth, but rather implies that growth will not cover mistakes as has been the case, that productivity increases will become increasingly difficult, and that there will be new types of difficulties for ordinary ways of doing business which will challenge the creativity of all sectors of the economy.[19]

There are two main factors which put limits on the growth of the U.S. economy.

Physical Limits

The first limit which must be faced is physical, based on natural resource availability. Growth became harder as production costs escalated, and if the world enters a recovery phase, the same process will occur, since previous growth was based on a profligate use of natural resources. This was so for four reasons.

First, exhaustible energy and natural resource prices have not reflected their true scarcity because the market system has not costed them out properly. The market price reflects today's cost of obtaining the resources and ignores that they may be exhausted tomorrow. The implicit assumption always has been that technology will provide a substitute and the result is an economy based on cheap energy and natural resources. As demand increases around the world the resultant scarcity will limit a continuation of this resource-using style of growth.

Second, corporations in the planning sector have compounded the problem by competing through product innovation and differentiation resulting in an emphasis on stylistic and physical obsolescence. When goods are designed to be "thrown-away" after use, or to be used less than their physical capacity because of style changes, or constructed to fall apart sooner than necessary, the result is increased wastage of energy and natural resources. Physical limits to the maintenance of this style of competition pose serious challenges to growth in the planning sector.

Third, economic growth has been based on the value of individual consumption. The awesome power of modern advertising has spread the free market gospel—the good life comes from increases in consumption of individually marketable goods and services. People are urged to believe they must have individual washers and dryers instead of laundromats, and private automobiles instead of public transportation. This phenomenon is particularly important when viewed in a worldwide context. The earth's resources simply could not sustain the world's adoption of this style of individualist-oriented consumption growth.

Fourth, pollution abatement poses physical limits to continued reliance on traditional economic growth. Corporations attempt to minimize private costs of production. Since the cost of polluted air and water have been borne by the public, production processes have tended to ignore social costs—i.e., pollution. As public awareness forces firms to internalize these costs, thus driving up the costs of production, further limits will be imposed on continued growth. This is what lies behind the conflict over acid rain which the Reagan administration avoided by asking for study after study. This is the issue that will have to be faced in cleaning up the Department of Energy's nuclear wastes and in dealing with the low-level radioactive wastes that no state wants to accept. At some point, however, their effects will have to be dealt with, and this will imply higher production costs. In 1988 it was revealed that the cost of cleaning up the waste material from military nuclear plants might approach $100 billion.[20]

These physical limits to growth pose difficulties and challenges to the planning sector and to the economy as a whole. They will tend to lower growth and thereby to exacerbate the underlying tensions over income shares.

Social Limits

A second set of limits to growth—social limits—pose even greater challenges because they strike to the heart of a market economy and of the enterprise culture promoted by the Reagan administration as the answer to the problems of the 1970s. These social limits are of two types. First, growth has been based on the production of "positional goods" which is self-defeating. Second, growth has relied on self-interest as its motor force. This, in turn, has undermined the general "moral base" necessary for the economic system to remain viable. Let us take up each of these in turn.

First, with affluence, especially the unequal affluence created during the Reagan administration, "positional" goods become an ever larger portion of total production. These are goods whose consumption is available only to those who have reached a certain economic position. Present-day Washington continually provides us examples: $1,000 suits, limousines, etc. But the pursuit of positional goods is self-defeating because by definition they can be enjoyed only if one has them and others do not. Donald Trump's yacht was the positional good of 1989. Growth allows others to obtain them, undermining the satisfaction of those who had the goods while adding little to the new owners, since the goods become less positional. There are two types of positional goods. Goods such as large diamonds or a one-of-a-kind designer dress are enjoyed solely for snob appeal. They set their owner apart from the crowd. Nancy Reagan's formal gowns are a good illustration. If everyone has access to them, they lose their ability to reflect supposed status. And the push to find ever newer positional goods in itself has become destructive as the abuse of the positional good par excellence, cocaine, has taken an ever heavier toll.

A second variety, quiet beaches, uncongested roads, servants, are unavailable if many have access to them. If we all can afford to take a vacation, the beaches will no longer be quiet. If we all can afford cars, the roads become congested. And if we all gained more income from growth, no one would have to be a servant. We now allow people to immigrate temporarily to provide this service.

The result is that expectations from growth are constantly disappointed. This drives people to seek new goods to capture "positional" advantages, leaving the majority constantly frustrated and reinforcing the resource-using nature of the economy. Furthermore, this constant frustration of peoples' dreams increases disharmony and conflict between social groups. One form this takes is an ever fiercer struggle among social classes and occupational groups for larger shares of per capita GNP. In terms of the goals of an economic system, this struggle obviously undermines fellowship and certainly forces a reconsideration of the meaning of free choice in consumption.

Social limits point out that traditional economics has forgotten one of Adam Smith's key insights. It is true he claimed that self-interest would lead to the common good if there were sufficient competition; but also, and more importantly, he claimed that this is true only if most people in society accepted a general moral law as a guide for their behavior, i.e., if there were a moral base for the society.[21]

The assumption that self-interest in a competitive environment is sufficient to yield the common good is an illusion. Policies and programs such as the CEIs which are based on "unleashing" our competitive instincts, of creating an enterprise culture, are similarly illusory. An economy, capitalist or socialist, where everyone—buyers, sellers, workers, managers, consumers, firms—constantly lied, stole, or committed fraud and violence would neither yield the common good nor would it be stable. Yet pushed to its logical extreme, individual self-interest suggests that it would usually be in the interest of an individual to evade the rules by which other players are guided. We have seen the unfortunate effects of bringing the rugged individualists to Washington and giving them control over the government. The resulting corruption in the Reagan administration must give us all pause.

Similarly, the "free-rider" concept suggests that it is in an individual's interest not to cooperate in a situation of social interdependence if others do cooperate, for they will obtain the same benefits without any sacrifice. Therefore, why don't individuals in societies always operate in this fashion? The answer is not fear of the police power of the state, but rather that our selfishness or tendency to maximize our material welfare at the expense of others is inhibited by a deeply ingrained moral sense, one often based on religious convictions.

Peter Berger reminds us that "No society, modern or otherwise, can survive without what Durkheim called a 'collective conscience,' that is without moral values that have general authority."[22] Fred Hirsch reintroduces the idea of moral law into economic analysis: "truth, trust, acceptance, restraint, obligation—these are among the social virtues grounded in religious belief which . . . play a central role in the functioning of an individualistic, contractual economy. . . . The point is that conventional, mutual standards of honesty and trust are public goods that are necessary inputs for much of economic output."[23]

The major source of this social morality has been the religious heritage of the precapitalist and preindustrial past. However, this legacy of religious values has diminished over time because of a twofold change: (1) the repudiation of the social character and responsibility of religion has meant its banishment to a purely private matter;[24] and (2) the elevation of self-interest as a praiseworthy virtue has undermined that privatized religious ethic.

The erosion of this preindustrial, precapitalist moral legacy proceeded slowly for two reasons: (1) economic growth was spread over a very long time period and (2) growth relied on decentralized decision making for the most part. This slow and seemingly natural process allowed popular acceptance and permitted adjustment in the moral base of the society, so that there seemed to be consistency between that base and economic behavior. However, the limits to this process are now being reached in the United States, and the present fervor for individualistic competition—market-place magic—is a last gasp effort to reverse history. This must of necessity produce conflict.

Capitalist development was far from conflict-free in the past. One of its advantages was the absence of an identifiable villain behind the disruptions which occurred. Such changes resulted from the decisions of thousands of persons acting independently. It appeared that no one could rig the rules for personal benefit, so inequalities appeared legitimate and the undermining of religious values had no identifiable cause. The rise of the large corporation and centrality of government today, however, provide a target for dissatisfaction. The policies of the last decade have clearly increased poverty and inequality. In such circumstances the legitimacy of inequalities and deterioration of values are open to question and to challenge. The gradual disappearance of the moral base of society forces government to attempt to act as a substitute and to provide a context which encourages principled action among the elite in the planning sector, while at the same time ensuring acceptance of the outcome by the majority.

Let us summarize the argument thus far. The erosion of the inherited moral base under the onslaught of continuous growth and spread of individualism has created the following situation: economic actors, especially the entrepreneurial elite, have been freed of the old religious and moral constraints; but the individualistic growth process has not provided any ready substitute social morality. Thus the previously effective inhibitions on lying, cheating, and stealing have lost their effectiveness and the functioning of both the public and private economy has suffered. The growth of the illegal components of the irregular sector are logical outcomes of the process. The outcome is the dramatic increase in the prison population of the country, from 200,000 in 1970 to 300,000 in 1980 and to 500,000 in 1987.[25]

The state's central role in managing the economy further exacerbates the social limits to growth. There is a central flaw in the current Keynesian approach which calls for the pursuit of self-interest by individuals in the private sector, but forbids it in the public sector. The expectation that public servants will not promote their private interests at the expense of the public interest reinforces the argument that the economy rests as importantly on moral behavior as self-interested behavior. As Hirsch wrote:

> The more a market economy is subjected to state intervention and correction, the more dependent its functioning becomes on restriction of the individualistic calculus in certain spheres, as well as on certain elemental moral standards among both the controllers and the controlled. The most important of these are standards of truth, honesty, physical restraint, and respect for law.[26]

The more that self-interest progresses and the more that the original moral base of the society is undercut, the less likely are these conditions to be met.

Attempts to rely solely on material incentives in the private sector, and more particularly in the public sector, suffer from two defects. In the first place, stationing a policeman on every corner to prevent cheating simply does not work. Regulators have a disadvantage in relevant information compared to those whose behavior they are trying to regulate. In addition, who regulates the regulators? Thus, there is no substitute for an internalized moral law that directs persons to seek their self-interest only in "fair" ways.[27] Secondly, reliance on external sanctions further undermines the remaining aspects of an internalized moral law.

In summary, the erosion of society's moral base under the onslaught of self-interest has important practical results. As Hirsch says:

> Religious obligation performed a secular function that, with the development of modern society, became more rather than less important. It helped to reconcile the conflict between private and social needs at the individual level and did it by internalizing norms of behavior. It thereby provided the necessary social binding for an individualistic, *non*altruistic market economy. This was the non-Marxist social function of religion. Without it, the claims on altruistic feelings, or on explicit social cooperation, would greatly increase, as was foreseen, and to some extent welcomed, by a long line of humanists and secular moralists. Less love of God necessitates more love of Man.[28]

The New Deal–Keynesian consensus suffered from these social limits and the CEI program to build an enterprise culture has accelerated the conflict. Any solution to the economy's problems will have to take a different tack, such as that suggested by the PKIs in the next chapter.

LOSS OF U.S. HEGEMONY IN THE INTERNATIONAL ECONOMY

The last factor in the decline of the New Deal–Keynesian consensus and the failure of the CEI restoration deserves separate treatment because of its importance. The position of the U.S. in the world economy has changed dramatically in the last two decades. Perhaps the most important change of the 1970s was the alteration from a Western system characterized by U.S. hegemony and independence to one in which the U.S. is interdependent or even dependent on other countries. The effect of this change has been profound: it has exacerbated the economic problems that originated in other areas and has further interfered with the effectiveness of orthodox policy.

Many of the major policy developments of the 1970s which finally shattered the domestic economic consensus were not taken autonomously by the U.S., but were forced on policymakers by external pressures. Two incidents stand out in this regard. The first was the August 15, 1971, bombshell of Richard Nixon in which he effectively removed the U.S. from the Bretton Woods currency arrangements and at the same time adopted a rigid program of wage and price controls, contrary to all of his pronouncements to that point. Of course Nixon was looking ahead to his reelection in 1972; however, the key factors in these decisions were international. For the first time the U.S. had begun to run deficits on its merchandise trade, which called into question the country's ability to redeem the massive amount of dollars that had been cycled through the international financial markets. And the Bank of England made it quite clear that it was no longer willing to absorb additional dollars to support their fixed value. Thus adjustment had to be made by the United States. This new reality forced the radical decisions which were taken and led finally to a reformulation of the manner in which the U.S. enters international capital markets.

This, in turn, had a major effect on the international economic system. International financial and commercial order is difficult to achieve among equals, and since the erosion of the United States' economic power after 1971, no single nation has been sufficiently powerful to impose order unilaterally. The breakdown of the Bretton Woods system resulted in floating exchange rates which, when coupled with recession in several major nations, posed a constant threat of an international commercial disintegration and, in turn, reinforced domestic recessionary forces.

The only mechanism which has been thrust into the Bretton Woods breach has been the annual economic summits among the seven major industrial countries. For the most part they have been

formal rather than substantive, though their 1985 agreement that
the dollar was overvalued did encourage its depreciation. Their
other clear effect, especially the 1988 Toronto summit, was to
reflect the loss of U.S. dominance and the growing role of the
Japanese.

The second case of an internationally induced domestic policy change was the revolution in interest rates which took place in
1979 when the Federal Reserve Board decided to deemphasize
interest rate targets and to concentrate instead on the growth of
the money supply. A key factor was the discontinuity between
U.S. and international interest rates. The U.S. money supply
growth rates and rates of inflation were also out of line with European countries. Paul Volcker, Chairman of the Federal Reserve
Board, went to Europe for consultations, and largely because of
the pressure and support of his counterparts, upon his return
called a Saturday meeting of the Board of Governors and adopted
the new strategy which completely changed the role of interest
rates in the economy.[29]

As noted above, this change pushed interest rates to historic
highs, but even more importantly it signalled the oligopolistic sector of the economy that their wage bargains would no longer be
ratified by the Fed. Coupled with international competition which
limited their price setting behavior, this encouraged the assault
on labor that has been the characteristic of the 1980s.

So in both instances of fundamental reformulation of domestic economic policy, the proximate cause was the vulnerability of
the U.S. economy to foreign economic pressure and influence.
This is a far cry from the hegemonic days of the 1950s and 1960s
where U.S. desires became reality, despite resistance by national-
ists such as Charles de Gaulle of France.

So there was a significant change in the external conditioning
factors vis-à-vis the U.S. economy; for the first time in the postwar
period, our economy became open to external economic pressures
and influences. During the 1970s and 1980s the U.S. economy was
quite successful in providing jobs as participation rates rose, especially among married women. Most of these jobs, in fact practically
all of them, were in wholesale and retail trade and the service
sector. The industrial and farm sectors produced few new jobs,
and those could not offset the major job loss in those sectors which

peaked in the 1982 recession. And over the period there was a substantial increase in part-time work and in discouraged workers who left the labor market.

The stagnation of the industrial or primary labor market is due to changes in the structure of the international economy. The creative-destructive nature of capitalism asserted itself through a continued process of uneven development. The rebuilding of Europe and Japan and the industrialization of Taiwan, South Korea, Singapore, Hong Kong, Brazil, among others, led to massive shifts in competitiveness in the world economy. These were exacerbated by the instability in exchange rates which greatly affected international competitiveness from one year to the next. Since the most advanced technology was used everywhere in the world, the old industrial centers, including the U.S., found themselves at a competitive disadvantage with their older plant and equipment and higher labor costs. The result was the closing of U.S. industrial plants or their relocation overseas, especially in the period of the overvalued dollar.

Thus the planning sector's ability to insulate itself from market forces has been destroyed by competition from abroad which in turn contributed to the assault on wages and on unions by employers in the sector. Yet it is the planning sector that has been the dynamo of the U.S. economy, as it is in other economies. Its stability and control over its environment has traditionally taken much of the risk out of economic operations, and has allowed a longer-term perspective. This encouraged R&D expenditures and new product and process innovations, and gave the U.S. its technological dominance. The only sector where this continues is in defense industries, and it would be unfortunate to have to rest the entire future of the economy on them.

The changed international situation of the U.S. becomes clearer when we look at a series of more specific indicators. The first is the continued inability of the U.S. economy to attain any degree of trade balance with Japan. In 1981 the deficit was $18 billion. This led to a series of efforts to control imports from Japan, the most notable the voluntary quota on automobiles and the 25 percent tariff on imports of small trucks. There had been similar steps taken in earlier years, such as the voluntary quota program on textiles or steel trigger prices. By 1987 the trade deficit with Japan had grown to $60 billion. Despite the rapid devaluation of the dollar against the yen since 1985, it is clear that in many key industries—autos, steel, much of electronics—currency adjustments are unlikely to result in competitiveness, and the U.S. has the choice of seeing the industry wither or protecting it in some fashion to allow an orderly adjustment.

At the base of the Japanese success is their ability to attain a domestic economic consensus which allows them to compete internationally. They do not draw the firm distinction between public and private sectors; rather both of them are Japanese and must collaborate for the economic security of the country. Thus government ministries to a large extent plot the competitive strategy for the country, and the large economic groups or conglomerates (keiretsu) carry out the plans. There is competition, but highly controlled. They do not have the hostile takeover or the business assault on labor variety of competition that characterize the U.S. economy, and they hardly encourage foreign competition in their domestic market. It took years of negotiating by the U.S. to get access to the Japanese market for our soda ash or our metal baseball bats—and then other forces entered to limit their sales.[30]

So the final effect of the loss of U.S. hegemony and the naive approach to international competition that has been followed by the Reagan administration is the significant increase in foreign influence in our domestic economy, and in our politics. The U.S. bond market now depends upon Japanese participation, and if they were to remove themselves as players, the effort to finance the federal deficit could only occur at much higher interest rates. There are growing holdings of real estate, of banking, and of industrial enterprises in foreign hands. And the foreign influence on public policy and opinion has grown dramatically as indicated by the public relations onslaught of Suzuki when its Samurai was criticized, and as the bevy of high-priced lobbyists in Washington for Japanese interests indicates.

CONCLUSION

This chapter has described the political-economic structure that formed part of the New Deal–Keynesian consensus and analyzed the forces that brought about its demise. In doing so it specified a particular view of the U.S. economy and the structures which undergird its functioning. It is here that the root of the current problems lie. It is also here and in this PKI analysis that the basis for an alternative set of polcies exists. The next and final chapter specifies them.

10. Toward a New Social Contract

What direction might our society move in order to construct a new social consensus to control the creative-destructive nature of uneven development under capitalism? This chapter suggests such directions.

In contrast with the supply-side approach so successfully sold to the voting public, these directions cannot be reduced to a simple diagram drawn on a napkin or to a few slogans such as "get the government off our backs." The U.S. economy is a complex mixed economy, and tracing a viable policy direction is, indeed, a difficult task. The Keynesian promise of full employment, low inflation, and continuous economic growth, achieved by manipulating monetary and fiscal policy, is no longer possible. That day is gone. The Reagan-CEI promise of rapid inflation-free growth, sparked by the dramatic increase in efficiency and productivity resulting from unfettering free enterprise, has also proven hollow. Recent economic performance has rested on the twin deficits in international trade and the federal budget; and beneath the image of an even-handed free market have hidden an unprecedented onslaught against labor and the margination of many Americans.

The legacy of these unfilled promises will be social strife; so any policy program must start with the conflict over income shares. This is the framework for the policies we suggest in the spirit of Post-Keynesian Institutionalism. These policies will further the goals we think most Americans share, while laying out a clear challenge rather than an easy promise. They try to deal realistically with social limits to growth, while confronting the struggle over income shares between workers and employers, and the conflict among nations, regions, and individuals which capitalism's uneven development has created.

The first section focuses on the nature of resource allocation mechanisms. All too often the choice is framed as *either* the market *or* bureaucratic control. Both must have some role, but there must be a carefully developed and maintained relation between them, and they must be subsidiary to a wider perception of the goals of the economy. The inevitable tension can be productive and creative if it exists in the context of three guiding principles—stewardship, jubilee, and subsidiarity—which can guide policy over the tightrope between the unproductive extremes.

The second section turns to specific policies and programs that we believe are necessary to re-embed the market economy into the social system. The proposals are grouped by the latent conflicts any new social consensus must overcome: between labor and capital, among nations, between sectors and regions, and between rich and poor. Each section suggests a number of policies which are consistent with the guiding principles and which can help fulfill our economic goals.

Such policies cannot, will not, and should not be adopted overnight. However, the proposals can be the basis for a new social consensus that will unite large segments of society in attempting to make the economy serve human beings.

MARKETS, BUREAUCRATIC CONTROL,
AND MORAL VALUES

A central concern of economics is how an economy allocates its resources—its raw materials, capital, and labor—among competing uses. Economists can often be classified by which of three mechanisms they emphasize in determining this allocation: markets, bureaucratic administration, or social values. Under a system of allocation by markets, individuals pursue their own self-interest and the market coordinates their decisions, resulting in society's resource allocation. In a bureaucratic control system, individual self-interest is again the motivating force but it is limited to a greater or lesser degree because citizens accept societal constraints, fear the consequences if they do not, or simply have a tradition of acceptance. In a system of allocation by social values, individual self-interest is limited and cooperation encouraged by a set of widely accepted moral values which in some way transcend the narrow self-interest of one individual.

CEIs place almost complete reliance on markets, and a central thrust of their policies has been to extend the market allocation mechanism into all possible areas, from school lunches to the environment to civil rights. There are exceptions, of course. The Reagan administration's social agenda of limiting abortion and punishing drug use, for example, generated many bureaucratic interferences in the market that were inconsistent with a libertarian stance. Also in an area like defense, CEIs accept bureaucratic control as unavoidable. Only at the level of the family is allocation by social value feasible or desirable. Of course such values are important for the society, but they should be left to charitable impulses of individual decision makers. Efforts to encourage allocation by social value are seen as self-defeating.

Keynesians also give markets a central role in resource allocation. However, they find numerous areas in which bureaucratic control is necessary to improve the functioning of markets. Pollution, occupational hazards, and discrimination all result if markets operate unfettered, so government must play a role. In addition the political process empowers government to place limits on self-interested behavior and bureaucratic allocation must be used to combat poverty, to prevent corporate wrongdoing, and to provide the many public goods the market will not. They do not place much emphasis on allocation by social values.

The PKI stance is that sole reliance on any one of these mechanisms is misguided, for each has flaws which prevent it from being completely successful in solving our economic problems. In addition this threefold classification of allocation mechanisms is insufficiently nuanced.

From Adam Smith to this day, mainstream economists, both CEI and Keynesian, have argued that the best way to allocate resources, to overcome scarcity, and to increase personal freedom is reliance on the individual's pursuit of self-interest in a private property system regulated by the forces of market competition. The government either acts as an umpire enforcing the rules of the economic game (CEI) or corrects for market failures (Keynesian). The Reagan economic policy simply placed much heavier emphasis on unfettering individual self-interest.

The shortcoming of this approach to creating a functioning economy and society can be illustrated by the scholarly work in economics over the past fifteen years that demonstrates that, under conditions of interdependence and imperfect information, rational self-interest leads to socially irrational results.[1] Traditional economic theory assumed independence of economic actors and perfect information. However, the more realistic assumptions that one's behavior affects another's and that each has less than perfect knowledge of the other's likely behavior give rise to strategic behavior, or what game theorists call "moral hazards." An example will be helpful.

A classic example of moral hazard, known as "The Parable of Distrust" was the real estate operator in the 1960s who attempted to earn a quick profit by selling a house in an all-white neighborhood to a black family, hoping that other homeowners would panic and sell at below market values to the realtor. The realtor then turned around and resold the houses at full market values to other black families. Each white owner attempted to deal with the threat of falling market values (real or imagined) by selling quickly before the price fell even more. If all attempted this strategy, prices declined faster. Most white owners would agree that the result was undesirable and irrational, but no household on its own would refuse to sell. In effect each household said hold firm only if all the others did as well. However, no agreement was concluded.

In this case the pursuit of individual self-interest resulted in the individuals and the group (white owners) becoming worse off than if they had cooperated. The problem is simple and common. The homeowners were interdependent and did not have perfect knowledge of what others would do, and the resulting lack of trust led to behavior that was self-defeating. Each homeowner would have been better off if they agreed not to sell. Since they did not trust the others to honor an agreement not to sell, each sold rather than be duped by being the only one not to sell.

Take the case of inflation. A labor union fights for a wage increase only to find that others also have done so and thus the wage increase is offset by rising consumer prices. No one union alone can restrain its wage demands and maintain the support of its members. Business firms are caught in the same dilemma. They raise prices to compensate for increased labor and other costs only to discover that costs have increased again. Distrust among unions, among firms, and between unions and firms makes impossible a cooperative agreement on price and wage increases.

The case of recession is similar. As aggregate demand in the economy declines, each company attempts to cope with its resulting cash flow difficulties through employee layoffs. However, if all companies pursue this strategy, aggregate demand will decline further, making more layoffs necessary. Most companies agree that the result is undesirable for each company and for the whole economy, but no one company on its own will maintain its workforce. In effect each company says it will not layoff its employees if all the others also do not layoff their employees. Yet, again, no agreement is concluded.

Such cases have two things in common. There is a group with a common interest in the outcome of a particular situation; however, when individuals choose their self-interestedly best available course of action, the result is not what any member of the group desires. Individualistic choices lead to undesired social and individual results. Smith's "invisible hand" not only fails to yield the common good, but in fact works malevolently.

Why is it so difficult for the individuals involved to make an agreement? The reason is basically economic—exit is cheap, but voice is expensive.[2] Exit means to withdraw from a situation, person, or organization and depends on the availability of choice, competition, and well-functioning markets. It is usually inexpensive and easy to buy or not, sell or not, and hire or fire on your own. Voice means to communicate explicitly your concern to another individual or organization. The cost to an individual in terms of time and effort to persuade, argue, and negotiate will often exceed any prospective individual benefit.*

In addition, the potential success of individual voices depends on the possibility of all members joining together for collective action. This presents the "free rider" problem. If someone

---

*Exit is much more difficult in Japan where the Confucian tradition is much more binding. As a result, with much greater emphasis on harmony and consensus at all levels, voice is more appreciated and cultivated.

cannot be excluded from the benefits of collective action they have no incentive to join the group. This is why union organizing is next to impossible in states that prohibit union shops, where a majority of the workers voting for a union means all workers must join and pay dues.

The problem is further complicated by the possibility that what started as a simply self-interested or even benevolent relationship will become malevolent. Face-to-face strategic bargaining may irritate the parties involved if others are perceived as violating the spirit of fair play. This can result in a response of hatred rather than mere selfishness. Collective action is unlikely if the members of the group are hateful and distrustful of one another.

Allan Schmid refers to these problems as a "social trap," a situation where "micromotives are not consistent with what individuals who share a common preference want to obtain as a long run result. . . . The micromotive is supplied when there is some act under the individual's unilateral control that promises to produce some welfare improvement for that individual. . . . The alternative line of action that would be consistent with the more preferred long run result is marked by the fact that no matter how hard the individual tries, alone he can produce no net benefits or fewer than in the dominant activity."[3] Social traps exist because the alternative line of action requires a level of trust to reach group agreement. In social traps, altruistic or cooperative behavior by one individual will achieve nothing unless it changes the actions of others.

Thus for an individual or organization to break out of a social trap requires a common consciousness of one's interdependence with others, the realization that, in fact, the group is more than a collection of individuals. This consciousness does not have to be benevolent or altruistic, though it undoubtedly would make collective action easier to attain. It certainly requires a degree of mutual trust. If malevolence arises, the trap will be strengthened. And it is here that CEI self-interested individualism fails, for social traps are prevalent in our modern mixed economy.

How can we spring the trap? The resolution of the problem is not easy, for the social traps are persistent and intractible. There are at least three possibilities: government intervention; group self-regulation; and cultural reinforcement of habits of noncalculating behavior.

Market failures such as pollution or monopoly have generally been seen as warrants for government intervention. However, there are ubiquitous market failures of the "moral hazards" variety in everyday economic life. In these cases private economic actors can also benefit from government measures for their protection, because interdependence and imperfect information generate distrust and lead the parties to self-defeating behavior. Certain kinds of government regulation—from truth-in-advertising to food-and-drug laws—can reduce distrust and thus economic inefficiency, providing gains for all concerned. However, government regulation has its limits. Where the regulated have concentrated power (i.e., electric companies) the regulators end up serving the regulated industry more than the public. In addition, there are clearly situations in which government operates to serve the self-interest of the members of its bureaucratic apparatus. CEIs would have us believe that such is always the case. We see a more mixed level of performance, one that indicates government will have a role, but that it cannot be the dominant mechanism for allocating society's resources. One key element in its limitations is that the ability of government to regulate is dependent on the willingness of people to be regulated.

The Kennedy administration's wage/price guidelines were a partially successful attempt to control inflation through public encouragement of labor and management cooperation to limit wage increases to productivity increases. The cooperation broke down because of the growing struggle among social classes and occupational groups for larger shares of GNP. More formal cooperation between labor and management, monitored by government, might reduce the distrust that cripples their relationship. In order to do so government would have to be accepted by all sides as above the fray and willing to encourage agreements that would benefit society. The experience of the 1970s in which government activity delivered less than it promised, and of the 1980s when it was used to serve the agenda of bureaucrats and to facilitate the goals of the powerful, imply a diminished capacity of government to play this role.

The second way to spring the trap is self-regulation. Sellers could voluntarily discipline themselves not to exploit their superior information. This has been the basis of professional ethics.

Surgeons, for example, have traditionally taken on the obligation, as a condition for the exercise of their profession, to avoid performing unnecessary operations, placing the interest of the patient at the forefront. The danger is that their professional association will end up protecting its members at the expense of others. In addition, changes in the nature of medical care and its financing have combined with access to very high incomes to erode the ethical base of the profession, weakening this mechanism.

This leads us to the final possibility—developing habits of non-self-calculating behavior, reinforced by cultural practices, so that short-run rewards become less important. The efficient operation of markets requires something beyond calculated self-interest. Barry Schwartz in *The Battle for Human Nature: Science, Morality, and Modern Life*[4] has illustrated this necessity in his experiments. He found that behavior encouraged by narrow reinforcements, such as money, led to routine and unimaginative behavior, rather than creative problem solving. This is a particular illustration of his claim that the "rational economic man" is created rather than an inherent part of human behavior. And since culture and society create this type of behavior, when it is no longer functional or desirable, culture and society should be able to encourage different human models, different patterns of behavior.

At this point in the development of our economic society, its effective functioning requires that we must more and more accept values that transcend the narrow self-interest of the economic model as the guide for individual behavior. Is it possible to rebuild a moral consensus wherein we relearn habits of non-self-calculating behavior? Yes, but we must rethink our view of people as simply self-interested maximizers. Economists have made a major mistake in treating love, benevolence, and particularly public spirit as scarce resources that must be economized lest they be depleted. This is a faulty analogy because, unlike material factors of production, the supply of love, benevolence, and public spirit is not fixed or limited. As Hirschman says: "first of all, these are resources whose supply may well increase rather than decrease through use; second, these resources do not remain intact if they stay unused."[5] These moral resources respond positively to practice, in a learning-by-doing manner, and negatively to non-practice.

A good example is a comparison of the system of blood collection for medical purposes in the United States and in England.[6] In the U.S. we gradually replaced donated blood with purchased blood. As the campaigns for donated blood declined, because purchased blood was sufficient, the amount of blood donated declined. In effect, our internalized benevolence towards those unknown to us, who need blood, began to atrophy from nonuse. In contrast, blood donations remained high in England where each citizen's obligation to others was constantly emphasized.

People are capable of changing their values. In fact a principal objective of publicly proclaimed laws and regulations is to stigmatize certain types of behavior and to reward others, thereby influencing individual values and behavior codes. Aristotle understood this: "Lawgivers make the citizen good by inculcating habits in them, and this is the aim of every lawgiver; if he does not succeed in doing that, his legislation is a failure. It is in this that a good constitution differs from a bad one."[7] A. K. Sen has noted that this tradition in economics has been lost and that the roots of the economic view of human nature derive from the Sanskrit tradition.[8]

Habits of benevolence and civic spirit can be furthered by bringing groups together to solve common problems. Growth of worker participation in management, consultation between local communities and business firms to negotiate plant closings and relocations, establishment of advisory boards on employment policy that represent labor, business, and the public, all are steps toward a recognition that self-interest alone is insufficient, that mutual responsibilities are necessary in a world where interdependence and imperfect information tempt individuals into strategic behavior that, in turn, generates distrust and self-defeating results.

The key point is that competitive situations generate strategic behavior and, in turn, distrust. In an environment of distrust, behavior based on individual self-interest leads to sub-optimal outcomes. For example, distrust between workers and employers leads to inefficient results, since neither side trusts the other to live up to the contract. As a result the worker has an incentive to shirk and the employer has to increase supervision costs to counter the possibility. If somehow workers would self-supervise, i.e., not shirk, productivity would be higher and all could benefit.

Changing the environment from a competitive one to a cooperative one might provide the trust necessary for people to alter
their behavior. This is not a call for altruism but is an argument
that it is possible to change the environment so that people will
realize that their long-term interests require foregoing their short-
term interests.

We conclude that no one allocative mechanism can successfully enable our economy to attain the three goals of basic material
needs, self-esteem, and freedom. The market, bureaucratic control, and social values all have their advantages and disadvantages
as mechanisms for directing society's resources toward those ends.
So some combination must be incorporated in any policies that are
undertaken to build a new social consensus. In addition they must
be complemented by an environment that encourages cooperative
behavior.

At the fundamental level, the economic problems of the current day originate in a moral crisis and in an inability to control
the resulting social conflict. The moral crisis has occurred because
of the erosion of the moral base of society. The promotion of an
individualistic culture of enterprise, the naive reliance on government power joined with its use for personal goals, and the shift in
distribution of income toward capital which have characterized
recent policies have destroyed any social consensus and have exacerbated social conflict.

There are two starting points for dealing with the contemporary economy. To deal with social conflict a new social consensus
must be created. For only if a new social contract can be negotiated
and agreed upon by the different classes of society can the economy and the society be revitalized.

Secondly, this will only be possible within a moral context,
one in which the too easy separation of moral values and economic
behavior is realized for what it is—impossible and destructive. So
a key starting point for dealing with our economic problems is a
moral stance consistent with our underlying value structure but
which can guide us in making our economic decisions, both individually and as a society.

There are many possible central moral values. We suggest
three which have direct linkage to the goals of society and which
could receive widespread acknowledgment as points of departure

for rethinking our own behavior and the functioning of our economy: stewardship, jubilee, and subsidiarity.

Stewardship. This is a profound moral value in the Judeo-Christian moral tradition. A steward or trustee conception of property differs from the market economy's theory. John Locke argued that private property was a necessary part of a good society and was justified by and derived from the labor of its owner. This labor theory of property came to be one of the crucial elements of the classical economic doctrine. Because someone had wrested the soil from the state of nature and had cut the trees and improved the land, the land should be theirs and they should be entitled to use it for whatever purpose they saw fit—and so should their children and grandchildren. The modern economy, with huge corporations the dominant form of property, is far removed from property creation in the sense of Locke. So in contrast to the Lockean theory of property, stewardship holds that private individuals may own and use property for their own interests, but only as long as it does not result in harm to the common good. For example, the need of a local community for employment must be weighed against a firm's property right to relocate a plant to a different community.

The specific implication of this moral canon is that society has a responsibility for the resources which are at its disposal, and they must be used well. If the system of automatic adjustment through markets cannot deal meaningfully with current problems, there is a mandate to interfere to ensure that economic performance improves. We do not suggest that property rights be interfered with capriciously; but where the evidence shows that some interference or change is necessary to improve the overall functioning of the economy, the demands of stewardship should rule.

Jubilee. Good human relationships do not thrive in the context of extreme competition, where self-esteem comes from one's position relative to others. An alternative approach to such hierarchial patterns is the biblical concept of jubilee which grew out of the practice described in Leviticus[9] when every fifty years was a time of celebration but also a time of restitution, remission, and release, where slaves were released and land and houses that had been sold reverted to the original owners or their heirs. In this fashion, society had a mechanism which allowed inequality (competition) but also redressed its detrimental tendencies in the interest of maintaining social cohesion.

The economy does not function better because of the substantial inequalities built into it, contrary to what CEIs and the Reagan administration would have us believe. Are workers' energies stimulated by the possibility of buying the $10,000 designer revolvers or the $95,000 chinchilla bedspreads that continued in popularity even during the worst of the 1981–82 recession? Would corporate chief executives quit to the quiet of their homes if their incomes were lower than the 1987 median of $762,000?[10] Hardly; they would still be rewarded well in monetary terms and in psychic income—pride, challenge, power, status.

A more successful approach economically and in terms of the goal of fellowship would be to build on an ethic of jubilee. This does not mean an immediate and massive redistribution of income, but the adoption of policies that provide, with dignity, an income guarantee and full employment for all who can work. In addition, basic goods, and especially housing, should be ensured to all.

These policies would not only increase the absolute level of income of the lower-income population but would reduce the relative income differences. A jubilee ethic would provide the motivation necessary for these policies.

Subsidiarity. Solutions to our economic problems will be found only if citizens are willing to cooperate in the difficult adjustments necessary to change the economy and build a new social consensus. That requires policies to be developed and implemented at the lowest feasible levels, an embodiment of the principle of subsidiarity.

Less than half of the eligible electorate bothered to vote in the last U.S. elections. Yet, there has been a proliferation of neighborhood groups. National institutions have become too large, too uncontrollable, too unresponsive. We must develop smaller institutions more responsive to individual needs.

U.S. society today is characterized by largeness of firms and government institutions. Exxon, GM, and IBM are all mega-institutions. Government agencies such as the Department of Defense are even larger. Socialist economies share this same characteristic. Their economic institutions are even larger and more bureaucratized than ours.

The development of the U.S. economy has created a fundamental division of social, political, and economic life. Put most simply, the dichotomy is between the mega-institutions and the private life of the individual. People could cope with these mega-institutions if the process had not so deinstitutionalized their private life. People have always found their identity through and, in turn, impressed their values on, the mega-institutions through what Peter Berger calls "mediating structures." This is where freedom is nurtured and protected, where the counter to bureaucracy lies, where moral values can play a role in resource allocation. However, this interlocking network of mediating institutions—family, church, voluntary association, neighborhood, and subculture—has been severely weakened by the growth of the mega-institutions that have taken over many of their traditional functions.

Keynesians will point at the corporations and the market as the dominant factor in the erosion of these instruments of subsidiarity, and will look to government for protection and countervailing power in the spirit of John Kenneth Galbraith. Conservatives such as Charles Murray will point the accusing finger at government itself, exonerating the private sector, and will look to individual effort for the source of rejuvenated mediating institutions.[11]

We feel that both approaches are partial and will be unsuccessful. The only possible road to success is to confront the inherent contradictions in the society and economy directly, and to search for a mode of bringing government and the individual into consonance. The goal is a social consensus in which individual needs and possibilities can be fully realized, and in which government can take its proper and important role. The large corporations will continue, of course, but much more restricted by the social consensus to serve the broader social needs. Further encouragement should be provided for the growth of not-for-profit organizations. Credit unions, employee stock ownership plans, neighborhood associations have all been grass-roots responses to the dichotomization of modern life. Thus, economic policy must foster not-for-profit organizations.

The underpinning of the whole effort must be the moral canons suggested above. For only if behavior is guided by moral concerns which transcend self-interest, and which call into question that self-fulfilling "myth of self-interest,"[12] can our society and economy be reconstructed so as to confront the conflicts than now exist.

ECONOMIC POLICIES FOR A NEW SOCIAL CONSENSUS

Government economic policies are not mere adjuncts to some primary economic base. As we know from the work of Polanyi, they are constitutive of the capitalist economy. Since economies are embedded in social systems, without some set of government policies, there would be no functioning capitalist society. While some policies are more effective than others, that can be discovered only by specific analysis of each policy.

This implies that there is more than one "capitalist road." Capitalism flourishes in a wide variety of institutional and policy settings, ranging from Social Democratic Scandinavia to authoritarian South Korea and Taiwan. The reality is that capitalist entrepreneurs and managers tend to be opportunistic and pragmatic. While they might prefer a laissez-faire economic policy, they will adapt to political and economic realities. Although they might not like the constraints they face, they will pursue profit within those limits. Thus they will build factories on a co-ownership basis in China or in the Soviet Union if that will yield profit.

The set of policies we propose are designed to establish the framework within which firms can pursue their profits. The requirements of the policies are that they be coherent, that is not contradictory, and that they guide firms into the type of behavior that promotes society's goals.

The creative-destructive nature of uneven capitalist development generates conflict among individuals, classes, regions, and nations. The great success of the CEIs has been their ability to attribute these conflicts to the imperatives of the market. But this is also their great failure, for the conflicts must now be faced: the budget and trade deficits must be dealt with, and the marginalized and impoverished are becoming ever more present. So any new social consensus must face up to this reality. In the remainder of this book we attempt to construct a set of policies to deal with those conflicts; they are rooted in the moral canons of stewardship, jubilee, and subsidiarity. They embody a recognition of the importance of cooperation and social values in addition to self-interest and public control, and they assume that all three elements must be present to make the economy function well.

Conflict between Labor and Capital

Incomes Policy. The implicit incomes policy of the 1980s has been to allow capital to impose its will on labor. This is clearly untenable over any period of time, and it leads to behavior such as the Eastern Airlines machinist strike which was supported by the pilots largely because of their disdain for Frank Lorenzo of Texas Air—even though it forced the airline into bankruptcy and led to wage cuts for all. In the long run an effective incomes policy requires an agreement about the fairness of income distribution— that is, a new social contract based on the stewardship mandate. However, in the short run, a governmentally inspired and societally supported program to discourage the extremes of wealth and to ensure that workers receive fair treatment in receiving part of what they produce could be effective. This is particularly the case if people believe it is a necessary first step toward implementing a whole new economic program that embodies a new social contract.

One policy would be an income tax that is progressive in its upper ranges. The promised outpouring of saving by the wealthy, from tax reductions, has not occurred; rather we have seen the burgeoning of the purchase of positional luxury goods. Why should this be supported through the tax system when there are so many needy? As a society we can indicate our admiration for those who earn much; but we can also expect them to contribute to the society more than others.

A second possible policy is the Tax-Based Incomes Policy (or TIP).[13] The crux of TIP is utilizing taxes as a means of tying increases in money incomes to increases in productivity. Suppose, for example, productivity were rising at an annual rate of 3 percent (the rule until recently). The program would prescribe a limit on wage and salary increases of, say, 5 to 6 percent per annum. This 2 to 3 percent over productivity gains would allow some leeway to firms with greater or lesser productivity improvements, but it would also cap inflation at some low level. If the norm were violated a stiff tax would be charged to the offending firm, thus providing strong incentive to stay within the limit. If this policy were applied to the 1000 or 2000 largest firms in the U.S. it would be a major contributor to controlling the conflict between labor and capital and thus preventing the resurgence of inflation.

All versions of incomes policies share the common objective of limiting inflationary increases in wages, salaries, and profit income and encouraging the maintenance of the existing income distribution. This common goal is consistent with the explanation of stagflation based on the inherent social conflict over income distribution. As we move into the 1990s, renewed inflationary pressures are likely, and fiscal policy has lost much of its ability to deal with them because of the rigidities of the structural budget deficit. This places a great onus on monetary policy which will be unable to stabilize demand and generate the proper level of investment to ensure optimum growth and full employment unless the struggle over income shares is confronted directly.

Attacks on workers and their incomes by business must be stopped. This would require the enforcement of existing laws on union organizing and on work and safety rules. It would ask corporations to find manners of respecting their workers' needs and of bringing them into the production process and the gains from efforts to improve productivity.[14]

The alternative is heightened social conflict as labor and management battle it out. This could be avoided by an explicit set of incomes policies, such as those discussed above, which shared out incomes. It would turn a zero sum game, where one must lose for the other to win, into a positive sum game, where both can win. A shared sense of justice in the distribution of income can only help productivity and labor-management harmony.

There also should be more direct ways for workers to exert greater control over their work lives and incomes. We turn to that next.

Worker Self-management. The problems of productivity and of social strife over income distribution can also be dealt with by encouraging new alternatives to our traditional corporate organization.

The most likely approach would be the encouragement of workers' self-management and worker ownership which provide

a direct link to productivity, as well as contributing to self-esteem
and fellowship. Of course, most firms and their managers do not
want to see democracy expanded in the workplace. They tend to
believe that efficiency and discipline require one absolute center
of control over work—their control. Nevertheless, in a number of
cases, managers are exploring ways to change the organization of
production to increase their workers' job satisfaction. Quality-con-
trol circles and profit sharing are becoming common management
responses to encourage employees to make their work contribution through the social group in the factory.[15]

The reason for these new management initiatives is clear—
under the old system, many workers expressed their boredom,
anger, and despair by working as slowly as possible, by appearing
at work irregularly, by doing poor quality work, by occasional acts
of sabotage, and by frequent job changes. The "efficient" system
of authoritarian discipline and minute division of labor has been
a contributing factor to declining productivity in the U.S. economy. Managers see profit sharing and other worker participation
devices not as a means of wage flexibility but as a means of establishing the more cooperative relationship with their employees
that is necessary to compete in the changing economic world.

Clearly workplace democracy and worker self-management
are important ingredients not only to esteem and fellowship but
also to productive efficiency. Federal legislation should require
corporations to establish factory councils or possibly reserve seats
on boards of directors for worker representatives in workplaces
where employees want them. A 1977 Swedish law requires corporations to include workplace participation as an issue in contract
negotiations with unions. Many U.S. unions are demanding part
ownership of firms in return for wage cuts. Federal chartering of
corporations could become another way of forcing companies to
discuss workplace democracy with their employees.

How can worker self-management be extended without waiting for government or employer initiatives? Only workers can decide on the changes they want, so there is no set formula. It is
useful, however, to look at some ways workers have tried to gain
control over their work situations. We summarize a particular
form of cooperation, worker management, and two specific instances, the Employee Stock Option Plan (ESOP) at Weirton Steel

in the U.S. and the industrial cooperatives of Mondragon in the Basque region of Spain.

Worker-owned and managed firms are relatively new on the national scene in the United States, though some have existed at the local level for many years.[16] They have become important for several reasons. It is becoming clear that profitable plants are being closed, not just unprofitable ones, and this is more common when the plant is a small part of a conglomerate holding company. The plant may be closed because even more profit can be earned if moved to a lower wage area, for a tax write-off, or for a variety of other non-production related reasons.[17] In these situations, purchase of the plant by the present employees preserves jobs, which makes it an attractive possibility. In addition, there is now a legal mechanism, Employee Stock Ownership Plan (ESOP), to facilitate employee ownership, and it provides significant tax incentives to firms.[18]

There is increasing evidence that worker-owned firms incorporating employee participation and workplace democracy have rates of productivity at least as high and frequently higher than traditional firms.[19] Thus worker-owned firms have been used to maintain employment at plants that otherwise would have closed *and* have been used to maintain and improve productivity as well as the quality of work life. In fact, they all appear to be linked. As employees become owners and managers, the old distrust that led to shirking and excessive supervision can often be reduced. The new environment enables workers to see that the short-run advantage of shirking is outweighed by the negative impact on long-run productivity and profits that they share in. Free riding is still possible, of course, if the employees never coalesce as a group.[20]

A 1988 report published in England indicates that stock ownership and profit-sharing schemes actually stimulate worker performance.[21] It analyzed the results of 414 companies in the period 1977–1985 and showed that those with such programs did consistently, and in some cases spectacularly, better than the others. Also, the smaller the firm, the more direct was the impact.

An interesting case in the U.S. is Weirton Steel. Since 1984, some 8,400 employees have owned the company under an ESOP, and have operated the plant profitably. Management and labor attribute this success—under the previous ownership of National

Steel the company was on the edge of bankruptcy—to the implementation of the ESOP. In the face of general decline in the steel industry, Weirton has expanded its employment from 7,800 when the ESOP began to 8,400. The company has paid out about one-third of its profits each year—$15–20 million—while reinvesting the remainder in plant modernization. R. Alan Prosswimmer, company vice-president and chief financial officer, attributes the company's turnaround to the ESOP: "Over $10 million in savings last year alone were attributable to our employee programs." Walter Bish, president of the Independent Steelworkers Union, added that the workers, since becoming owners, "are much more aware of the fact that quality is important." Rank and file workers speak similarly saying that the ESOP has resulted in "a lot of attitude changes," because previously workers "were working for National Steel and the profits went there. Now the profits are staying here."[22]

Of particular interest as a model for employee-owned and managed firms are the industrial cooperatives of Mondragon in the Basque region of Spain.[23] Their achievements are quite impressive. The first of the Mondragon cooperatives was established in 1958. Twenty years later the 100 cooperatives together had sales close to $1 billion, one-fifth of which was exported to other countries. Among the many goods produced are refrigerators and other home appliances, heavy machinery, hydraulic presses, steel, semi-conductors, and selenium rectifiers. Among the cooperatives are the largest refrigerator manufacturer in Spain, a bank with over $500 million in assets, a technological research center, a technical high school and engineering college, and an extensive social security system with health clinics and other social services.[24]

The ownership and management structure of the Mondragon cooperatives are of particular interest. Every new member must invest a specified amount in the firm where they are employed. At the end of each year a portion of the firms' surplus or profit is allocated to each worker's capital account in proportion to the number of hours worked and the job rating. The job rating schedule allows for a quite narrow 3:1 ratio between the highest and lowest paid workers. The result is a pay scale quite different from that prevailing in private industry. In comparison with the industry average, lower-paid workers earn more in the cooperatives, middle-level workers and managers earn the same, and top managers earn considerably less. Each cooperative's board of directors is selected by all the members and, in turn, the board appoints the managers. There is a social council made up of elected representatives of the lowest-paid workers which negotiates with the board over worker grievances and other issues of interest.

The purely economic results are impressive. When both capital and labor inputs are accounted for, the Mondragon cooperatives are far more productive in their use of resources than private firms in Spain. One comparison with the 500 largest firms in Spain found that in the 1970s the average cooperative used only 25 percent as much capital equipment per worker but worker productivity reached 80 percent of that in private industry.[25]

How might we explain this highly efficient labor force in the Mondragon cooperatives? Clearly worker motivation plays a major part.[26] As workers became owners and participated in management decisions the incentives to shirk were lessened. It was not that workers became more altruistic; rather the structural environment made it easier for trust to develop. Thus strategic behavior declined as workers saw that their short-term individual interests could conflict with their long-term interests. Shirking might benefit them here and now but productivity would benefit them over the long haul. Bradley and Gelb conclude from their study, "that co-operation could theoretically contribute to efficiency in at least two ways: by rendering more effective traditional 'vertical control' by reducing resistance, and by generating pressures towards horizontal reinforcement. Mondragon plausibly does both. Vertical control is improved by the generation and sustaining of consensus and high-trust relationships within the enterprise. Horizontal reinforcement is induced through dispersion of shareholdings and appreciation of the role of effort in the success of the enterprise."[27]

The free rider problem was controlled by the growth of group consciousness which may make it difficult to transfer the Mondragon experience. Basque solidarity clearly has been an important factor in its success.[28] However, this may be a chicken-egg problem. Must we have the group consciousness first or will the experience of ownership and management help create that consciousness? We do not know, but the continued deterioration of our industrial structure is creating the conditions for worker buyouts which, if combined with the philosophy of stewardship, could be used to build a new social consensus.

Bradley and Gelb point out other factors that inhibit the transferability of the Mondragon experiment. They conclude that ties with local communities and limited labor mobility appear important to the success of the cooperatives. In the United States, where there is more labor mobility and weaker ties of community, the group consciousness may be more difficult to generate. This is one of the challenges that must be met by new policy designs.

Conflict between Rich and Poor

In an economy marked by wide extremes of income and wealth distribution, competition in markets means some go hungry and homeless while others use their buying power to have luxuries produced. Some feel proud and successful, others feel defeated and inadequate. Esteem and fellowship do not thrive in the context of extreme competition, where esteem comes from one's position relative to others.

Corner Solutions, Crime, and Negative Externalities. To understand the problem better, let us explore those situations where the free market solution is what economists call a "corner solution."[29] Market economists see the market system as a process of solving maximization and minimization problems, maximizing some output with given inputs, or minimizing the cost of inputs to obtain some given output. Any solution in which one or more of the inputs or outputs are given a zero value is called a "corner solution" because, in mathematical terms, it lies at the corner of the set of all possible solution values.[30]

The free market system's optimal solution to the problem of maximizing society's output given input resources may be a corner solution in which the incomes of some workers may be zero (or at least below the poverty level). It may not be profitable for any employer to hire a certain type of labor at a positive (or above the poverty level) wage; for given their skills, these workers are not needed to produce maximum output. In very poor, labor surplus economies efficiency dictates paying unskilled labor a zero or near zero wage. The market economy's optimal solution, therefore, is a corner solution where some workers face starvation for the sake of economic efficiency.

To a lesser degree the same phenomenon exists in the United States. Left to itself the free market yields efficient results that leave some workers with zero incomes (unemployed) and others working but with poverty level incomes. In the U.S. during 1987 there were on the average 7.5 million people unemployed, most receiving zero income from the economy. If their dependents are added, more than 20 million people were in this situation. In addition, 8.8 million people were employed and earned incomes that left them below the poverty line.

The possibility of corner solutions causes a number of problems for a market economy with its foundation of rational decision making by individual actors. First, there is the probability of high unemployment rates and large-scale poverty.[31] Second, the individually rational response of "corner dwellers" to their plight may be socially disruptive. Economic theory usually goes silent at this point. Certainly many go on public assistance since it is better than no income, and some who could get below poverty level jobs choose to stay on welfare if its total benefits exceed that of the possible job. The major welfare program, Aid for Dependent Children, uses income-support formulas that give an incentive for people to stay on welfare. The recent reductions in Medicaid, eliminating the working poor from the program, have created another incentive to stay on welfare. In addition, there is another perfectly rational alternative which avoids capitalism's deadly sin of sloth and which is consistent with the ethic of the entrepreneurial society. After weighing all of the gains, costs, and risks, corner dwellers can choose to allocate part of their labor to illegal activities such as prostitution, gambling, burglary, shoplifting, running numbers, selling drugs, and mugging. The moral base of society has been eroded at the upper reaches of the income distribution, why should we expect it to be any different in the lower echelons?

Of course, when wages fall below some minimum level, not everyone heads for the welfare rolls or becomes a criminal. This is the common fallacy of "blaming the victim" which is as old as the debate on the Poor Laws. Nonetheless, there is certainly some relation between the number of people on welfare or the amount of crime committed and the balance between unskilled labor's wages and welfare benefits or the gains from criminal activity. This reality provides an additional warrant for intervention in the free market economy.

The welfare and crime externalities of zero or near zero wages of a corner solution concern society as a whole, and not simply the workers involved. "Low wages themselves generate an externality, crime, that may be a rational response to the set of market wages."[32] Unfortunately, this externality usually is ignored as are welfare costs of unemployment and low wages.

Whether desperate people are driven to go on welfare or commit crime by poverty or weak people are enticed into welfare because the benefits are too high and into crime because the risks are not high enough, the fact remains that crime creates enormous costs for the community in the form of negative externalities—loss of life and property, costs of law enforcement, and the psychic costs of fear and insecurity. And the total costs of welfare programs are significant. These are cases where the free market simply fails. Public intervention is called for.

The 1988 welfare reform bill recognized this in some degree by providing training funds for those on welfare and by encouraging on-the-job training in hopes of developing the skills which would facilitate gainful employment. A number of state programs have been successful in this regard, but only in the presence of a booming economy. So making employment at above poverty wage levels our top policy priority could pay for itself by reducing the relative value of anti-social behavior and of welfare.

Education, Anti-Poverty Programs and Positive Externalities. Free market economists such as Milton Friedman have long recognized that education is a special commodity that requires government intervention.[33] It has positive externalities, i.e., education has a greater value to society as a whole than to the individual alone. For example, an educated person makes a better voter and a citizen more able to contribute to our modern, complex society. The recognition of this reality has led to educational improvement programs in virtually all of the states and to George Bush's desire to be known as the "Education President."

Many commodities besides education possess positive externalities. Health is another example. Preventing or curing workers' illnesses or preventing accidents not only benefits the workers but society also avoids the lost output. Preventing communicable diseases and illnesses has benefits to all who are exposed, so subsidizing some parts of the health system can have the same benefits as education. One effect of CEI market policies applied to a noncompetitive industry, health care, has been a dramatic rise in costs, most of which has fallen on private employers. Chrysler estimates that health-care costs are $700 per vehicle produced, far above the $375 in France, $337 in Germany, $246 in Japan, or $223 in Canada. Their response has been to begin to shift those costs to their workers; but there is also growing business interest in national health insurance as a means of keeping their costs competitive internationally.[34]

The argument can be extended. Why not subsidize other basic needs such as food, clothing, and shelter. The free market answer is that these commodities do not have positive externalities, their total value is captured by the individuals who consume them. Free market economists also argue that people's incentive to help themselves would be destroyed, that the possibility of failure, as well as success, is a necessary incentive for people to work hard and become productive and economically responsible. Government programs lessen these incentives and result in increased poverty.[35]

However, this is a shortsighted argument if a portion of the population are corner dwellers and are driven to obtain their food, clothing and shelter through criminal activity which generates negative externalities. In addition, there is an output loss of the underskilled, undernourished, and discouraged that affects all of us.

A recent study provides evidence that equal opportunity laws and affirmative action programs are beneficial to workers traditionally discriminated against *and* that a company's overall productivity and profits can be improved by such measures.[36] The study found that without such measures, "severely disadvantaged workers tend to drop out entirely. Taken separately, equal opportunity laws prove quite effective in increasing the effort levels of discriminated-against workers. This increase causes workers to realize greater earnings and the profits of the firm also increase. One of the reasons this is so is that the workers who were previously discouraged by discrimination now find it worth their while to try and try hard. This causes all workers to try harder in response."[37]

A successful approach in terms of the goals of meeting basic material needs and of self-esteem and fellowship would be to have an ethic of jubilee. Redistribution of income, *per se,* is not the issue. Rather the key is the adoption of a full-employment program, coupled with equal opportunity and affirmative action, for all who are able to work, and social welfare policies that provide, with dignity, basic material needs (especially food, housing, and health care) to those not able to.

These policies would not only increase the absolute level of income of the lower-income population but would reduce de facto the relative income differences. Such a jubilee ethic would provide the conditions necessary for esteem and fellowship to flourish.

Full-Employment Policy. Unemployment is more than a statistic. Lurking behind the statistics are real people whose human dignity has proven to be inseparable from their employment. One study found that as unemployment increases, there are corresponding increases in the suicide rate among middle-aged males, incarcerations in state prisons, new admissions to mental hospitals, and infant mortality rates in urban areas.[38] One of the somber effects of the 1981–82 recession was a dramatic increase in child abuse cases in areas hard hit by unemployment.[39]

Dr. Sidney Cobb of Brown University and Dr. Stanislav Kasl of Yale have done extensive research on the health and behavioral effects of unemployment caused by plant closings.[40] Over the thirteen-year period of their study they found a suicide rate among unemployed workers which was thirty times the national average. They also found a higher incidence of a whole series of diseases (e.g., heart disease, hypertension, diabetes, peptic ulcer) among the unemployed than among employed workers. They found that job losses had serious psychological effects such as extreme depression, tension, anxiety, insecurity, and loss of self-esteem. This result is not surprising because in a market economy, employment—or access to wealth—is necessary to one's identity as a human being. We don't ask someone, "Who are you?" but rather "What do you do?" I am a professor or a carpenter. I work for General Motors or the University of Notre Dame. We have imbibed the individualist tradition with its emphasis on achievement and attribution of responsibility to individuals. At its most extreme the argument assumes that workers are unemployed because they are lazy, lack skills, or demand wages that are too high.

These psychological effects are compounded by the real material problems unemployment causes. Employment is the only source of income for most people and income is necessary to lead a life of dignity. Food, clothing, housing, education, recreation all cost money.

Unemployment is one of the main structural problems of a market economy. CEIs assume unemployment is a natural phenomenon and is the price of a free economy. Keynesians argue that it is the unfortunate but perhaps unavoidable by-product of controlling inflation. In reality unemployment exists because in our economy a majority own no land, tools, or capital, and have only their labor to sell. A minority own all of the land, tools, and capital and then hire labor to work with the capital. The owners hire when it appears profitable and do not hire when profit expectations are low. Employment is a by-product of profit making; and there is no reason to believe this will result in full employment. Except during wartime the U.S. economy rarely has had unemployment rates below 4 percent.

Since private economic institutions cannot provide full employment the responsiblity rests with society. But so far we have been unwilling to guarantee useful employment for everyone able and willing to work (the Humphrey-Hawkins Act of 1978 is a full-employment bill, but it is toothless). Rather we put people on welfare which further lowers their self-esteem and assaults their dignity. The real immorality of unemployment is our unwillingness to modify defective economic institutions and to pay the price necessary to eliminate the cause of the sufferings. The unemployed and millions of others, including all those urban youth who never have had a job, bear the costs of technological change, plant relocations, and government cutbacks in spending. We as consumers benefit in lower prices, and the owners of corporations benefit in higher profits.

Whether through a public employment program or job tax credits to the private sector, a top policy priority must be to guarantee a job to everyone willing and able to work. We should also provide adjustment assistance to those who lose their jobs because of changes in competitive position, and should make every effort to keep open plants that can be operated efficiently. The need for a full-employment policy has long been recognized, but never implemented. President Truman's last *Economic Report* in January 1953 stated:

> It means full utilization of our natural resources, our technology and science, our farms and factories, our business brains, and our labor skills. The concept of full employment values ends as well as means; it values leisure as well as work; it values self-development as well as dedication to a common cooperation. Full employment means maximum opportunity under the American system of responsible freedom.

> And it is a concept which must grow as our capabilities grow. Full employment tomorrow is something different from full employment today. The growth of opportunity, with a growing population and an expanding technology, requires a constantly expanding economy. This is needed to abolish poverty and to remove insecurity from substantial portions of our population. It offers the prospects of transforming class or group conflict into cooperation and mutual trust, because the achievement of more for all reduces the struggle of some to get more at the expense of others.

> Although our dedication to full employment has made great strides within recent memory, we cannot afford to be complacent. We cannot assume that henceforth what needs to be done to promote the maintenance of full employment will be done. None of us—regardless of party—should let the idea of full employment degenerate into a slogan bandied for narrow political advantage. Like freedom, it needs to be guarded zealously and translated into action on a continuing basis. Moreover, if we fail in this, our very freedom may be placed in jeopardy.[41]

A full-employment guarantee is sometimes opposed on the ground that it would hinder labor productivity. However, countries such as Japan that have much greater employment security have had more rapidly increasing productivity for decades and now have surpassed us in labor productivity. If fear of unemployment causes restrictive work rules, the job security created by guaranteed full employment may enhance rather than retard productivity.

One mechanism which could facilitate this policy would be more consultation among the main economic actors. The Employment Act of 1946 called for close cooperation and frequent consultation among industry, agriculture, labor, and all levels of government in implementing the goals of the act. Committees of these groups should be established and meet regularly with the Council of Economic Advisers and other appropriate government offices. It is difficult to say in what precise form the policy-making process would emerge from these consultations. A host of other policies could emerge from joint consultation: targeted jobs programs, education and training programs to equip workers with the skills needed for the future, day care centers for employed parents, and so on. The key point is to supplement the workings of the market with a consultative process to develop policies to generate the desired results.

In addition, a wage subsidy to employers who hire new employees and train them makes economic sense. Firms have little incentive to train workers because the new employees can take their acquired skills and go to work for other employers. This is a classic case of market failure, though if society covers part of the cost there are gains for all. The employee acquires better skills and becomes more productive, thereby earning higher income. The firm gets a more productive work force and the reduction in unemployment and the higher productivity levels of workers would add up to substantial gains for society as a whole. The cost of unemployment benefits would decline, not an insignificant matter: since its inception in 1935, over $200 billion has been paid out in unemployment claims, nearly $30 billion in 1982 alone.[42] The higher productivity of the labor force means greater output for all. All benefit as each becomes more productive.

Guaranteed Basic Material Needs. Employment must be the major means of obtaining basic material needs. As a last resort public service jobs must be made available on a standby basis. Receiving welfare undermines self-esteem and nothing is produced. Paying people to work, even in public service jobs, maintains their self-esteem and something is produced.

In addition to the full-employment policies outlined above the following types of policies are needed:

1. For those unable to work—the handicapped, the sick, women with small children—a fair and efficient income transfer payment system is needed. Work incentives must be built into the system—training and placement for the handicapped; day care centers for working mothers; phased reduction of public aid over a brief (2–5 year) period to encourage job placement for those physically able to work.

2. Basic Needs: medical care and housing. A full-employment policy coupled with an income supplement program can provide for the basic needs of all, while maintaining freedom and self-esteem. However, two elements of basic material needs loom so large in people's budgets that special policies are necessary.

In health care, a long-term plan for the education of more medical personnel of different types including paramedical personnel is important. A movement away from the present emphasis on high-cost, capital-intensive treatment toward less hospitalization and more outpatient treatment is crucial to contain rising treatment prices. Present insurance schemes have apparently also contributed to rapid price increases, so the way health care is paid for must be resolved. Group practice modeled on the Kaiser Permanente model is one possibility. Many other specifics must be worked out—for example, resolving the right and obligation to remove people from life support systems; and provision of pre-natal care to the poor.

Because of its high cost relative to a household's annual income, housing problems are not easily solved by merely giving families more income and allowing the market to work. In addition a significant portion of the housing stock in our older cities has been allowed to deteriorate.

CEIs have a ready solution to the housing problems facing many older cities in the Northeast and the Midwest: leave the city alone and it will eventually rehabilitate itself. That is, if urban stress is allowed to continue unabated, over time the price differentials between urban residential sites and suburban residential sites will become so large that investors will find it profitable to redevelop the city.

This process of "market" revitalization has to some extent

already begun in some cities, and the process has been accelerated by the impact of inflation on the suburban housing stock. However, we must recognize that if we are to depend solely upon this mechanism to solve our urban housing problems, some neighborhoods must wait ten, twenty, thirty years or more before the price differential appears attractive to the potential investor. In the meantime sound housing stock is literally thrown on the scrapheap for lack of maintenance expenditures—a perversion of the idea of stewardship—and more importantly millions of families must suffer the effects of urban neglect as they wait to see whether it will be the wrecking ball or the investor who will displace them.

Thus to the poor who are concentrated in urban places, the market solution is not very appealing. Indeed, for them, the market solution is defeatest in nature. It assumes that housing decay will roll like a wave from the urban core toward the suburbs, pushing prices up in front of it and lowering prices in its wake. When prices are low enough, reinvestment will take place. But that is not the end of the process, eventually decay will attack the weakest rehabilitated neighborhood, and start the cycle anew.

This unadulterated market process is unacceptable, but we cannot ignore market influences in our search for equitable solutions to the housing problem. This is particularly true since the electorate seems disinclined to spend from tax revenues the hundred of billions of dollars necessary to revitalize our cities and their housing stock. Thus at this point we must in large part depend upon private investors for the needed funds.

These funds will be forthcoming if public policy is appropriately designed and implemented. However, in our haste to leverage these funds from the private sector, we cannot neglect our basic goals of providing for basic material needs, extending freedom, and fostering esteem and fellowship. Unfortunately, these goals have been largely ignored in the past. Public housing, whether in the dehumanizing high rise, high-density version or in the more recently popular scattered-site version, sacrificed freedom and esteem for the attainment of a minimum standard of housing for the poor. That is, those who are forced to reside in public housing must forfeit their right to choose where they will live and in the process they are branded by their housing unit as a public housing resident. Thus they are aliens to the larger society.

This need not be the case. We propose a radical change in federal housing policy. At present the principal public housing subsidy is a tax subsidy, an unlimited mortgage-interest deduction from taxable income. This is a subsidy to the middle and wealthy classes since the deduction increases with the size of mortgage, and interest on a second house, such as a beach house, also can be deducted. This is estimated to have cost taxpayers $40 billion in 1988.[43]

We suggest that this subsidy should be capped at an amount to buy a basic house (what used to be called a "homestead allowance"). This could be set at a figure such as the median house price. This would increase tax revenues anywhere from $10 to $20 billion a year that could be targeted to subsidize lower-cost housing construction and rehabilitation. Private housing contractors and financiers could be given subsidies for building new houses and rehabilitating existing houses that could be sold for less than 50 percent more than the median price of housing in that area, with the subsidy to vary inversely with the price. At present the main activity in low-income housing programs is through non-profit community groups, and they should be given preference in these programs.[44] This would increase the housing stock in the lower price range while also holding-down its price level, making houses more affordable for both the poor and lower middle classes.

Some portion of this housing subsidy could be allocated to aid renters. An existing federal program, the Housing Allowance Program, is founded on two basic propositions. First, the poor should not be forced to spend more than 25 percent of their income on housing. Second, the housing subsidy should be the difference between 25 percent of the family's income and the average rental value of a standard home (no code violations) which is of the appropriate size for the family in question. Thus if the income of a family of four is $500 per month and the average rental value of an appropriately sized standard home is $300 per month, this family would receive a subsidy of $175 per month, which can be used to rent or pay the expenses on any home or apartment which is free of code violations. If the family prefers less ample surroundings, it is free to select such a place of residence as long as it is free of code violations. In our example, the family would still receive the $175 per month subsidy, however, its contribution would be less than 25 percent of its income. On the other hand, if a family preferred a higher than average quality of housing, it must supplement the subsidy with a greater share of its income.

Studies of housing allowance experiments indicated that the programs are less costly than present programs and have a beneficial impact on existing housing stocks.[45]

The freedom of choice of these two programs will lead to a heightened sense of esteem and fellowship on the part of the participants. Since the poor are not forced to reside in public housing units, they decide which community they will join. Some, no doubt, will choose their old neighborhoods where friends remain, the culture is comfortable, and acceptance is immediate. Others may prefer to join upwardly mobile neighborhoods. Still others, such as the elderly, may wish to return to high-density housing where companionship, shopping, and essential services are not too distant.

With a set of full-employment policies supplemented by income maintenance, medical care, and housing programs, basic material goods should be assured, freedom of choice expanded, and esteem and fellowship enhanced. In the process, the realities of the market have been neither ignored nor allowed to work severe hardships on those least able to cope. The jubilee ethic gives very different possibilities from the competitive ethic.

Conflict among Regions

Conflict and competition between the Northeast-Midwest and the South-Southwest, between the "rustbelt" and the "sunbelt," needs to be directed onto more productive paths.

Community Full Employment. As a beginning, policies must be developed that have community full employment as their objective. That is, instead of merely setting an aggregate goal—say, 4 percent unemployment—policies should target that level of unemployment at the community level.* This will require economic pol-

---

*The definition of community will have to be flexible. For example, the Ohio Valley region might be defined as a community because of its economic integration and geographic proximity. In other cases Standard Metropolitan Statistical Areas—basically a city with its suburbs—might be used.

icy, both at the national and community levels, to be effective. A number of policies are necessary.

First, social cost-benefit studies must be done of ailing industries and of plant relocations. These are the two major sources of local unemployment once a full-employment level of expenditures is achieved at the national level. Care must be taken not to subsidize firms that should go out of business. On the other hand many small firms, which are very efficient, fail because they cannot obtain loans in competition with planning sector firms. This is where a policy of credit rationing can be useful. In a market economy, credit is rationed to the highest bidder.[46] This rigs the game in favor of the largest and most powerful firms. A specific policy of allocating some percentage of total credit to small firms would be a step toward revitalizing local communities.

Plant relocations from one community to another are a much more serious problem. Most relocations are done by planning sector firms. From their private cost-benefit analysis it is efficient to close operations in South Bend, Indiana and move them to North Carolina. A social cost-benefit analysis might indicate that the move is inefficient. The social costs include the idled factory buildings, schools, sewer systems, and other social infrastructure left behind in the old community (typically in the Northeast or Midwest) and the increasing costs of providing all these services in the new community (frequently in the sunbelt). The result is a deterioration in the elements of the old infrastructure and a failure to build adequate new ones. Thus Toledo's roads and sewers fall apart and Phoenix does not build enough. In addition, there is the unemployment insurance and welfare benefits cost of those left behind. And this leaves out the human suffering of those unemployed or forced to sever their roots and migrate to seek work.

Second, community-targeted full-employment policies require the capacity to anticipate plant shutdowns in given industries. This, in turn, requires the development of early warning systems and forecasting models that yield predictions about the private sector. In addition, it requires that the Council of Economic Advisers or some other federal body provide accurate forecasts of ongoing and new areas of public investment such as mass transit. For both the private and public sectors projections of skill requirements will be needed if retraining programs are to be successful.

Third, community revitalization requires that the national economic consultative process design incentive policies to encourage the allocation of capital among specific industries and geographic regions.

Fourth, public investment and direct purchases from the private sector must be used by the federal, state, and local governments to obtain community full employment. Thus one important consideration in the letting of government contracts should be community need. In addition, changes in telecommunications have now made it possible for a significant decentralization of the largest economic entity in the country, the federal government. It should be possible to begin to move portions of the Federal government to other areas of the country and to maintain the communication that is necessary to operate departments efficiently. A starting point might be to close the unneeded military bases, which all can agree upon, and to move other federal agencies or portions of agencies into them. This could not only maintain the local communities but could increase the efficiency of the federal government.

Ironically, this type of public planning for community revitalization and full employment may be the only way small-scale, local business firms survive in the face of competition from the large corporations.* In one of his novels, Charles Dickens said, "Every man for himself said the elephant as he danced among the chickens." Planned government intervention might help the chickens to survive.

Revitalizing Local Communities. Solutions to community-level economic problems and to the resulting regional conflicts will be found only if citizens are willing to cooperate in the difficult readjustments necessary to revitalize the economy. And that requires policies guided by the principle of subsidiarity be developed and implemented at the lowest feasible levels. In this context, the mediating institutions which are so important to individuals' sense of fellowship and self-esteem can be sustained.

---

*One potential by-product of the leveraged buyout craze may be a return of some of the subsidiaries to local control when the debt-ridden firm is forced to sell off its assets. The key will be the ability to obtain financing for the locally based initiatives.

There is also a direct relation between the decline of local communities and the social limits to growth. The moral base of society has progressively been undermined.[47] This collective conscience or moral law has generally operated through the community-based mediating institutions of private life. Because of their remoteness and sheer size, the mega-institutions are "consumers" not "producers" of this type of morality. A general moral code cannot rest on the activities of individuals either. The experiments with "life-styles" of "consenting adults" is too unstable and unreliable as a basis for the generation and maintenance of a collective conscience. However, without such a moral base, the ethic of stewardship, the possibility of fellowship, and the reality of freedom become problematic. Here again community revitalization is important.

Our modern political philosophies—liberalism, conservatism, socialism—have failed precisely because they have not understood the importance of mediating institutions. Liberalism has constantly turned to the state for solutions to social problems while conservatism sought the same in the corporate sector. Neither recognized the destructiveness to the social fabric of relying on mega-institutions. Socialism suffers from this same myopia. Even though it places its faith in renewed community it fails to see that socialist mega-institutions are just as destructive as capitalist ones.

Ways must be found to revitalize community-based mediating institutions from the bottom-up. The new forms of organization such as workers' ownership could play a positive role in this regard.

An encouraging note in a generally grim picture is the growth of not-for-profit organizations. Credit unions, ESOPs, neighborhood associations have been grass-roots responses to the dichotomization of modern life. Thus, an important part of economic policy must be to foster not-for-profit organizations. As an example, let us focus on one such not-for-profit, mediating institution—the neighborhood association.

Growing numbers of urban residents realize that if their neighborhoods are to remain stable, they must act together and capitalize upon the uniqueness of their "sub-urban" communities. Thus more and more neighborhoods are represented by formal or informal neighborhood associations. In some cities such as Pittsburgh and Birmingham, all neighborhoods within the city have been identified and neighborhood organization has begun. In other cities such as Las Vegas, Wichita, and Madison, Wisconsin, an impressive number of neighborhoods have been identified and organized. All indications point to a growing number of neighborhood associations in the future. They have been quite successful in a number of important areas: (a) They have provided a mechanism for residents to develop real participatory democracy; (b) They have been used extensively to influence local governmental decision-makers; (c) Local residents, business concerns, and most importantly the media are beginning to think and act in terms of neighborhoods; and (d) Federal agencies have demonstrated an increasing willingness to recognize neighborhoods for analytical and policy purposes.

By definition, the collective action of neighborhood residents recognizes that each individual in the community—the rich and the poor alike—are affected by the actions of others in the community. These third party effects or spillovers from individual actions determine the quality of life in a neighborhood. Thus, if a neighborhood association can instill confidence in the future, individual residents will risk new investments in their property, which in turn will raise the value of surrounding property. Or if a neighborhood association can instill pride, there will be a corresponding reduction in vandalism and other criminal behavior. In both cases a successful neighborhood association which induces positive spillover effects improves the quality of life in the neighborhood which in turn helps to guarantee the basic human need for safe adequate housing.

In a like manner, neighborhood associations can protect the freedom of choice of those who reside in urban neighborhoods. Historically, the poor have had limited housing choice, generally restricted to the housing stock that the affluent no longer wanted. Thus, if the affluent wished to return to the inner city, the poor would be simply pushed aside. This no longer needs to be the case. Collective action on the part of neighborhood residents can protect them from the ill effects of "gentrification" and can allow them to share in the benefits of this process.

Lastly and most fundamentally, neighborhood associations foster directly the third goal of esteem and fellowship. Sharing problems, finding solutions, working on projects, all develop a spirit of responsibility not only to the individual but to the neighborhood. It is this cooperative nature of neighborhood associations which ultimately generates the confidence and pride which is essential to community preservation.

Solving community problems and the conflict between different communities cannot rely solely upon decisions made at the national level. That will create more mega-institutions. Certainly national policies are necessary to ensure full employment, stable prices, and the implementation of social policy. A careful balance must be maintained between the national economic policies necessary to control the macroeconomy for the commonweal and the decentralization necessary to make worker self-management, local government, and community-based mediating institutions foster freedom of choice and fellowship.

Rebuilding Social Infrastructure. Most of the deteriorating infrastructure, discussed previously, is specific to local communities—subways, bridges, streets, sewer systems. Certainly there is a need for federal financial help. A small tax on each gallon of automobile gasoline sold would provide the needed funds. However, this is an area where public jobs programs could be utilized efficiently and productively. During the 1930s, the Civilian Conservation Corps, a New Deal public works program, built most of the sidewalks in the Midwest and the campgrounds in the West to name a few of their projects. This is also an area in which local community organizations could participate, helping to facilitate their solidarity.

Public policy has tended to favor new projects, the water projects of the West or the transportation project such as the Tennessee-Tombigbee waterway. While maintaining existing infrastructure may be less glamorous, from an economic standpoint it may be at least as efficient a use of resources.

Conflict among Nations

The creative-destructive nature of free market capitalism is nowhere more clearly demonstrated than in the international economy. Every problem in the U.S. economy—from the price of sugar to unemployment in Youngstown—is in part a reflection of what is occurring internationally. And this has become more true during the last fifteen years when the world economy moved toward ever greater market coordination. From the end of World War II until 1971, the organizing principles were those agreed upon at Bretton Woods. Since that time, free markets have played an ever greater role. In the process there are two areas of international conflict which have arisen and whose solution will affect the outlines of the world economy in the coming decades.

Trade Imbalances. The large trade deficits of the 1980s coupled with significant loss of industrial jobs is the most serious challenge the U.S. economy faces. There is presently an active call to protect our industries against foreign competition and/or to increase our international competitiveness by raising productivity. The U.S. has become more productive with each passing year but other countries—particularly Japan, West Germany, South Korea, Taiwan, and Brazil—have had even faster rates of productivity growth. Thus they have become ever more competitive with the U.S., especially when the dollar was overvalued before 1986.

This is natural. At the end of World War II the U.S. stood alone as the only significant industrial country to escape the ravages of the war. Japan, Germany, and the rest of Europe were in ruins. The British economy was exhausted from the war effort. U.S. dominance of the world economy was established. The U.S. dollar became the international currency and the U.S. set the rules for an international trade regime based on the nineteenth century liberal principles of free flows of capital and goods. While often violated in practice this was the spirit animating trade negotiations—emphasis on procedures and not on results.

The system operated well, and the U.S. was a very positive hegemon; the recovery of Europe and the acceleration of Third World growth were two results of our leadership. However, as the other countries began to rebuild, the dominant position of the U.S. could not survive. Japan, Germany, and others rebuilt with the latest technologies, giving them a more up-to-date industrial structure than the U.S. Their lower wage levels combined with newer plant and equipment to make them high-productivity producers. The process was speeded up as countries such as South Korea and Taiwan began to industrialize, combining the latest technologies with exceptionally low wage levels. The result was strong competition for the rest of the world, the normal process of uneven development under a capitalist world system.

The result is an international economic system where the only difference in costs are labor costs, since transportation costs have rapidly declined and since capital is exceptionally mobile. Unless firms receive some formal or informal protection, as in Japan, firms in high-wage countries are forced to reduce costs, either by cutting wages or becoming even more productive. Under the Reagan administration, the tactic was to attack wages.

The alternative of becoming ever more productive is not much better for it is a self-defeating race as each country counters with new competitive strategies. The problem is that competition increases productivity but in the process creates losers—those who are out-competed. This is both a creative and destructive process. In the long run it creates expanded productivity and wealth, though unevenly, while in the short run it destroys firms, jobs, and communities.

This normal process of uneven development is compounded for the U.S. by an additional factor. The economies that rebuilt after World War II did so with substantial protection against foreign competition. They all protected agriculture and utilized various tariff and non-tariff means to protect selected industrial products. For example, Japan through the 1960s imposed formal tariff and non-tariff barriers against foreign competition while building a highly centralized economy based on networks of firms and banks. When the trade barriers were lowered in some degree, these networks of firms continued to buy among each other even when foreign products were cheaper. So the economy built by the Japanese was not a replica of the free market economy as understood by economists, but was predicated on the assumption that survival of the networks of firms is the most important goal, not mere profit. Under these circumstances, the effect of a tariff reduction will be quite different in Japan and in the U.S. The result has been tremendous Japanese trade surpluses reaching almost $90 billion dollars in 1987. The surplus with the U.S. grew from $17 billion in 1982 to almost $60 billion in 1987.[48]

Countries correctly utilize governments as the social institution to soften the destructiveness of the process of uneven development while doing minimal damage to the creative side of the process. In the case of the international economy, governments have attempted to protect the interests of their respective countries while reaping the gains from participating in trading relations.

To formulate a program to overcome the international problems facing the U.S. we must discard the dichotomy between free trade and protection. The real world is a continuum where most countries utilize a combination of partial openness where it benefits them, and subsidies, export promotion, and import restrictions in other areas. The following listing demonstrates the asymmetrical trade openness of countries in the world economy:[49]

1. *United States:* most open and least regulated of large industrial countries; uses some protection (textiles, etc.) and limited subsidies; industrial firms tending to locate abroad in search of lower wages; large trade deficits with threat of extensive deindustrialization; earnings on investments abroad no longer sufficient to cover excess imports, indeed in 1988 payments exceeded investment receipts for first time; large borrowing and capital investment from abroad covering deficit.

2. *European Economic Community and European Free Trade Area:* mainly open markets but agriculture protected; considerable use of subsidies for manufacturing and growing use of voluntary import restraint agreements; moderate export of capital.

3. *Japan:* highly controlled and only partly open markets with substantial subsidies and export-oriented financing; strong tradition of networks of industrial firms and banks, of industry-government cooperation, and of a national strategy of manufacturing exports and raw material imports; growing capital exports and plant relocations abroad, in search of lower wages.

3. *Newly Industrialized and Less Developed Countries:* limited market openness with widespread use of subsidies and regulations to protect domestic industries against foreign imports and to encourage new industries and expand exports; some neo-liberal countries in Latin America have very open markets.

4. *Eastern Bloc Countries:* mainly controlled through state-owned trading companies with minor openness, difficult import access, large-scale foreign borrowing and technology imports, and subsidized exports to earn foreign exchange.

In sum, the real world of the international economy is characterized by widespread use of industrial policies and export subsidies; extensive surpluses, discounting, and dumping in world markets; and quotas, tariffs, and import restraints. It is in the context of this world, not the free market world envisioned by economists, that policy must be formulated.

The least promising approach to an international policy is a continued reliance on converting our trading partners to free trade. It is naive to think they will embrace policies that result in our exports undermining their industries and jobs. State control mechanisms are entrenched in newly industrialized countries, less developed countries, and even industrialized countries, particularly Japan. Western Europe is becoming ever more concerned with unemployment and protecting its manufacturing plants and jobs. Latin America and Africa carry large external debts and need to expand exports and restrict imports.

Greater dollar devaluation is no more promising. The devaluation since 1985 was needed and has kept the trade deficit from being even worse. However, by itself devaluation cannot revitalize U.S. exports and reduce imports. Newly industrialized countries such as South Korea peg their currencies to the dollar, use extensive export subsidies and import restrictions, and use the power of government coercion to maintain low wage levels.

Another factor compounding U.S. problems are the military obligations assumed after World War II and the onset of the Cold War with the Soviet Union. The U.S. committed its political, economic, and military might to protect Europe and Japan. Over the subsequent years of the Cold War other areas were added—South Korea, Israel, South East Asia, Central America. The financial cost of doing so was sustainable during the early years since our export surplus was so large. As countries rebuilt, substituted for our imports, and became competitive in export markets, our trade surplus declined until by the early 1970s it became negative. Thus maintaining troops around the world and providing military aid to competitor countries contributes to the balance of payments deficit.

There must be a greater sharing of these costs, and the U.S. must realize that it is not a world hegemon. This would allow us to avoid such silly policies as guaranteeing Japanese oil shipments through the Strait of Hormuz at an estimated cost to us of some

$200,000 per barrel, not to speak of the other costs in terms of U.S. and civilian lives lost. This might also allow us to avoid the astronomical future costs of building and maintaining a 600 ship navy to rule the waterways of the world.

So instead of pursuing the chimera of free trade, we should attempt to find fair ways of righting the present imbalances, without resorting to unthinking protectionism. More promising policies include sharing of military expenses; imposition of a VAT-waiver corrective tariff and other offsets to foreign subsidies and dumping; adoption of an industrial policy; and increased trade adjustment assistance.

First and most important, the U.S. must force its allies to accept a more equal share of the mutual defense burden. At present defense expenditures in the U.S. are about 7 percent of GNP. Among our NATO allies it averages 3.5 percent and in Canada and Japan about 1 percent. This is what enables them to have higher rates of investment than the U.S. And since billions of dollars flow overseas to maintain our troops, the balance-of-payments suffers. The best policy would be to convince the countries to pay their own defense costs including supporting our troops abroad. If they refuse, bringing U.S. troops home would force the issue. The savings are certainly in the tens of billions of dollars. If this is politically too drastic then an alternative possibilty would be to apply an across-the-board revenue tariff of 10–20 percent on the imports of the relevant countries—mainly Western Europe, Japan, South Korea, and Taiwan.

The recent changes in the Soviet Union and Eastern Europe may make a reduction in overseas military costs more feasible. This is an opportunity to work out new arrangments with our allies.

Second, most industrial countries and newly industrializing countries have Value-Added Taxes (VATs) in the 12–15 percent range which they waive on exported products. This is an export subsidy. The U.S. should impose a VAT-corrective tax equal to the exporting countries domestic VAT. An alternative would be to introduce a VAT system in the U.S. This is discussed in the last section of the chapter. Other penalties and surcharges should be held in ready to discourage cases of dumping, discounting, and other flagrant uses of import and export controls. Obviously there would need to be negotiations to establish acceptable exceptions.

Third, we as a society must face up to certain choices. Do we want a steel industry? Do we want an electronics industry? Do we want whatever the marketplace gives us or do we want to guide that market system, through the agency of government, to give us what we consciously choose as a society? If so, we are forced to develop an industrial policy. That is, we must decide that we want to maintain certain levels of certain industries even if that requires subsidies or import restrictions. In light of the previous paragraph, such decisions need to be communicated to and negotiated with our trading partners. Otherwise tit-for-tat policy responses could reduce everyone's welfare. There should be room for this type of negotiation because every country has industries it wants to maintain. Very likely the ideal of multi-lateral trade will have to be replaced with more reciprocal arrangements. The growth of international trade will probably slow down but hopefully will be reestablished on a sounder basis. Countries will develop a wider range of economic activities, consistent with their capabilities. International trade will become an adjunct to the domestic economies. Over the long term this will enable countries to control the destructive elements of uneven development better.

Finally, despite the above policies, there will still be many industries that are hurt by international competition. To soften the human suffering in those cases of massive dislocation, trade readjustment aid needs to be increased. Retraining programs for displaced workers, relocation allowances, and subsidies to help the impacted communities attract new businesses, in addition to helping to reduce human suffering and increase economic efficiency by providing access to new skills and encouraging mobility of resources.

Order out of Chaos: New International Agreements. The Bretton Woods system deliberately interfered with the workings of international markets. Exchange rates were fixed, resources were to be provided to countries whose investment needs were greater, and countries that ran into international payments difficulties could obtain temporary adjustment loans. Keynes had wanted even more intervention with greater provision of funds, in the interest of providing liquidity and demand to aid world growth.

Even in its less ambitious form as pressed by the U.S., the Bretton Woods system performed well for almost thirty years.

There was unprecedented economic growth throughout the world, World Bank funds provided for modernization of whole sectors of countries, and the IMF generally seemed to be able to bring stability to exchange rates, though the costs were often very high.

The move to organizing the world economy on market principles has been far less successful. World economic growth has slowed, and in many areas of Africa and Latin America has actually become negative during the 1980s. Trade imbalances have become extreme. Instability of exchange rates has become endemic in many areas, particularly Latin America where depreciations of currencies by 200 or 300 percent in a matter of months is not at all uncommon. Even the U.S. exchange rate has seen changes of over 100 percent in a space of years, with consequent impact on domestic producers. And the international debt owed by many countries, now including the U.S., can only have a severe constricting effect in years to come.

Only some of the East Asian countries and Germany have been able to handle these changes with relative ease, largely because of their governments' monitoring and control of the economies and because of their dedication to exports. And the slowing of growth in the world hurts all countries. For example, Latin American imports fell by almost $50 billion when the crisis hit in 1982, and their trade with the U.S. turned from almost balanced in 1981 to a surplus of almost $20 billion in 1986, as they attempted to generate the trade surplus dollars necessary to pay their debts.

The world needs more stability. We need first of all to deal with the debts of Third World countries on a basis that will allow them to resume growth. There are many possibilities, and the Brady proposal is a welcome movement toward debt forgiveness and away from the unsuccessful case-by-case approach of the earlier Baker plan. The Europeans and especially the Japanese are leading in this area. Next we must attempt to move back to more stable exchange rates by reaching international agreements on ranges of rates and mechanisms to support them. The industrial countries have done this with some success for the dollar, but it should be extended to other currencies. The only way this will work is if we begin to deal with international capital flows, making them less fluid by regulating them and beginning to tax them. The goal of free capital flows is to move capital to where it can contribute most to production. In fact, however, capital flows for speculative and financial reasons that often have little to do with productivity. And in the case of capital flight from Third World countries, it makes any efforts at development they might undertake unlikely to succeed.

So the international conflicts which exist, as seen most clearly in the trade imbalances and the retrogression in developing countries, must be met head-on. We need the courage and foresight of 1944 when a system was developed which led to sustained and stable economic change in the world.

Conflict between Economic Growth and Environment

The most dangerous conflict and the most difficult to resolve is that between traditional patterns of economic growth and environmental systems. Any program for future economic improvement must be based on a wiser use of natural resources and more attention to the impact on environmental systems. At this point particular attention must be paid to reducing fossil fuel burning and to safer disposal of toxic waste.

Increased taxation of gasoline is necessary to force conservation in its use. At the same time this could facilitate dealing with the federal budget deficit. It could also aid subsidies to public transport to make it cheaper than private transport, thereby aiding energy savings.

The movement toward international agreements can be aided by meaningful attention to the issues of acid rain and to policies which can lessen its effects. This must be a constitutent element in the effort to develop closer economic ties with Canada as represented by the free trade agreement between the two countries.

There is an ever-growing awareness of the fragility of the environment, and adoption of a stewardship ethic can only encourage this. Positive steps have been taken in swapping portions of their debts to create natural wilderness preserves in Bolivia and Costa Rica. The World Bank now requires an environmental assessment of all of its projects, which will incorporate that issue into

Third World policy making. Collaboration on limiting chlo-
rofluorocarbon emissions is worldwide. So while there is much to
be done, the movement appears quite positive. It must be encouraged further.

PIE-IN-THE-SKY OR OPTIMISTIC REALISM: HOW TO PAY?

We have accused CEIs and Keynesians of being unrealistic.
We claim to have a more realistic view of how the economy actually
operates. They might counter with the claim that our policy proposals are pie-in-the-sky—how are they to be paid for? We have
already mentioned some ways of financing our program: limiting
the interest deductions against income on tax returns; having a
truly progressive income tax; forcing our allies to share the mutual
defense burden or the imposition of a 10–20 percent tax on their
exports as an alternative; and the military which bloated unpro-
ductively during the Reagan years can certainly be put on a diet.
Operating the economy at full employment will increase actual tax
revenues.

These are important but insufficient. Clearly taxes must be
raised. The Reagan tax cuts of the early 1980s were ill-advised.
In addition, expenditures on certain government entitlement programs must be controlled.

As mentioned earlier, most industrial countries use a value-
added tax in the range of 12–15 percent. The introduction of such
a tax without appreciably reducing existing personal income taxes
would go a long way to cover the costs of expanded programs. It
would be easy to share the VAT revenues with states and local
governments to carry out many of the programs. In addition, the
tax would fall on consumption not on income. This would provide
an incentive for savings and a disincentive for consumption.

Probably the greatest mistake of social policy in the 1970s was
the failure to control for the possible escalation of entitlement
expenditures. For example, the full indexing of social security
payments through the passage of a cost-of-living adjustment
(COLA) has resulted in social security expenditures of $207 billion
in 1987, second only to military spending in the federal budget.

With the aging of the population this will get worse. Reducing the COLA to 60 percent of the Consumer Price Index would cut federal expenditures about $150 billion per year by the year 2000. Another $50 billion annually could be saved by gradually raising the retirement age, taxing benefits in excess of contributions, and reducing initial benefits to higher income individuals.[50] We run the risk at this point of opening a new phase of conflict, between the generations. It will take real political will and leadership to deal with this problem, which will only grow over time.

Even more important is a reevaluation of federal retirement programs including the military. At the least these should be taxed above some minimum exemption. And as discussed earlier, cost containment rules must be developed for the various health programs including medicare. Of crucial importance is to establish the right of patients or their heirs to decide when life-support equipment should be removed.

The road ahead is not easy and the precise directions of change are still ambiguous. It is clear that we cannot rely only on policies at the national level. While necessary they must be balanced by policies and programs at the local and state levels. An economic system in which jobs are guaranteed will require an increased level of democracy in order to function effectively. When workers are freed of the fear of losing their jobs, cooperation will need to replace fear as the motive for working. As the destructive side of capitalism is controlled in order to obtain our three goals of basic material goods, self-esteem, and freedom, care must be taken that the creative side is not crushed by bureaucracy, inefficiency, and lack of incentives.

To be sure, the direction we point to will not be followed immediately, and if it were, it would not result in a miraculous transformation of the economy. However, it is less improbable than the full restoration of laissez faire contemplated by CEIs or the complete transformation of society envisioned by radicals, and it can lead to a more humane society than the existing one.

Notes

1. Introduction

1. Joseph A. Schumpeter, *Capitalism, Socialism, and Democracy*, 3d ed. (New York: Harper & Brothers, 1950), p. 83.

2. Richard A. Easterlin, "Does Economic Growth Improve the Human Lot? Some Empirical Evidence," in *Nations and Households in Economic Growth* (New York: Academic Press, 1974).

3. See Paul L. Wachtel, *The Poverty of Affluence: A Psychological Portrait of the American Way of Life* (New York: Free Press, 1983).

4. Denis Goulet, *The Cruel Choice: A New Concept in the Theory of Development* (New York: Atheneum, 1971), pp. 241–45.

5. Tibor Scitovsky, *The Joyless Economy: An Inquiry into Human Satisfaction and Consumer Dissatisfaction* (New York: Oxford University Press, 1976).

2. Free Enterprise and Laissez-Faire Economics

1. Adam Smith, *The Wealth of Nations* (New York: Modern Library, 1947).

2. Thomas Malthus, *On Population* (New York: Modern Library, 1960).

3. See J. R. Poynter, *Society and Pauperism: English Ideas on Poor Relief, 1795–1834* (London: Routledge and Kegan Paul, 1969). Also see Guy Routh, *The Origin of Economic Ideas* (White Plains, N.Y.: International Arts and Sciences Press, 1975).

4. See Poynter.

5. Malthus, p. 33.

6. Ibid., p. 54.

7. Ibid., pp. 8–10.

8. Thomas Malthus, "A Summary View of the Principles of Population," *Three Essays on Population* (New York: Mentor, 1960), pp. 33–34.

9. Malthus, *On Population,* pp. 69, 75.

10. Ibid., p. 75.

11. Ibid., pp. 591–92.

12. Thomas Malthus, *Principles of Political Economy* (Boston: Wells and Lilly, 1821), and Jean Baptiste Say, *A Treatise on Political Economy* (Philadelphia: J. B. Lippincott, 1867), pp. 134–35.

13. W. Stanley Jevons, "Economic Policy," paper read before Section F of the British Association for the Advancement of Science, September 1870. Published in *Essays in Economic Method*, ed. R. L. Smith (London: Duckworth, 1962), pp. 27–28.

14. Alfred Marshall, *Principles of Economics* (1890: London: MacMillan, 1959), p. 149.

15. Ibid., pp. 144–69, 574–77.

16. For a more detailed treatment of this claim see Charles K. Wilber and Jon Wisman, "The Chicago School: Positivism or Ideal Type," *Journal of Economic Issues* 9, 4 (December 1975): pp. 665–79.

17. For a fascinating study of this period see Robert Keller, "Supply-side Economic Policies during the Coolidge Mellon Era," *Journal of Economic Issues* 16 (September 1982): 773–90.

18. See Alexis de Tocqueville, *Democracy in America* (New York: Vintage Books, 1945) and Robert N. Bellah et al., *Habits of the Heart: Individualism and Commitment in American Life* (Berkeley: University of California Press, 1985).

19. It should be noted that work on the microtheory of individual markets continued with further steps in mathematizing the theory, in developing optimization techniques such as linear programming, and in extending results in other areas such as trade theory. It is in analyzing the whole economy, the macroeconomy, that laissez-faire theory moved to the background during that period.

3. The Triumph of Keynesianism

1. Gottfried Haberler, *The World Economy, Money, and the Great Depression, 1919–1939* (Washington, D.C.: American Enterprise Institute for Public Policy Research, 1976), p. 9.

2. Ibid.

3. Goronwy Rees, *The Great Slump* (London: Weidenfeld & Micolson, 1970), p. 85.

4. Guy Routh, *The Origins of Economic Ideas* (White Plains, N.Y.: International Arts and Sciences Press, Inc., 1975), pp. 267–68.

5. Edwin Cannan, "The Demand for Labour," *Economic Journal* 42 (1932): 357–69; cited in Routh, *Origins of Economic Ideas*, p. 268.

6. Indeed, Roosevelt had run on a campaign criticizing Hoover's deficits, saying, "Let us have the courage to stop borrowing to meet continuing deficits. Stop the deficits." Quoted in Robert Lekachman, *The Age of Keynes* (New York: Random House, 1966), p. 43.

7. Mario Einaudi, *The Roosevelt Revolution* (New York: Harcourt, Brace, 1959), pp. 76–97.

8. Lekachman, p. 123.

9. Ibid., p. 220. Joan Robinson, a post-Keynesian, referred to the American branch as "bastard Keynesians" because she felt they had lost much of Keynes's insights by obscuring the inherent problems of a market economy behind the hopes for government stabilization policies.

10. Ibid.

11. Ibid.

12. Ibid, p. 24.

13. Herbert Stein, "Fiscal Policy: Reflections on the Past Decade," in *Contemporary Economic Problems: 1976,* ed. William Fellner (Washington, D.C.: American Enterprise Institute for Public Policy Research, 1976), pp. 55–84.

14. Murray Weidenbaum, Martin Feldstein, and Beryl Sprinkel chaired the council under President Reagan, and Michael Boskin under President Bush. However, politics eclipsed economic analysis and the locus of economic policy shifted to the Department of Treasury and the Office of Management and Budget.

15. Robert Solow and Paul Samuelson, "Analytical Aspects of Anti-Inflation Policy," *American Economic Review* 50 (May 1960): 177–94.

16. Franco Modigliani, "The Monetarist Controversy or, Should We Forsake Stabilization Policy," *American Economic Review* 67, 2 (March 1977): 17–18.

17. Paul McCracken, "Reducing the Inflation Rate," *Wall Street Journal,* 15 July 1977, p. 10.

18. Frank E. Morris, "A Fed President Views the Money Supply," *Wall Street Journal,* 23 June 1982, p. 30.

19. Rudiger Dornbusch and Stanley Fischer, *Macroeconomics* (New York: McGraw-Hill, 1978), p. 289.

20. Ibid., p. 290.

21. Robert Eisner, *The Total Incomes System of Accounts* (Chicago: University of Chicago Press, 1989).

4. The Assault on the Keynesians:
Free Enterprise Once Again

1. The books are published as John Kenneth Galbraith, *The Age of Uncertainty* (Boston: Houghton Mifflin, 1977) and Milton and Rose Friedman, *Free to Choose* (New York: Harcourt Brace Jovanovich, 1979).

2. Melvin Reder, "Chicago Economics: Permanence and Change," *Journal of Economic Literature* 20 (March 1982): 1–38.

3. Milton Friedman and Anna Jacobson Schwartz, *A Monetary His-*

tory of the United States, 1867–1960 (Princeton, N.J.: Princeton University Press, 1963).

4. Milton Friedman, "National Economic Planning," *Newsweek*, 14 July 1975, p. 71.

5. See George Gilder, *Wealth and Poverty* (New York: Basic Books, 1981) and Charles Murray, *Losing Ground: American Social Policy 1950–80* (New York: Basic Books, 1984).

6. Milton Friedman, "The Role of Monetary Policy," *American Economic Review* 58, 1 (March 1968): 11.

7. Beryl Wayne Sprinkel, *Money and Markets: A Monetarist View* (Homewood, Ill.: Richard D. Irwin, 1971), p. 166.

8. See Robert Nozick, *Anarchy, State, and Utopia* (New York: Basic Books, 1974).

9. Friedman, "National Economic Planning."

10. Herbert Stein, "Some 'Supply-Side' Propositions," *Wall Street Journal*, 9 March 1980.

11. Ibid.

5. The Reagan Years: CEIs and the Haunted Prosperity of the 1980s

1. Empirial proof of any economic theory is very scarce, especially when the reference point is natural science. Donald McCloskey, *The Rhetoric of Economics* (Madison, Wisc.: University of Wisconsin Press, 1985) finds the empirical basis for economic propositions quite weak and shows that their acceptance within the economics profession is based on much broader considerations of "rhetoric."

2. There are a number of cogent criticisms which can be made of this starting point. Amitai Etzione's interesting book *The Moral Dimension* (New York: Basic Books, 1988) builds an entirely different theory by assuming that there is also a "moral rationality" which guides behavior as well as this "economic rationality." Others point out that behavior always carries with it an important social dimension which is not represented in the individualistic calculus. See E. Michael Himes and John Himes, "The Myth of Self-interest," *Commonweal* (November 1988), pp. 20–21.

3. Laissez-faire theory is not alone in its habit of shifting from short-run empirical propositions to long-run tautologies when confronted with contradictory evidence. The structure of both Marxism and Rostow's stages-of-growth theory lend themselves to this form of defense. See Paul Streeten, "Strength Through Tautology," *The New Republic* (September 4, 1971), pp. 27–29.

4. One of the more damning kiss-and-tell books about the Reagan administration documents this well. See Clyde Prestowitz, Jr., *Trading*

Places: How We Allowed Japan to Take the Lead (New York: Basic Books, 1987).

5. These and the following statistics are computed from the figures in the *Economic Report of the President, 1989* (Washington, D.C.: United States Government Printing Office, 1989).

6. William Greider, "Annals of Finance: The Price of Money," *The New Yorker* (November 9, 16, 23, 1987).

7. One estimate found that 47.7 percent of the decline in inflation from 1980 to 1983 was due to the slack caused by the recession. Another 33.7 percent resulted from lower international food and energy prices, while the remaining 18.6 percent occurred through a recalculation of the home ownership component of the index. See John Palmer and Isabel Sawhill, *The Reagan Record: An Assessment of America's Changing Domestic Priorities* (New York: Ballinger, 1984), p. 80.

8. Certainly the frustration with this experience contributed to labor's effort to bring Frank Lorenzo and Eastern Airlines to its knees through the costly and possibly counterproductive strike of March 1989.

9. An extensive summary of these changes is included in Sam Rosenberg, "The Restructuring of the Labor Market, the Labor Force and the Nature of Employment Relations in the United States in the 1980s," manuscript (1988).

10. These income distribution figures are from U.S. Department of Commerce, *Current Population Reports,* various issues.

11. See the article by Michael Evans, "The Bankruptcy of Keynesian Econometric Models," *Challenge: Magazine of Economic Affairs* (January-February 1980): 13–19.

12. Harry Anderson and Richard Thomas, "Stockman's Ladder," *Newsweek* (February 9, 1981), p. 66.

13. The quotes are from William Greider, "The Education of David Stockman," *Atlantic Monthly* (December 1981), pp. 27–54.

14. The numbers actually understate the magnitude of the deficit, for they include the surplus in the Social Security Trust Fund which was over $50 billion in 1988. This surplus will disappear in the coming decade as retirements increase. In addition, the federal outlays to stabilize the Savings and Loans will probably be financed "off budget," so that the federal outlays will not appear in the deficit figures.

15. Peter G. Peterson, "The Morning After," *Atlantic Monthly* (October 1987), p. 44.

16. Walter W. Heller, "Activist Government: Key to Growth," *Challenge: Magazine of Economic Affairs* (March-April 1986): 8.

17. Peterson, pp. 47–48.

18. Douglas Dalenberg and Randall Eberts, "Public Infrastructure and Economic Development," *Economic Commentary-Federal Reserve Bank of Cleveland* (January 15, 1988).

19. For additional treatment see National Council on Public Works

Improvement, *Fragile Foundations: A Report on America's Public Works* (Washington, D.C.: U.S. Government Printing Office, 1988).

20. Prestowitz, p. 11.

21. Gary W. Loveman and Chris Tilly, "Good Jobs or Bad Jobs: What does the Evidence Say?" *New England Economic Review* (January-February 1988): 46–65.

22. Calculation from *Economic Report of the President, 1988,* Table B-25.

23. See Charles Murray, *Losing Ground* (New York: Basic Books, 1984)

24. J. Larry Brown, "Hunger in the U.S.," *Scientific American* (February 1987), p. 37.

25. Ibid., pp. 40–41; Food Research and Action Center, *Food and Nutrition Issues in the Food Stamp Program* (Washington, D.C., 1981); *Report of the President's Task Force on Food Assistance* (Washington, D.C.: U.S. Department of Agriculture, Food and Nutrition Service, January 1984).

26. Children's Defense Fund, *American Children in Poverty* (New York: 1984).

27. *Hunger Reaches Blue Collar America: An Unbalanced Recovery in a Service Economy* (New York: Physician Task Force on Hunger in America, 1987).

28. The source for these statistics is Jonathan Kozol, "The Homeless and Their Children—I and II," *The New Yorker* (January 25 and February 1, 1988).

29. The data in much of the following sections are taken from Kim Hopper and Jill Hamberg, *The Making of America's Homeless: From Skid Row to New Poor* (New York: Institute for Social Welfare Research, Community Service Society, 1984). They drew upon the Censuses of 1970 and 1980. When the data from the 1990 Census become available, we would expect a continuation and perhaps even an acceleration of the trends they note.

30. Ibid., pp. 32–33.

31. Ibid., p. 39.

32. Ibid., p. 47.

33. *South Bend Tribune,* March 9, 1989.

34. *Sourcebook of Criminal Justice Statistics, 1987,* p. 484.

35. Heller, p. 9.

6. Cycle Theories: Watch and Hope

1. Nikolai Kondratieff, "The Long Waves in Economic Life," *Review of Economics and Statistics* 17 (1935): 105–115. Reprinted in *Readings in Business Cycle Theory* (Philadelphia: Blakiston, 1944), pp. 20–42.

2. Quoted by George Garvey, "Kondratieff's Theory of Long Cycles," *Review of Economics and Statistics* 25 (November 1943): 204.

3. The exact quotation from J. W. N. Watkins, a follower of Karl Popper, is, "This is a sort of blasphemy." The target of this attack is the idea that a long wave could cause people to do anything. See J. W. N. Watkins, "Ideal Types and Historical Explanation," in *Readings in the Philosophy of Science,* ed. H. Feigl and M. Brodbeck (New York: Appleton-Century-Crofts, 1953).

4. Geoffrey Barraclough, "The End of an Era," *New York Review,* 27 June 1974.

5. Quoted from Burns and Mitchell by Robert A. Gordon, *Business Fluctuations,* 2d ed. (New York: Harper, 1961), p. 249.

6. Lange is quoted by Ernest Mandel, *Late Capitalism* (London: New Left Books, 1975), p. 140

7. Maurice Lee, *Macroeconomics: Fluctuations, Growth and Stability,* 5th ed. (Homewood, Ill.: Richard Irwin, 1971), p. 36.

8. There are many sources which treat cycles. One nice summary is in R. Gordon.

9. Kondratieff, p. 32

10. See his criticisms in Garvey, pp. 216–19.

11. Quoted in Mandel, pp. 128–29.

12. Kondratieff, p. 35.

13. Ibid.

14. Schumpeter's work can be found in Joseph Schumpeter, *Business Cycles: A Theoretical, Historical, and Statistical Analysis of the Capitalist Process* (New York: McGraw Hill, 1939) and "The Analysis of Economic Change," in *Readings in Business Cycle Theory,* pp. 1–19.

15. The major work by Kuznets was Simon Kuznets, *Secular Movements in Production and Prices,* (1930: New York, A. M. Kelley, 1967). Rostow's work appears in "Kondratieff, Schumpeter, and Kuznets: Trend Periods Revisited," *Journal of Economic History* 35 (1975): 719–53; and "Long Swings in the Growth of Population and in Related Economic Variables," *Proceedings of the American Philosophical Society* 102, 1 (1958): 25–52.

16. Mandel, presents his views in chapter 3 of *Late Capitalism.*

17. David M. Gordon, "Up and Down the Long Roller Coaster," in *U. S. Capitalism in Crisis* (New York: Union for Radical Political Economics, 1978), pp. 22–35.

18. See W. W. Rostow's review of Tibor Vasko, ed., *The Long Wave Debate* (Berlin: Springer, 1987) in *Journal of Economic Literature* (December 1988): 1759–61.

19. Paul Samuelson, "Interaction between the Multiplier Analysis and the Principle of Acceleration," *Review of Economics and Statistics* 21 (May 1939), pp. 75–78.

20. At this point we start drawing heavily on James Gleick, *Chaos: Making a New Science* (New York: Viking, 1987).

21. Ibid., p. 86.

22. Ibid., p. 304.

23. Nathaniel J. Mass, *Economic Cycles: An Analysis of Underlying Causes* (Cambridge, Mass.: Wright-Allen Press, 1975).

7. Marxism: Inherent Cycles and Inevitable Crises

1. Some examples are Joseph Schumpeter, Wassily Leontief, Joan Robinson, Martin Bronfenbrenner, J. K. Galbraith, and Robert Heilbroner.

2. Karl Marx, *A Contribution to the Critique of Political Economy* (New York: Charles H. Kerr, 1904), pp. 11–12.

3. Ibid., p. 11

4. Karl Marx, *The Eighteenth Brumaire of Louis Bonaparte* (New York: International Publishers, no date), p. 13.

5. Marx, *Critique,* pp. 12, 13.

6. Karl Marx and Friedrich Engels, *Manifesto of the Communist Party* (New York: International Publishers, 1932), p. 9.

7. Ibid., pp. 9, 12.

8. Ibid., pp. 16, 21.

9. Marx, *Critique,* p. 13.

10. Marx and Engels, *Manifesto,* p. 9.

11. Karl Marx, *Capital* (Moscow: Foreign Language Publishing House, 1961), Vol. 1, pp. 170–71.

12. Karl Marx, *Value, Price and Profit* (New York: International Publishers, 1935), p. 40.

13. Ibid., p. 41.

14. Marx, *Capital,* Vol. 1, p. 235.

15. Ibid., Vol. 1, p. 639.

16. Ibid., Vol. 1, p. 209.

17. Ibid., Vol. 1, p. 209.

18. Ibid., Vol. 1, pp. 152–53.

19. Ibid., Vol. 1, p. 595.

20. Ibid., Vol. 1, p. 760.

21. Ibid., Vol. 1, pp. 762–63.

22. Ibid., Vol. 3, p. 241.

23. Paul M. Sweezy, *The Theory of Capitalist Development* (New York: Monthly Review Press, l956), pp. 191–92.

24. James O'Connor, *Fiscal Crisis of the State* (New York: St. Martins Press, 1973).

25. In a provocative and well-argued book, *Schooling in Capitalist America: Educational Reform and the Contradictions of Economic Life* (New York: Basic Books, 1976), Samuel Bowles and Herbert Gintis point out the conspiratorial side of public education by arguing that in the public schools each class of people is taught according to what will be expected of them later in life. Working-class children are taught to respect authority and to carry out tasks given them by obliging teachers. The children

of the upper class, on the other hand, are taught to use their creativity and analytical powers, for these will be useful to them when they begin to manage production. In such ways class stratification and often animosity is strengthened and perpetuated.

26. Robert L. Heilbroner, *The Worldly Philosophers*, 4th ed. (New York: Simon and Schuster, 1972), p. 154.

27. Paul A. Baran and Paul M. Sweezy, *Monopoly Capital: An Essay on the American Economic and Social Order* (New York: Monthly Review Press, 1966).

28. See Samuel Bowles and Richard Edwards, *Understanding Capitalism* (New York: Harper & Row, 1985); Samuel Bowles, David Gordon, and Thomas Weisskopf, *Beyond the Waste Land: A Democratic Alternative to Decline* (New York: Doubleday, 1983): Michel De Vroey, "A Regulation Approach Interpretation of Contemporary Crisis," *Capital and Class* 23 (Summer 1984): 45–66; David Ruccio, "Fordism on a World Scale: International Dimensions of Regulation," International Conference on Regulation Theory, Barcelona, 16–18 June 1988; *Marxism Today* 32, 10 (October 1988). The entire issue is devoted to the subject of "New Times and Post-Fordism Capitalism."

29. This section draws heavily from Bowles and Edwards, and Bowles, Gordon, and Weisskopf.

30. Bowles and Edwards, pp. 94–95.

31. Ibid., p. 95.

32. Ibid., pp. 96–97.

33. Reprinted from Bowles and Edwards, p. 98.

34. Leonard A. Rapping, "The Great Recession of the 1970s: Domestic and International Considerations," in *Alternative Directions in Economic Policy*, ed. Frank J. Bonello and Thomas R. Swartz (Notre Dame, Ind.: University of Notre Dame Press, 1978), pp. 152–79.

35. Raford Boddy and James Crotty, "Class Conflict and Macro Policy: The Political Business Cycle," *Review of Radical Political Economics* 7, 1 (Spring 1975): 1–19.

36. Roger E. Alcaly, "An Introduction to Marxian Crisis Theory," in *U.S. Capitalism in Crisis* (New York: Union for Radical Political Economics, 1978), p. 17.

37. David M. Gordon, "Capital-Labor Conflict and the Productivity Slowdown," *American Economic Review* 71, 2 (May 1981): 34.

8. Toward a New Political Economy
Methodological and Historical Considerations

1. I. M. D. Little, *A Critique of Welfare Economics*, 2d ed. (Oxford: Clarendon Press, 1957); and Milton Friedman, *Essays in Positive Economics* (Chicago: University of Chicago Press, 1953).

2. The discrepancy between this promise of economics and the

reality is the source of most "economist" jokes, e.g., if you laid all economists end to end you'd never reach a conclusion.

3. See Milton Friedman and David Meiselman, "The Relative Stability of Monetary Velocity and the Investment Multiplier in the United States, 1897–1958," in *Stabilization Policies: Commission on Money and Credit* (Englewood Cliffs, N.J.: Prentice-Hall, 1963).

4. Albert Ando and Franco Modigliani, "The Relative Stability of Monetary Velocity and the Investment Multiplier," *American Economic Review* 55 (September 1965): 693–728; and Michael De Prano and Thomas Mayer, "Tests of the Relative Importance of Autonomous Expenditures and Money," *American Economic Review* 55 (September 1965): 729–52.

5. Milton Friedman and David Meiselman, "Reply to Ando and Modigliani and to De Prano and Mayer," *American Economic Review* 55 (September 1965): 753–85.

6. See also Martin Bronfenbrenner, *Macroeconomic Alternatives* (Arlington Heights, Ill.: AHM Publishing, 1979), pp. 185–88; and Peter D. McClelland, *Causal Explanation and Model Building in History, Economics, and the New Economic History* (Ithaca: Cornell University Press, 1975), pp. 132–35.

7. William Poole and Elinda B. F. Kornblith, "The Friedman-Meiselman CMC Paper: New Evidence on an Old Controversy," *American Economic Review* 63 (December 1973): 908–17.

8. Some standard economists have come to the same interpretation but draw different conclusions. See Franco Modigliani, "The Monetarist Controversy or, Should We Forsake Stabilization Policies?" *American Economic Review* 67 (March 1979): 1–19; and William J. Baumol and Alan S. Blinder, *Economics: Principles and Policy* (New York: Harcourt, Brace, Jovanovich, 1979), pp. 257–71.

9. The initial quote is from the *New York Times*, 1984; the second is in an article by Louis Rukeyser, *The Observer*, March 15, 1988.

10. Donald N. McCloskey, *The Rhetoric of Economics* (Madison: University of Wisconsin Press, 1985).

11. See Charles K. Wilber and Robert S. Harrison, "The Methodological Basis of Institutional Economics: Pattern Model, Storytelling, and Holism," *Journal of Economic Issues* 12 (March 1978): 61–89; Paul Diesing, *Patterns of Discovery in the Social Sciences* (Chicago: Aldine Atherton, 1971); and Benjamin Ward, *What's Wrong with Economics?* (New York: Basic Books, 1972). Philosophers of science long ago moved beyond logical positivism as a viable methodology, even in the natural sciences.

12. We should recall an earlier distinction. The American followers of Keynes took from Keynes the belief that the economy could be fine-tuned with little need for structural change. However, a large segment of British economists and growing numbers in the U.S. find the key to Keynes in his belief that the economy was inherently unstable. It is this

branch we find most amenable and they are termed the Post-Keynesians. Institutionalist analysis has a long tradition in the U.S. tracing to Thorstein Veblen and John R. Commons in the early twentieth century.

13. K. William Kapp, "The Nature and Significance of Institutional Economics," *Kyklos* 29 Fasc. 2 (1976): 209–30.

14. John Kenneth Galbraith, *Economics and the Public Purpose* (Boston: Houghton Mifflin, 1973).

15. Warren J. Samuels, "Interrelations between Legal and Economic Processes," *Journal of Law and Economics* 14 (October 1971): 435–50, and "The Coase Theorem and the Study of Law and Economics," *Natural Resources Journal* 14 (January 1974): 1–33.

16. Willard F. Mueller, "Antitrust in a Planned Economy," *Journal of Economic Issues* 9 (June 1975): 159–80.

17. Charles Craypo, "Collective Bargaining in the Multinational, Conglomerate Corporation: Litton's Shutdown of Royal Typewriter," *Industrial and Labor Relations Review* 29 (October 1975): 3–25.

18. P. B. Doeringer and M. Piore, *Internal Labor Markets and Manpower Analysis* (New York: Lexington Books, 1971).

19. See the articles in Alfred S. Eichner ed., *A Guide to Post-Keynesian Economics* (White Plains, N.Y.: M. E. Sharpe, 1978).

20. See many of the works by Thorstein Veblen and Wesley Clair Mitchell.

21. "The hedonistic conception of man is that of a lightning calculator of pleasures and pains, who oscillates like a homogeneous globule of desire of happiness under the impulse of stimuli that shift him about the area, but leave him intact. He has neither antecedent nor consequent. He is an isolated, definitive human datum, in stable equilibrium except for the buffets of the impinging forces that displace him in one direction or another. Self-imposed in elemental space, he spins symmetrically about his own spiritual axis until the parallelogram of forces bears down upon him, whereupon he follows the line of the resultant. When the force of the impact is spent, he comes to rest, a self-contained globule of desire as before." Thorstein Veblen, "Why Is Economics Not an Evolutionary Science?" in *The Place of Science in Modern Civilization* (New York: B. W. Huebsch, 1919; Russell & Russell, 1961), pp. 73–74.

22. See Wilber and Harrison.

23. This is not storytelling in the pejorative sense, but scientific; see Ward, *What's Wrong with Economics?* chapter 12.

24. Cited in Wilber and Harrison, p. 73.

25. Alfred S. Eichner, "A Look Ahead," in *A Guide to Post-Keynesian Economics,* p. 171.

26. Ibid., p. 174.

27. Ibid., p. 171.

28. See Karl Polanyi, *The Great Transformation* (New York: Farrar and Rinehart, 1944).

29. Ibid., pp. 115–16.

30. See Karl Mannheim, *Freedom, Power, and Democratic Planning* (New York: Oxford University Press, 1950), p. 191.

31. Polanyi, pp. 72–73.

32. Ibid., p. 73.

33. Ibid., p. 76.

34. Ibid., p. 134.

35. Ibid., p. 231.

9. Structure and Operation of the U.S. Economy:
The PKI View

1. See for example the East Asian economies described in Roy Hofheinz and Kent Calder, *The Eastasia Edge* (New York: Basic Books, 1982) in which the symbiotic relation of the two sectors blurs any distinction and there is little of the adversarial relation which characterizes the sectors in our economy.

2. See U.S. Bureau of the Census, *Statistical Abstract of the United States, 1988* (Washington, D.C.: Government Printing Office, 1987), for most of the data in this section.

3. One interesting study which concentrates on clearly illegal activity is Carl Simon and Ann Witte, *Beating the System: The Underground Economy* (Boston: Auburn House, 1982).

4. John Blair, *Economic Concentration* (New York: Harcourt Brace Jovanovich, 1972).

5. See Damon Darlin, "Most U.S. Firms Seek Extra Profits in Japan, At the Expense of Sales," *Wall Street Journal*, 15 May 1987, pp. 1, 6.

6. Ibid., p. 6.

7. Hobart Rowan, "A Real and Present Danger," *Washington Post, National Weekly Edition*, 13–19 February 1989, p. 5.

8. See, for example, Sidney Weintraub, "Missing Theory of Money Wages," *Journal of Post Keynesian Economics* (Winter 1978–79): 59–78. For discussions of dual labor markets see L. C. Thurow, *Generating Inequality* (New York: Basic Books, 1975); P. B. Doeringer and M. Piore, *Internal Labor Markets and Manpower Analysis* (New York: Lexington Books, 1971); and M. Reich, D. Gordon, and R. Edwards, "A Theory of Labor Market Segmentation," *American Economic Review* (May 1973).

9. Eileen Applebaum, "Post-Keynesian Theory: The Labor Market," *Challenge* 21, 6 (January-February 1979): 45–46.

10. Burton A. Weisbrod, *The Voluntary Nonprofit Sector* (Lexington, Mass.: Lexington Books, D. C. Heath and Co., 1977), p. 21. Also see Barry P. Keating and Maryann 0. Keating, *Not-For-Profit* (Glen Ridge, N.J.: Thomas Horton and Daughters, 1980).

11. This approach is consistent with work such as Robert N. Bellah et al., *Habits of the Heart: Individualism and Commitment in American Life* (Berkeley: University of California Press, 1985) and Michael Himes and

Kenneth Himes, "The Myth of Self-interest," *Commonweal,* 23 September 1988, pp. 493–98.

12. A. Allan Schmid, *Property, Power, and Public Choice: An Inquiry into Law and Economics* (New York: Praeger Special Studies, 1978), p. 240.

13. See Robert H. Hayes and William J. Abernathy, "Managing Our Way To Economic Decline," *Harvard Business Review* (July-August 1980).

14. A good example was the toothpaste producers: "marketers are pegging their hopes on minor changes in product appearances, packaging, scents or flavors and the companies are spending tens of millions of dollars to advertise those changes." See Bill Abrams, "Warring Toothpaste Makers Spend Millions Luring Buyers to Slightly Altered Products," *Wall Street Journal,* 21 September 1981, p. 27.

15. Lester C. Thurow, "Why Productivity Falls," *Newsweek,* 24 August 1981, p. 63.

16. *Wall Street Journal* 12 July 1982, p. 1.

17. A talk delivered in April 1988 and quoted in *The South Bend Tribune,* 2 April 1988.

18. There were 259 LBO's in 1987 with a total of $37 billion in assets transferred. In 1989 the RJR Nabisco LBO totalled close to $25 billion. Studies of the phenomenon are David Ravenscraft and F. M. Scherer, *Mergers, Sell-offs, and Economic Efficiency* (Washington, D.C.: Brookings Institution, 1987) and Allen Michael and Israel Shaked, *Takeover Madness: Corporate America Fights Back* (New York: Wiley, 1986).

19. An extensive treatment of the change in the growth path of industrial countries, its explanation, and its implications is contained in Ajit Singh, "The Golden Age," manuscript.

20. An excellent treatment of these issues is published every year as Lester Brown, ed., *The State of the World* (Washington, D.C.: Worldwatch Institute).

21. See Adam Smith, *Theory of Moral Sentiments* (London: Henry Bohn, 1861) and A. W. Coats, ed., *The Classical Economists and Economic Policy* (London: Methuen, 1971). It is interesting that Milton Friedman, in his *Essays in Positive Economics* (Chicago: University of Chicago Press, 1966) has a similar starting point when he says "Differences about policy among disinterested citizens derive predominantly from different predictions about the economic consequences of taking action . . . rather than from fundamental differences in basic values" (p. 5).

22. Peter Berger, "In Praise of Particularity: The Concept of Mediating Structures," *Review of Politics* (July 1976): 134.

23. Fred Hirsch, *Social Limits to Growth* (Cambridge, Mass.: Harvard, 1978), p. 141. We owe him the idea of social limits to growth.

24. See R. H. Tawney, *Religion and The Rise of Capitalism* (New York: Harcourt, Brace & World, 1926) and Charles K. Wilber, "The New Economic History Re-examined: R. H. Tawney on the Origins of Capitalism," *American Journal of Economics and Sociology* 33, 3 (July 1974): 249–58.

25. *Sourcebook of Criminal Justice Statistics* (Washington, D.C.: 1987).

26. Hirsch, pp. 128–29.

27. This casts new light on the recent attempts to construct theories of justice that are acceptable to all. See John Rawls, *A Theory of Justice* (Cambridge, Mass.: Harvard University Press, 1971) and the literature spawned by that work. The whole endeavor can be seen as an attempt to create a substitute moral law based on rationality rather than religion.

28. Hirsch, pp. 141–42.

29. The entire fascinating tale is one key element of the story of the Federal Reserve in William Greider, "The Annals of Finance," *The New Yorker* (November 14, 21, 28, 1987).

30. See Clyde V. Prestowitz, Jr., *Trading Places: How We Allowed Japan to Take the Lead* (New York: Basic Books, 1987).

10. Toward a New Social Contract

1. See George A. Akerlof, *An Economist's Book of Tales* (Cambridge: Cambridge University Press, 1984); Kenneth E. Boulding, *The Economy of Love and Fear* (Belmont, Calif.: Wadsworth Publishing, 1973); Fred Hirsch, *Social Limits to Growth* (Cambridge, Mass: Harvard University Press, 1978); Albert O. Hirschman, *Exit, Voice, and Loyalty: Responses to Decline in Firms, Organizations, and States* (Cambridge, Mass: Harvard University Press, 1970); Andrew Schotter, *Free Market Economics: A Critical Appraisal* (New York: St. Martin's Press, 1985), pp. 47–88; A. Allan Schmid, *Property, Power, and Public Choice: An Inquiry into Law and Economics* (New York: Praeger, 1978).

2. See Hirschman, *Exit, Voice, and Loyalty* and Albert 0. Hirschman, *Rival Views of Market Society* (New York: Viking, 1986), pp. 77–101.

3. Schmid, pp. 162–69.

4. Barry Schwartz, *The Battle for Human Nature: Science, Morality and Modern Life* (New York: W. W. Norton, 1986).

5. Hirschman, *Rival Views of Market Society,* p. 155.

6. See Richard M. Titmuss, *The Gift Relationship* (London: Allen and Unwin, 1970).

7. *Nicomachean Ethics,* 1103b.

8. A. K. Sen, *On Economics and Ethics* (Berkeley: University of California Press, 1985).

9. *Leviticus* 25:8–55.

10. *Forbes* (May 30, 1988), p. 155.

11. Charles Murray, *Pursuit of Happiness* (New York: Simon and Schuster, 1988).

12. See Michael J. Himes and Kenneth R. Himes, "The Myth of Self-interest," *Commonweal* (September 23, 1988), pp. 493–98.

13. See, for example, Sidney Weintraub with Henry Wallich, "A Tax Based Incomes Policy," in Sidney Weintraub, *Keynes and the Monetarists* (New Brunswick, N.J.: Rutgers Press, 1973); for further discussion

of TIP, see Laurence Seidman, "Role of a Tax Based Incomes Policy," *American Economic Review* (May 1979): 202–206; also Richard Slitor, "Implementation and Design of Tax Based Incomes Policies," *American Economic Review* (May 1979), 212–15.

14. See David Kirkpatrick, "What Givebacks Can Get You," *Fortune* (November 24, 1986), pp. 16–20.

15. Michael J. Piore, "A Critique of Reagan's Labor Policy," *Challenge* 29, 1 (March-April 1986): 48–54.

16. The best known and most studied of these firms are the plywood cooperatives in Oregon and Washington. See K. Berman, *Worker-Owned Plywood Companies* (Pullman, Wash.: Washington State University Press, 1967).

17. Barry Bluestone and Bennett Harrison, *The Deindustrialization of America* (New York: Basic Books, 1982).

18. U.S. Congress, Joint Economic Committee, *Broadening the Ownership of New Capital: ESOPs and other Alternatives,* 94th Congress, 2nd session (Washington, D.C.: Government Printing Office, 1976).

19. Henry M. Levin, "Issues in Assessing the Comparative Productivity of Worker-Managed and Participatory Firms in Capitalist Societies," in *Participatory and Self-Managed Firms,* ed. D. Jones and J. Svejnar (Lexington, Mass.: D.C. Heath, 1982); R. Oakeshott, *The Case for Workers' Coops* (London: Routledge & Kegan Paul, 1978); K. Friden, *Workplace Democracy and Productivity* (Washington, D.C.: National Center for Economic Alternatives, 1980).

20. See B. Thurston, "South Bend Lathe, E.S.O.P. on Strike Against Itself?" *Self-Management* 8 (Fall 1980): 19–20.

21. *Profit Sharing and Profitability* (London: Kogan Page/IPM, 1988). Also see the newsreport, "Letting Workers in on the Share-Out," *Sunday Times(London),* 22 January 1989, p. E1.

22. Pete Sheehan, "A New Model of Economic Democracy: The Workers of Weirton Steel," *New Oxford Review* 54, 10 (December 1987): 13–17.

23. See Henry M. Levin, "The Workplace: Employment and Business Intervention," in *Handbook of Social Intervention,* ed. E. Seidman (Beverly Hills, Calif.: Sage Publications, 1983); A. G. Johnson and W. F. Whyte, "The Mondragon System of Worker Production Cooperatives," *Industrial and Labor Relations Review* 31, 1 (1977): 18–30; H. Thomas and C. Logan, *Mondragon: An Economic Analysis* (Boston: George Allen & Unwin, 1982); and William and Kathleen Whyte, *Making Mondragon: The Growth and Dynamics of the Worker Co-operative Complex* (Ithaca, N.Y.: ILR Press, 1988).

24. Most of the data are from Levin, pp. 511–12.

25. Henry M. Levin, "Raising Employment and Productivity with Producer Co-operatives," in *Human Resources, Employment and Development, Vol. II,* ed. P. Streeten and H. Maier (New York: St. Martins's Press, 1983).

26. See Keith Bradley and Alan Gelb, "Motivation and Control in the Mondragon Experiment," *British Journal of Industrial Relations* 19, 2 (June 1980): 222–25. Their survey and interview studies indicate that cooperative organization is significantly associated with Mondragon's commercial success.

27. Ibid., p. 225.

28. However, Bradley and Gelb claim that it is not very important. See their " The Replication and Sustainability of the Mondragon Experiment," *British Journal of Industrial Relations* 20, 1 (March 1982): 22–33, 30–31.

29. This material is drawn from Andrew Schotter, *Free Market Economics: A Critical Appraisal* (New York: St. Martin's Press, 1985), pp. 65–80.

30. A good illustration of a simple corner solution is the old army nutrition problem. Assume we want to provide a group of soldiers with a minimum daily requirement of protein (70gm) and iron (10mg) at the least cost. There are three foods available to do so and that vary in costs per ounce: peanut butter (40gm, 4mg, $0.20), Spam (20gm, 3mg, $0.50), and Jello (60gm, 1mg, $0.30). One result is immediately evident. No Spam would be purchased because, ounce per ounce, peanut butter gives more protein and iron and is cheaper. Thus Spam would have a zero value in the final solution of this cost minimization problem.

31. In the absence of corner solutions, the assumptions of economic theory make it almost impossible for there to be involuntary unemployment. There is always a wage level low enough to make it profitable for some firm to hire workers willing to work at that wage. The theory also assumes a high degree of substitution among workers. The reality of the "underclass" in our society makes this a less tenable assumption.

32. Schotter, p. 77.

33. Milton Friedman, *Capitalism and Freedom* (Chicago: University of Chicago Press, 1962), pp. 85–107. Some would question Friedman's consistency and motives but that is a different question.

34. *Wall Street Journal*, "National Health Plan Wins Unlikely Backer: Business," 5 April 1989.

35. This is the basic thesis of Charles Murray, *Losing Ground: American Social Policy 1950–80* (New York: Basic Books, 1984).

36. Andrew Schotter and Keith Weigelt, "Affirmative Action and Equal Opportunity Laws: Some Experimental Evidence," Working Paper, C. V. Starr Center, New York University, 1987. The results were generated using techniques from the relatively new field of experimental economics in which carefully controlled laboratory tests attempt to simulate real-world economic situations. In a series of experiments, 200 participants were used to study "unfair" games that investigated the effects of equal opportunity laws and "uneven" games that studied the effects of affirmative action programs.

37. See the report in the *C. V. Starr Newsletter* 6 (1987), pp. 7–8.

38. Harvey Brenner, *Mental Illness and the Economy* (Cambridge, Mass.: Harvard University Press, 1973).

39. "Child Abuse Seems to be Increasing in Areas with High Unemployment," *Wall Street Journal* 6 August 1982.

40. Cited in Don Stillman, "The Devastating Impact of Plant Relocations," *Working Papers for a New Society* (July-August 1978), pp. 48–49.

41. *Economic Report of the President* (Washington, D.C.: Government Printing Office, 1953).

42. Robert Kuttner, "A Great American Tradition: Government Opening Opportunity," *Challenge* 29, 1 (March-April 1986): 22.

43. Ibid., p. 24.

44. See Peter Dreier, "Nonprofit Housing: Local Success Stories," *Commonweal* (April 7, 1989), pp. 201–202.

45. Ira Lowry, "Experimenting with Housing Allowances," Rand Corporation (April 1982).

46. In fact this is not quite accurate, a reality which the wheeling and dealing that brought the demise of many Saving and Loans only serves to emphasize. Lenders engage in their own form of credit rationing. Imperfect information regarding borrowers' ability to pay back loans causes lenders to use other criteria in addition to the interest rate to decide to whom to extend credit. These other criteria—collateral, general credit rating, etc.— favor large firms over small local ones.

47. The importance of such a moral base has been widely recognized. Gary Wills ("Benevolent Adam Smith," *New York Review* 9 February 1978) finds a moral system based on cooperation as central to Smith's views. Edward Banfield *(Moral Basis of a Backward Society* [Glencoe, Ill.: Free Press, 1958]) located the moral base in small groups, in this case the family. James C. Scott *(The Moral Economy of the Peasant: Rebellion and Subsistence in Southeast Asia* [New Haven: Yale, 1976]) finds it in a subsistence insurance ethic and shows that its destruction is likely to lead to rebellion.

48. The many ramifications of this story are told in Clyde Prestowitz, Jr., *Trading Places: How We Allowed Japan To Take the Lead* (New York: Basic Books, 1988).

49. See William A. Lovett, "Solving the U.S. Trade Deficit and Competitiveness Problem," *Journal of Economic Issues* 22, 2 (June 1988): 459–67.

50. Peter G. Peterson, "The Morning After," *Atlantic Monthly* (October 1987), pp. 43–69.

Index